Guildford

Uniform with this volume

NOTTINGHAM *Geoffrey Trease*

SOUTHAMPTON *A. Temple Patterson*

READING *Alan Wykes*

In preparation

CHELTENHAM *Simona Pakenham*

TYNESIDE *David Bean*

LEICESTER *Jack Simmons*

Guildford

A BIOGRAPHY

E. R. Chamberlin

Macmillan

First published 1970 by
MACMILLAN AND CO LTD
London and Basingstoke
Associated companies in New York Toronto
Dublin Melbourne Johannesburg and Madras

Printed in Great Britain by
WESTERN PRINTING SERVICES LTD
Bristol

Contents

List of Plates

Between pages 150 and 151

Photographs 27 and 28 are reproduced by courtesy of the University of Surrey. All other photographs, with the exception of those taken by Reginald Jackson, are by courtesy of Guildford Borough Council and reproduced by T. A. Wilkie.

LIST OF MAPS

Acknowledgments

THE author is indebted to A. Campbell and the Royal Historical Society for permission to quote from Mr Campbell's translation of the *Encomium Emmae Reginae*; to Ian Nairn, Nikolaus Pevsner and Penguin Books Ltd for permission to quote from *The Buildings of England: Surrey*, to Enid M. Dance and the Surrey Record Society for permission to quote from Dr Dance's introduction to *Guildford Borough Records 1514–1546*, and to Christopher Fry for permission to quote from his *Prologue* written for the opening of the Yvonne Arnaud Theatre. Grateful thanks are also due to the Directors of the *Surrey Advertiser* Group for unrestricted access to their invaluable files of local newspapers.

The inductive historian is very much in the position of the architect who fashions his own structure from bricks made by other men. This is particularly true in the field of local history where the results of years of work may, perhaps, be expressed in half-a-dozen privately printed pages. The bibliography on pages 220–4 indicates at once the scope of the author's indebtedness to those who have preceded him and acts as acknowledgment of their labours.

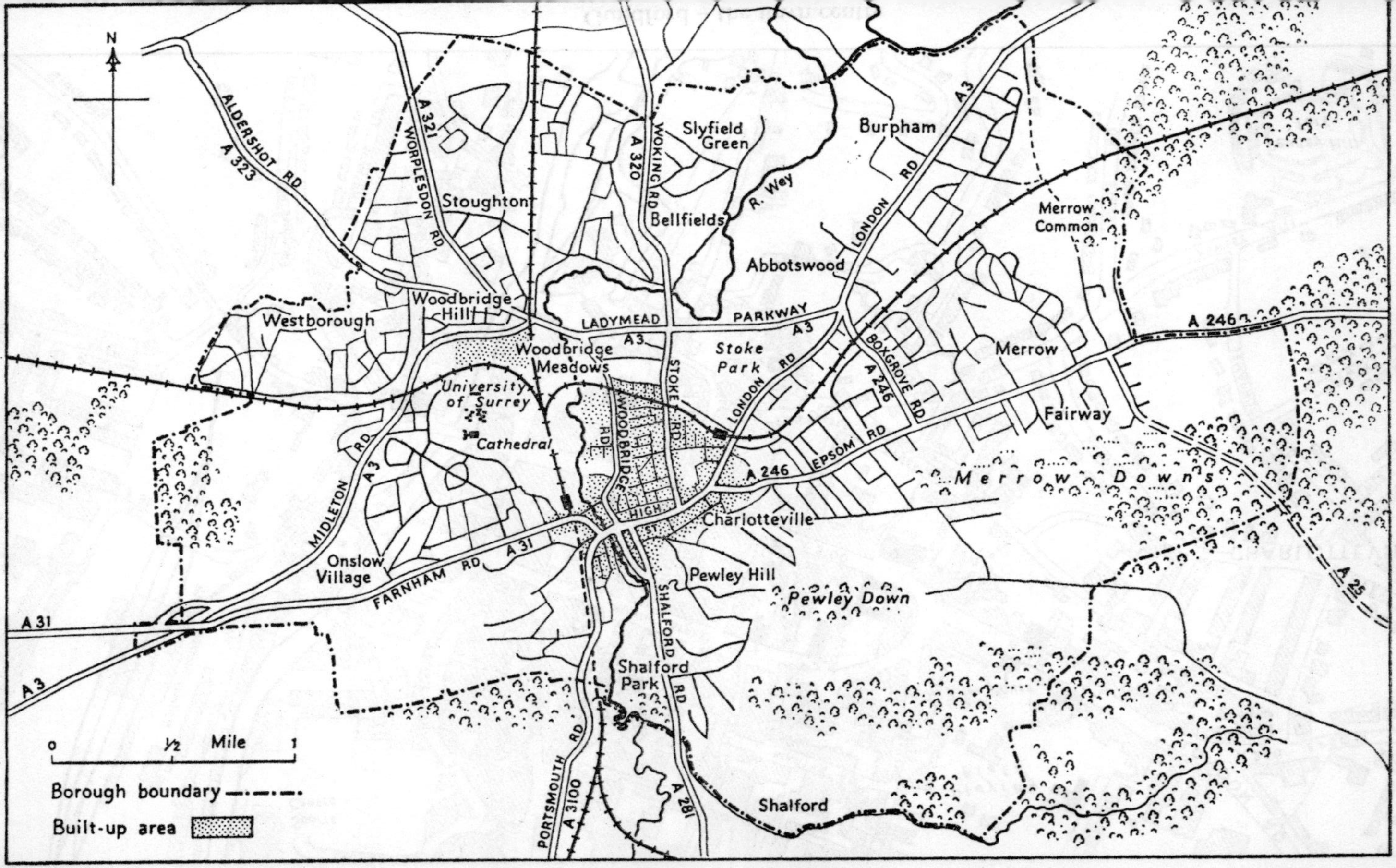

Guildford and environs

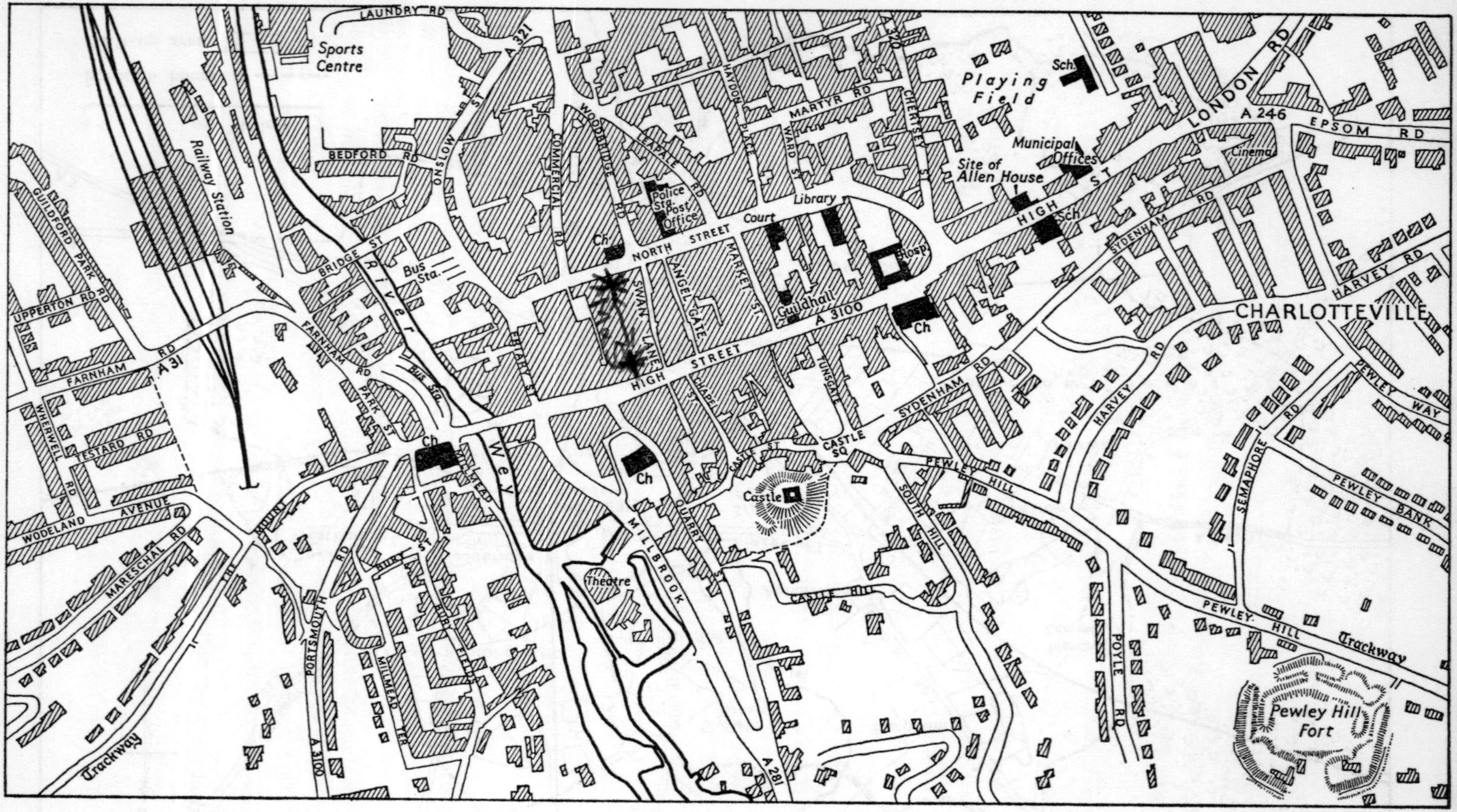

Guildford – the town centre

CHAPTER ONE

Commuter Country

At Waterloo the recorded music echoes in the high vaults, its mood gay or soothing according to the hour of the day. In the evening rush theoretically it urges the thousands onward into their predestined channels to be sucked out of London as, eight hours earlier, they had been sucked in. By 6 p.m. the immense transient population is at its maximum, some 40,000 people passing through the concourse at this peak hour, gathered in this dispersal point for the fan-shaped area to the west that Waterloo serves. On average, a train leaves the station every fifty seconds at the peak. Guildford, beyond the girdling Green Belt of London, is accorded main-line status, but trains run to it with metropolitan frequency for the town has two stations, products of the exuberant self-confidence of the railway age, and two lines serve them, giving a choice of trains, the one suburban with its terminus at Guildford, and the other long-distance, with Guildford merely a stopping-point.

The routes divide at Surbiton, the suburban line swinging south-east to pass through ancient villages each with the characteristic bulge created by the attraction of the railway. The line rapidly becomes rural, meandering, the train stopping at every station so that by the time Guildford is reached there is only a tiny handful of passengers. On this approach the town is seen as a mass of trees, the deep cutting through the last slope of the southern hills becoming a green tunnel, and the station itself is quiet, in springtime bright with the blossoms of the over-arching chestnuts.

The main line sweeps in a great south-western curve, passing communities as ancient as those on the line of its twin, but these have been overwhelmed by the flood of brick. Open country starts hesitantly at Weybridge but almost immediately succumbs to the sprawl of Woking, created entirely by the railway and now a dead finger of London poking into the heart of the country. Suburban travel stops at Surbiton: from thereon the train belongs to long-distance commuters, among them the 2,000 from Guildford, some 8 per cent of the town's working population. The number of season tickets issued is an index of the range of possible daily travel and the total therefore declines steeply as the distance from London increases – in 1968 44,000 were issued for travel to Woking, 25,000 for Guildford, 13,000 for Haslemere, 8,000 for Portsmouth. Less than eight miles separates Woking, the last outpost of London, from Guildford, but a great heath between still acts as a fragile barrier. The hills rise from out of the heath and the town becomes visible on their slope.

The train passes through the landscape, irrelevant, but the road is an integral part of it and, following the road, the amoeboid nature of London's growth is made apparent. Apparent, too, is that mundane miracle of human organisation, the ability to check that potential for unlimited growth whose laws are clearly shown by the fossilised communities embedded in the capital. Without that check Guildford and its fellows on the encircling ring of towns would long since have been engulfed, along with those communities that lie within the ring. The degree of absorption is arbitrary so that the heart of Richmond remains intact but only a thin skin of Twickenham fringes the river. Paradoxically, the closer that a once independent community lay to the heart of the capital, the more it seemed able to defend at least some of its characteristics. In Southwark the great George Inn survives essentially unchanged even though the Tabard is only a plaque on the wall. At Clapham houses cluster around a small town-square and a church stands free on the Common; but Balham and Tooting are only names. Throughout the entire area the boundaries between boroughs as ancient as Guildford and far greater in size are invisible except to the technical eye. To most inhabitants, the locality is identified by the name of the council appearing on the rates-demand, to the traveller by the names of the district branches of national organisations emblazoned on fasciae.

The A3 is born just south of Wandsworth and swings south-east to avoid the mass of Kingston, immemorially the rival of Guildford for the title of county town. The road becomes submerged in the featureless sea of Malden, achieving open country at Esher, from there onwards running roughly parallel with the suburban railway line. The Kingston By-pass accelerated the building-flood, but in the open country it becomes clear that it was the railway that was the greatest stimulator of brick. At every station the fields on one side of the line disappear under buildings, but the villages through which the road runs develop decorously. In places, such as at Cobham, where the road comes comparatively close to a station, the intervening area is filled in, creating a locality that is neither town nor village.

Theoretically, it should be possible to commute by bus on a trunk road less than thirty miles long, and the Transport Board does issue weekly tickets. But the service is leisurely compared with the railway, on average one bus an hour running from central London as against a train every fifteen minutes or so. A high average speed can be maintained beyond Esher, but within the conurbation the traffic chaos reduces speed so drastically that the average journey-time is more than ninety minutes, more than twice that of the railway. The private car is used as a commuting vehicle only as far as the outer fringes of London: beyond that, the problem of parking added to the insuperable problem of traffic density makes its use a wholly impractical luxury.

The A3 enters the town limits at the quondam village of Burpham, and over the next three-quarters of a mile is given a dramatic demonstration of Guildford's fate if the by-pass had not been constructed. There was once an independent community here, and at the main road-junction a massive shopping-centre in the standardised neo-Georgian gives at least continuation of purpose. But, beyond, the A3 has totally destroyed the organic links of the village with its neighbouring town. It is no longer a road but a conduit down which a stream of lethal metal hurtles unimpeded. The new building-developments draw back from the road or turn their backs upon it: the old, which were created by it, are now isolated, rendered sterile or derelict. A modest Methodist chapel with handsome terracotta tiles, proudly built in 1888, is now a derelict warehouse, the land around a dreary waste of nettles and rubbish. A tiny seventeenth-century pub has islanded itself in an immense car-park. A row of nineteenth-century cottages stands looking dusty, battered and weary as well it might under the unceasing assault of noise, dust and vibration. On this stretch of the road human figures are rare and appear incongruous: there is no crossing so the pedestrian has the choice of either walking the purgatorial length or taking a chance with the two-way traffic.

Then, at the junction with the by-pass, an immediate change in the nature of the traffic is apparent. The lunatic stream careers off to the right, taking with it the vast articulated lorries, the pantechnicons, the salesmen's cars, the giant transporters. Local traffic, filtering through, dominates the last stretch of the road – private cars, in day-time mostly driven by women and so moving at a civilised pace; ice-cream vans; coal lorries; grocers' vans. The houses drift back to the verge so that the road is again intimately linked with the community and passes on to enter the town at the top of its high hill.

ered track in Farnham and, following the low sandy hills
that lie south of the Hog's Back, comes the river from possibly
The faint of this lower track is marked by several footbridges and
nown...

CHAPTER TWO

The Shaping of the Town

(i) THE OLD ROAD

SWEEPING in from the west is a long ridge of satisfying proportions with a homely but descriptive name – the Hog's Back. A long
spine of chalk, in part thinly covered with turf, in part wooded,
it begins to emerge from the general level near the town of
Farnham, some ten miles away. The land falls away on either
side to north and south with increasing steepness, but the crest is
wide enough to maintain a broad and natural road. At the river,
the ridge ends abruptly so that the road is forced to descend
steeply – so steeply that not until the land hunger of the twentieth
century will houses appear along it.

Further to the south, the river is comparatively broad and
deep, and passes through marshy ground, but here in the gorge
it has carved for itself through the ridge it is narrow with firm
banks and approaches, making an ideal crossing. The natural
road crosses it and immediately begins to ascend again. But
instead of continuing the straight line of march onward over the
lower ground it veers to the right and immediately begins to
climb steeply again, for its goal is not London, upstart among
southern cities, but Canterbury and the Kentish coast. For this is
the Old Road, the trackway following the crest of the North
Downs from the natural arrival-point of immigrants from the
Continent, onward to the open plains of Wiltshire.

A short distance to the south of this high ridgeway, and
running parallel to it, is another track marginally less ancient but
still of great antiquity. Coming up from Winchester, it joins the

primeval track at Farnham and, following the low sandy hills that lie south of the Hog's Back, crosses the river independently. The route of this lower track is marked by sacred buildings, and romantics of the nineteenth century sought to link it exclusively with the pilgrimages to Canterbury. The fact that the river crossing is aligned between two chapels, isolated and dominant on their sudden hills, gives dramatic emphasis to the story; but, though the track was undoubtedly used as a pilgrims' way, long before Christianity had set its seal on Canterbury this lower road saw its own steady stream of travellers.

The development of a dual trackway over many miles of open country is curious and, despite a century of sometimes heated debate, its causes are even now not wholly understood. A long-standing theory argued that the high way was the path taken in winter when the lower way would have been less attractive owing to mud – but that theory was fatally weakened by the simple demonstration that long stretches of the ridgeway were composed of a flint and clay mixture which becomes sticky in bad weather[1] making progress far more difficult than on the lower, sandy track. Belloc, who applied his distinctive pragmatic scholarship and walked the Road as he walked the road to Rome, saw the high ridgeway as the path naturally taken by a flanking party of armed men protecting the travellers on the lower road.[2]

In due course, the western extension of the high ridgeway onward from Farnham became forgotten as the centre of civilisation moved from Wiltshire, but that section of the Old Road which ran along the Hog's Back so ideally met the changing requirements of road transport over the centuries that it retained its ancient identity. It was this section which ensured that a town would come into being, and flourish, at the place where the river cut through the ridge.

It was inevitable that a community of some kind would develop here, for the locality possessed all the essentials to support human life. The river, though modest, was navigable, clear, fast-moving and abounding in fish. In the beginning it could supply the elemental needs of food and drink: later, it could supply a source of energy for a civilisation otherwise dependent on muscle-power – a source so important that the town mill would automatically be the King's mill. The country, though too heavily forested for the primeval travellers with their tools of limited function, proved hospitable enough to men with tools of wood and iron. The surrounding hills sheltered it from the prevailing winds and in time provided fields open to the sun. But other communities along the river enjoyed similar advantages and yet never emerged from the status of hamlet or village: the community at the ford enjoyed one great additional advantage – the ability to trade. In addition to the great east–west natural road, two other roads developed running southward, one on each side of the river. The community became a natural staging-post for men journeying between the cities of the south-east, and though agriculture provided its basic needs it was as a caravanserai that it flourished. Its small industries rose and fell but the travellers' needs remained constant.

There are no legends to account for the moment when a few casually placed huts crystallised into an urban nucleus: no giant or hero or god performed some eccentric action at the ford and so gave his name to the community. In the fifteenth century Malory, dredging through the debris of half-remembered legends to clothe his *Morte d'Arthur*, brought Sir Lancelot 'to Astolat, that is Gilford' where the King was in residence – a story thereafter consistently ignored save that in the twentieth century it furnished a name for the odd commercial enterprise. After Malory, antiquarians seeking to pin down the Noviomagus of the Antonine Itinerary – a place as elusive as Atlantis – somewhat half-heartedly claimed that it might be situated on this river crossing. The township does not emerge from absolute darkness into at least the twilight of a name and identity until the tenth century when, baldly, it figures in the will of King Alfred surnamed the Great – 'To Ethelwald, my brother's son, I bequeath the manor at Godalming and at Gyldeford and at Steyning.'

Superficially, the historical name of the town seems adequate index to the reasons for its foundation, and as late as 1933 a mayor of the town could give official blessing to a story which appeared again and again from the nineteenth century onwards.

'Right back to those [Anglo-Saxon] times the name of "Guildford" was traceable, proving that it was always a town which had a guild – that getting together of citizen traders.'[3] But there are few studies more full of traps than that of place-names, where things are rarely what they seem and where the clearer the apparent derivation the greater the likelihood of error in interpretation. No esoteric reasoning is needed to demolish the 'guild at the ford' legend, however: before there was a guild there had to be a community which presumably had a name, and the one indubitable thing about the name 'Guildford' is that it has always been attached to the township on the River Wey, even as 'Guildown' has always been the name of the green shoulder of the Hog's Back that looms over the town.

At the other extreme of semantics is the austere argument that the name immortalises the true early name of the river itself. This, the argument runs, was once known by some variant of the name 'Guilou' but possibly became 'Wey' out of association with the primeval trackway itself.[4] More attractive in aesthetics and as tenable in logic is the derivation which bears the august seal of the *Oxford Dictionary of Place-names*. Here, 'Guildford' is the Golden Ford, ultimately taking its name from the profusion of marsh marigolds scattered about the banks of the river. Such is the current, and probably final, theory – although the captious can still argue legitimately that the concept of 'golden' might better be derived from the bright yellow sands that mark the lower crossing of the river.

The strong topography of the Surrey Hills created the township and defended its physical identity during the immense changes of the nineteenth and twentieth centuries. The Hills are modest in height and with gentle slopes, but so clearly delineated that it seems as though a mountain area had been scaled down to act as a topographical model. Even if the entire area had fallen victim to the building-fever of the past century it would still be possible to see, with an enduring and unusual clarity, the factors that produced the town where it stands. The axis has changed, responding to the immense social changes that made megalopolis of London, so that the eastward road no longer follows the crest of the Downs but has swung towards the capital. The pivot remained, unchanged until the mid-twentieth century, at the primeval point where the road crossed the river. Asphalt covers part of the marshy southern approaches along the river valley, but that approach still narrows abruptly where the chalk spine once impeded the flow of water. The Old Road within the town limits has been degraded to footpath or suburban street, but its line along the Hog's Back is still followed by traffic, moving with a velocity unthinkable to the first travellers but, like them, bringing prosperity to the towns in its path as a by-product of movement.

(ii) THE PEOPLE

Matthew Richardson of Guildford in Surrey accountant and surveyor, voluntarily makes oath that he did this month [September 1739] diligently and faithfully take an account of all the families and inhabitants then resident in the said corporation and outskirts thereof, as far as the south-west prospect of Guildford . . . and verily believes there are just 536 families and 2574 souls therein *viz* 1149 males and 1425 females according to the strictest computation he this deponent has been able to make.[5]

Such is the clearest surviving indication of the size of the town before the methodical census of 1801 established a basis for positive comparison. There had been at least one over-all census of the town made before Richardson's painstaking attempt. In 1086 the clerks of the Conqueror had swept through England on their stock-taking tour but they, like most other census-takers before the nineteenth century, had been primarily interested in money: who owned what and therefore could be expected to pay what. 'In Gildeford King William has 75 *hagae* wherein dwell 175 homagers' was their bald assessment. Like so much else in the enigmatic treatise called Domesday, the term *hagae* allows of a number of interpretations – a simple house, a complete messuage with outbuildings and land, or, possibly, a close. Close, the interpretation preferred by the *Victoria County History*, is a loose but convenient term which can embrace that concept of two or more households living in a complex which is clearly implied in the assessment – further on it states that a certain 'Randulph the clerk has 3 *hagae* where 6 homagers dwell'.[6]

Domesday gives the number of men in the town who held property, and it is reasonable to assume that these men were also the heads of households. But how many were there in a household? Domesday gives no certain clue, and multipliers ranging from $3\frac{1}{2}$ upwards have been suggested as a means of arriving at an estimate of total population. The currently accepted figure is 5, which would give Guildford a population of some 900, excluding slaves, in 1086: curiously, that multiplier is close to the one which Richardson used over 600 years later to arrive at his total of 2574 people grouped in 536 families. Assuming that 900 is a reasonable approximation to the population in 1086 and that Richardson's figures were correct, the town had taken over 600 years to treble its size.

But this is a very large assumption for, despite his display of precision, Richardson's accuracy is more apparent than real. Doubtless he was as diligent and faithful to the existing system as he claimed to be, but he was hampered by the same insuperable problem that hampered all his predecessors in census-taking – the lack of a unified system which could be applied over the widest possible area in the shortest possible time. His deposition was dated 28 September and so his statement that 'he did this month . . . take an account' could mean that it was spread over several days or, possibly, even weeks. The population was admittedly static compared with a similar area in the twentieth century, but there was still considerable movement. The diary of his local contemporary William Bray shows how frequent and casual were trips made to London: the wealthier citizens spent days at a time in the capital. What kind of provision did Richardson make to account for those absent on business or pleasure? A graver embarrassment is the fact that the outskirts to which he referred were presumably extra-municipal, and their population figures therefore padded out the total for the town itself.

The probability is that the population in 1739 was considerably lower than that calculated by Richardson: the census of 1801 returned 2634 – an increase of only 60 on Richardson's total, whereas the ensuing censuses showed a steady decennial increase in excess of 300. Even allowing for the over-all rise in population and the fact that the census of 1801 was by no means a precision instrument, it is extremely unlikely that the Guildford population had increased on average by only 10 persons a decade between 1739 and 1801. All in all Matthew Richardson's survey, though priceless by its local rarity, can be used only as a reference point and not an absolute figure.

Between Domesday and Richardson the total of the fugitive references to the town implies that it suffered a decrease in size. In 1611 Speed remarked, 'It had been far greater than now it is, when the palace of our English kings was therein set'[7] – a clear case of cause and effect, for the town had been abandoned as a royal residence a little over a century before and the consequent loss of employment must have had a drastic effect upon the still small community. More serious was that decline of the town's wool industry in the sixteenth century which led George Abbot, Archbishop of Canterbury and the town's greatest benefactor, to make his hesitant proposals in 1624 for 'the making of stuffes as they call them, as say, serge, dorincks, durance, perpetuana and other of that kind, which might ymploy the wooll groweing thereabout and exercise the people in labour'.[8] His well-meaning effort to redeploy the labour of his native town had little effect in the long run for, as he well knew, 'it is a great attempt to alter the trade of a towne so farr from the former course thereof'.

But, though manufactures suffered, trade, the constant stay of the town's prosperity, increased. In 1602 the Corporation thankfully noticed that 'whereas the marketts of this towne of late yeares (thanks be to God) have much increased and . . . are dailie like to be greater and greater' it was necessary to enlarge the existing provisions for the wheat market.[9] By the early seventeenth century there were five great inns of national reputation down the few hundred yards of the High Street. John Aubrey, a seasoned traveller, remarked that the town 'has always been famous for its good Innes and excellent Accomodation for Passengers – the best perhaps in England. The Red Lion particularly can make fifty beds: the White Hart is not so big but has more noble rooms.'[10] Fifty guests meant a corresponding number of horses to bring them there, creating employment for ostlers, grooms, corn-chandlers, saddlers: the guests themselves would spend money not only at the inn but also in the town itself. There is little wonder that the number of inns and taverns increased until, by the early nineteenth century, nineteen of them jostled each other in the same short stretch of highway.

The lack of population figures over the greater part of its history makes it extremely hazardous to plot the early rise and fall of the town's prosperity. A tentative graph would perhaps show a steady increase during the four centuries following the Conquest – the compilers of Domesday noticed that the value of the town was greater than it had been, despite the heavy damage inflicted on its neighbouring communities by the Conqueror's soldiers. The departure of the royal household and the collapse of the wool industry brought about a steady but unspectacular decline until the natural advantage of the town's trading-position served to check the fall. After levelling out, the graph would show the beginnings of a rise again, marked by the erection of the handsome Guild Hall in 1683 – although it is noticeable that a wealthy local family, the Onslows of Clandon, contributed a very large part of the cost. At about the time of Richardson's survey there are again indications of declining prosperity. In 1740 the churchwardens of Holy Trinity, 'imprudently engaged in new-building of the church [but] the deficiency of money being so great, it remained many years unfinished', divine service not being celebrated in the church until 1763.[11] Admittedly, Dissent had appeared in the town but it is significant that the citizens could not find the money to rebuild their ceremonial town-church even though the Onslows had again contributed hand-somely.

The accurate population-statistics that become available in the nineteenth century make explicit what had always been implicit: the town's prosperity was governed entirely by outside factors, making of it a mirror that reflected faithfully the changing conditions of south-east England. And the greatest, most enduring of those changes was that created by the railway, for it translated into technological terms the same factors that had created the town aboriginally. The railway rejuvenated.

It was a common urban experience, its effect most clearly shown on that ring of towns, of which Guildford is exemplary, which circled London at some twenty or thirty miles. The railway acted like a hormone stimulator wherever it touched, brick and mortar multiplying at a greater rate than ever before known. In some cases – at Slough and Woking in particular – the stimulation proved disastrous, reacting upon communities too small adequately to withstand it and so producing a species of urban elephantiasis. At the other extreme, where the railway failed to touch at all, such as at Hertford and Old Woking, the town grew by natural increase alone and therefore appeared to be stagnating. But where, as at St Albans and Guildford, the railway approached to within reasonable distance of an established community a controllable increase produced prosperity and yet enabled the town to retain its identity.

The identity of those towns ten miles or so from London was doomed, for the railway merely increased the already terrifying growth-potential of the capital itself. In a desperate attempt to alleviate the social pressures in inner London, Parliament passed the Cheap Trains Act of 1883, reducing duty on passengers travelling between 6 p.m. and 8 a.m. The Great Eastern Railway immediately took advantage, issuing workmen's tickets which, for a shilling a week, would take the traveller twelve miles out from central London at night and bring him back in the morning. Other companies were forced to follow and, inexorably, the tide of houses followed the tracks of the workers' trains.

In 1844 the terminus of the London and South-Western Railway was at Woking – or, rather, at some two miles from the town whence it derived its name. The speculators had dumped the station on an open heath, but so great was the generating power of the railway that the raw community which mushroomed around it usurped the name and identity of the ancient town so that, dowager-like, it acquired a prefix and was known as Old Woking. The new town was an impressive example for Guildford, badly in need of stimulation. In 1845 a contemporary recorded the melancholy pass to which the town had come: 'The present trade of Guildford offers a wide contrast to the view we have taken of its former commercial character. It is now principally famous as an Agricultural emporium. . . . Its grain market has supplanted the woollen mart: its celebrity as a clothing town has passed away: of its manufacture only the name remains: and even its boasted thoroughfare seems on the decay.'[12] But the potential advantage of its site as a focal point of communication was undiminished, and the coming of the railway was only a matter of time. In June 1844 an enterprising company obtained an Act for the extension of the railway from Woking, having raised £55,000 for the purpose, and in the following May the first station at Guildford was opened. That line was later continued on to Portsmouth and, with the establishment of the east–west routes by 1865, the town was again at the centre of a vital network.

Initially, the railroad brought no prosperity to the traders of the town, the great inns, in particular, suffering from the ill effect of a transport system that swept potential clients past the town at a great speed. But building and its ancillary trades again came into their own, first with the construction of the railway itself and then with the construction of the houses that inevitably followed. In 1870 a local directory gave the first clear indication of the role the town perforce was adopting. Stressing the advantage of Guildford as a railway centre it pointed out, 'City men may find in the suburbs of Guildford elegant residences within an easy distance of their place of business. . . .' Guildford, it seemed, was to become dormitory to London, and over the next three decades this was to be one of the major attractions emphasised in the town's self-advertisements, particularly those put out under the influence of landowners and builders. The tendency, established by the presence of a station only partly intended for local traffic, was confirmed and exaggerated when a terminus was built. In 1885 the 'New Line' from Surbiton to Guildford via Cobham was opened. It had one overriding purpose: the conveyance of men who worked in the capital to and from their homes in the green country many miles away. The term 'commuter' might still be limited to a financial transaction but the species had undoubtedly arrived. Following that inexorable law whereby the iron railroad generated brick, houses appeared in virgin land along the line, but here they appeared not in the formless flood that lapped London but decorously, individually, for they were the homes of men wealthy enough to travel the greater distances.

In Guildford the new station, accidentally but appropriately named London Road, caused a brief but massive invasion of labour. Unlike the main-line station, which stood at the beginning of the expanse of heathland that stretched to Woking, the new station was built on comparatively hilly ground and the cuttings approaching it and the embankment connecting it with the main station required the labour of some 1200 navvies. When they had finished, they had created something that curiously resembled a city wall for the high, grassy embankment swept round in a great curve, dictating the ensuing pattern of development. The new station gave, too, a balance to the town, for now the large and handsome villas began to appear on this, the eastern side as well as on the western side where the main station stood.

The town did not wholly welcome the new race of semi-citizens. Later, as community after community fell victim to the long-distance influence of London, the objections were based on the social fear that Guildford, too, would be smothered by the mass of residential brick, but initially the protests were financial. It was observed that the villas tended to be built just outside the town limits, contributing nothing to the corporate wealth even as their inhabitants contributed little to the prosperity of traders. In 1893, the long-drawn-out argument over the future site of the cattle-market produced a lively attack by a councillor on the habits of those citizens who earned their living in London. The market had for centuries odorously jammed the High Street and, eventually, had been moved to the parallel North Street. There, its hygienic conditions became, if anything, worse; and under strong pressure from the Board of Agriculture the Council was forced to consider its future. Common sense dictated its removal from a highway, but a vociferous minority protested that neighbouring shopkeepers would be badly affected. Smells were inseparable from markets, and no one had objected to a little dung on the street until the coming of a daintier class of citizen. And who were these people? 'Principally [they] consisted of the class who daily drove to the station to go to London and, as a rule the majority of that class brought back with them all the necessaries of life from London instead of giving their support to the tradesmen of Guildford.'[13]

But the tide increased and the population, after taking at least a century to double its size between Richardson's census and the coming of the railway, nearly trebled itself between 1861 and the end of the century. Most of that increase was by immigration, the birth-rate of the town being consistently below the national average. For a new class of citizen was becoming established – professional people who, having earned their living elsewhere and supplied now with generous pensions, sought to spend their declining years in congenial surroundings. The coastal resorts were only just beginning to exert their attraction on the elderly: the prevailing ideal was a 'country town' that anomalous term which comprehensively sums up the English attitude to urban society. And, despite an expansion unprecedented in its history, Guildford was still such a town. 'At mid-day, you could fire a cannon down the High Street and hit no one,' a resident later recalled of the town in the 1890s. But it was also connected by fast and frequent trains to London – the City for a man who was working, Town for the man who had retired and yet, still active, needed occasional contact with the wider world. The numbers of retired increased – the Army and Navy in particular contributing a high proportion – until by 1930 the local Medical Officer of Health could state as an incontrovertible fact that they formed a good third of the population.

The expanding proportion of commuters and pensioners, together with a low birth- and death-rate, could have led to the erosion of the very base of the town's identity, substituting for an organic community a dormitory peopled by the elderly during the week and, at the weekend, by part-time citizens whose vital interests lay elsewhere. The fact that it did not was due in part to the national crises of the Depression and the Second World War, and in part to the viability of a community which, though small, had been able to root itself before the immense social changes of the nineteenth and twentieth centuries struck it. In his report for 1911 the Medical Officer stated, again as an incontrovertible fact that the town was a residential area. But the potential for healthy growth was evidently not yet swamped for, turning to the problem of housing, he urged the Council to push ahead with the new experiment in council housing because 'A very large extension of motor manufactory is taking place in the Borough, with consequent influx of workers'.[14] The manufacturers were the Dennis brothers, an enterprising couple of young men who, in 1895, had established their Universal Athletic Store to take advantage of the current craze for cycling and then, with considerable foresight, had turned to the development of automobiles at the turn of the century.

The existing traditional crafts of brewing and printing were joined by other industries, born of the technological revolution, which began to contribute their weight as a corrective to the social imbalance. The Gas Company, virtually a traditional industry itself for it had been established in 1824, was expanding and received a check only by the appearance of the Electricity Supply Company in 1891. This flourished so rapidly that it cost the Corporation £80,000 to acquire it in 1921 – and yet proved one of the major sources of income for the town until the Company was engulfed by the national organisation. Public works made their tardy appearance. The borough appointed its first surveyor in 1864, and he immediately tackled the task of paving the still medieval streets at an over-all cost of some £11,000. It was not a large sum, but much of it went where it was most needed – in paying the wages of unskilled and semi-skilled men who might otherwise have drifted from the town. A massive draining-scheme was initiated in 1892, whose cost of £35,000 proved to be only a prelude to other, more extensive, sewage schemes. Public baths and recreation grounds came into being: private building continued unabated. The sum of all these activities was the maintenance of a growth potential which could provide employment not only for townsmen but, surprisingly, for some of the distant victims of the economic collapse of the early thirties.

After years of steady increase, the population declined slightly in the period immediately following the First World War, the unsettling effect, perhaps, of war service on a generation thus abruptly shown wider horizons. Thereafter the increase continued, steadily but undramatically, until it dropped slightly in 1930 and then, in just twelve months, leaped by over 2000, an astonishing figure for a community which measured its annual increase in the lower hundreds. The new rate of increase continued until the mid-thirties, when it tapered off but still remained at a far higher level than before the decade. In 1933 a report on education noticed that schools in the poorer part of the town were suddenly becoming crowded and put it down to a recent influx of workers: 'One large local firm that formerly employed 600 men now employs 1100'.[15] Three years later the Medical Officer of Health gave it as his opinion that the majority of the immigrants were from the distressed areas, seeking the employment 'which this fortunate town is able to provide'.[16]

Guildford endured its own unemployment crisis, the peak occurring in 1932 when the Mayor, William Harvey, launched his highly original rescue operation that formed a prototype for schemes in other areas. But the peak was of comparatively short duration and, for the individual, unemployment, though frequent, was relatively short-lived. The biggest single source of employment was the construction of the by-pass which had fortunately begun in 1929 and continued through the worst years of the Depression. The government grant which enabled most of the work to be carried out was allocated only on condition that fifty per cent of the labour force was recruited from the distressed areas of the north and west. In addition to the steady intake of office commuters and pensioners, the community now received skilled manual workers from Wales and the North of England. Many eventually returned, but many stayed, reinforcing the permanent labour-pool. The building trade, worst hit of all at the beginning of the crisis, was the first to recover, for houses were still required for that very large proportion of the Surrey population whose incomes were unaffected. In Guildford, the presence of the large body of people living upon private pensions probably had a stabilising effect. A fixed income might be a liability in a booming economy but under the prevailing conditions even small but regular pensions became a distinct asset both to the individuals and, in their sum, to the community as a whole. Retail trade, still the staple of the community though gradually being overshadowed by the developing industries, was largely unaffected. The official minutes of the Chamber of Trade showed no particular alarm even during the most critical period: food, clothing and furniture still had to be bought and the shopkeepers of Guildford were spared the terrible dilemma of shopkeepers in other localities – whether to turn away a hungry man or subsidise him at the risk of joining him in the dole queue later.

By the time that normality returned, the population was stabilised at the highest point in the thousand years of the town's recorded history. Despite the protests of the Medical Officer, the Registrar-General still declined to invest the town with the magical figure of 40,000, the official estimate in 1938 being 39,840. But in that same year the census for the supply of gasmasks, harbinger of the coming war, showed a population of 42,000. The Second World War saw another steep rise, the greatest in 1941 when, following the bombing of London, refugees swelled the population to nearly 50,000. It fell the following year but continued still at a high rate of increase, following the pattern of the thirties whereby many of those who were forced to come, liked what they saw and stayed. The birth-rate, too, increased, moving up from the 14.53 per 1000 of 1939 to 16.42 in 1945. It still remained slightly below the national average, even in the phenomenal 'baby boom' of 1946 when it reached 20.75 births per thousand – doubtless due, the Medical Officer thought, to the return of servicemen to civilian life in 1945 – but, in conjunction with the influx of younger workers, it was sufficient to redress the balance of ages in the community. Despite increasing longevity the proportion of the elderly declined from

the ominous one-third of 1930 to less than a quarter in 1966, the
last occasion upon which a gerontological survey was made.
At 19.6 per cent of the population, the proportion was still higher
than for the United Kingdom as a whole but, since then, the
establishment of the University alone has probably brought the
figure down to the national average.

Until the twentieth century population was the almost universal
index of urban prosperity: on that simple scale the town had
surpassed itself, for in 1939 the population was more than
sixteen times greater than it had been exactly two centuries before
when Richardson made his survey, whereas the national increase
was only sevenfold. But as the figures mounted so there came the
awareness, as in other communities, that there was an optimum
level: below it lay stagnation but above it lay suffocation. From
the 1930s onward professional planners made their cautious
estimates as to this ideal local population, but their only common
denominator was the tacit admission that the ideal and the
practical were virtually synonymous, that towns obeyed an
organic rhythm of their own. Addressing the new Guildford
Society at its inaugural meeting in 1936 Professor Abercrombie
advocated that the town's upper limit should be about 40,000:
the population then stood at a little over 38,000. In 1945 the
Jellicoe Plan for the borough proposed a population of some
53,000 substantiated a little later by the Greater London Plan
which proposed 51,800: the population then stood at a little
under 45,000. In 1966, when the population stood at about
55,000, the Surrey Development Plan, taking a deep breath, foresaw a rise 'fairly rapidly during the plan period to approximately
61,000 by 1971 and to 67,500 by the mid or late seventies'.[17]
There seems no particular reason to suppose that another ideal
figure will not be announced some time in those mid or late
seventies.

(iii) THE LAND

Matthew Richardson's census of the town's inhabitants was only
a part of his work: more important, both for contemporaries and

posterity, was the survey he made of the town itself, which was published in March 1739 under the resounding title of *The Ichnography or Ground Plan of Guldeford*. The only surviving plan of the town prior to this beautifully executed work was the crude survey, published in 1607, in which the town appeared as an appendage to the Royal Park. The 1607 survey showed a handful of conventionally drawn houses clustering along a highly simplified road-system and was quite useless for a citizenry grown increasingly conscious of property rights.

Boundaries of common lands in particular were hazy – how hazy was well shown by the high-handed action of a citizen, William Wyntershull, who, taking advantage of the fact that a previous citizen had been granted permission temporarily to store timber on waste ground in the North Town Ditch, successfully enclosed an acre of the land himself. He occupied it for some years and would have undoubtedly established himself ultimately as the proprietor had it not been for the long memories of some of his fellow citizens. In 1598 a succession of elderly witnesses came forward to swear that the land 'is and tyme out of mynd hath bene parcell of the wast ground belonging to this town', some of them going back fifty years and more to find childhood memories that would substantiate the claim. 'John Smalpece aged 80. When he was a boy . . . the said parcel of ground lay wast, upon which ground beares were used to be baited: which he better remembereth because that at that tyme hee was there present with many other boys at a beare baytinge. And the beare breaking loose, many boys . . . for fear fell downe into the ditch. An that then hee saw timber there.' Joan Bannister, a baker's widow aged eighty, remembered the occasion when the bear broke loose, she being ten or twelve years old at the time. Among the witnesses was a certain John Derrick who earned for his deposition a species of immortality. He not only remembered the time when bears were baited on the site but also declared that 'When he was a scholler in the free school of Guldeford, he and several of his fellows did runne and play there at crickett and other plaies' – supposedly the first recorded mention of the game of cricket in the English language.[18]

The standard of the *Ichnography* was such that eventually it found its way into the official records. Doubtless it came as a flash of light after the obscure appeals to octogenarian memories, but even so it relied heavily upon personal knowledge of necessarily transient landmarks in order to define the town limits. The itinerary to which a jury swore in 1741 began clearly enough and could be followed in the present century: 'The boundaries of the said Corporation do begin between master Allen's mansion-house and brew-house, then across the high street directly to the north-west end of the duke of Somerset's house leaving the well there on the west side. Then in a straite line by the west side of the duke of Somerset's garden wall into school-house lane. . . .' But thereafter the choice of many of the landmarks was an invitation to later litigation – 'an old elm tree in the hedge of mrs Ede's garden . . . a pollard tree next the London road . . . a cross cut in an elm board. . .'. In the open fields compass directions were given in a manner that would have taxed the ability of a mariner – 'west of mr Steer's field, then turn a circular corner north-west, then walk eastward on the north side of the south hedge. . .'.[19] In the nature of things most of the landmarks would decay in time, or be removed – not always innocently – so that the laborious task of beating the bounds was a very real civic necessity for very many years after Richardson had accurately surveyed the town centre.

A comparison between the *Ichnography* of 1739 and the Ordnance Survey Sheets of the same area for 1963 reveals in graphic form what was implicit in the written records: the town was astonishingly resistant to change, its centre entering the late twentieth century in a form that had endured for at least three centuries on the evidence of the buildings, and for a far greater period on the evidence of the road system. A twentieth-century traveller could find his way across the heart of the town using the *Ichnography* alone, for it was based on a street plan that was dictated by the changeless power of topography. The primeval entrance from the west appears, under the name of The Mount, in both plans: its exit on the south-east has become the Road to Dorking on the *Ichnography* and Pewley Hill, ending in a footpath, on the Ordnance Survey. In the twentieth, as in the eighteenth, century, the only entrance from the south still runs below the Castle which once guarded it: only its last few hundred yards were realigned – as late as 1961 – to rationalise the entrance according to current concepts. On the east the road forks and, bearing the same names, continues to the same destinations: the north-east entrance, too, remains unchanged though somewhat diminished in importance. Only on the north-west has the logic of the system been totally destroyed, for here the long-protected lands of the Royal Park and the Friary left a vacuum which was inevitably filled in the building fever of the nineteenth century. The railway itself, though greedy of land, was clear-cut in its depredation: the destruction of continuity was caused by a road system imposed on a small and already mature area. The steep descent from the Hog's Back, though negotiable by a horseman or a man on foot, proved dangerous for coaches, and in the late eighteenth century the natural road was diverted slightly to descend by the easier slope on the north side of the ridge. There it encountered the ancient road to the king's manor house and so entered the town decorously enough. But in 1882 a second bridge was thrown across the river to develop the suddenly valuable open lands of the Friary. The once decorous road from Farnham was swollen, the area was chopped up to accommodate the increased volume of traffic, and what remained viable has been obliterated by a bus station.

Along the line of the High Street the great inns have disappeared, with the exception of the Angel, but their long narrow sites influenced the design of the buildings, ensuring a continuity of plan. Distinctively, gardens remain and their survival is, perhaps, the most remarkable of all and the most powerful evidence of the slowness of change. Each of the three churches maintain their God's Acre in the ancient form, though burials in the town ceased in 1855 and a footpath goes past the tombs of Holy Trinity to the looming car-park. But the immense power of religious emotion would necessarily keep the graveyards intact, while the gardens were defended by nothing more than their owners' liking for a touch of green, and should have fallen easy victim to the building boom. But it was cheaper to build on virgin land only a few minutes' walk away from the built-up area and so the gardens survive in a variety of forms, but still relevant to the buildings they graced. The garden of the Duke of Somerset's house is a tiny paved square at the foot of a tumbling wilderness: the riverside gardens that swept down from Quarry Street have been islanded by the new road: the garden of the Grammar School is asphalted in part: that of the Town Hall seems like a window box, so set around is it by brick walls, but each adds its quota to the sum of green and of continuity.

Of the major buildings the Friary and the Spital House alone have disappeared, though the beautiful gardens of the Spital with their immense trees survived until 1934; and the Friary Yard remained, though as a decrepit area littered with temporary hutments, until 1970. The siting of the major buildings, though initially dictated by the shape of the town, now acts as a kind of splint to the High Street for, antiquarian piety preserving what religious piety or commercial pride erected, the Street must continue to run between them. The curious dog-leg of the Upper High Street – created by the aligning of smaller buildings with the greater masses of the Grammar School and Somerset House – has been smoothed but is still discernible. The *Ichnography* gives two names for this section of the High Street, regarding it as quite distinct from the lower half, and though the names have been abandoned the differing character is maintained, intangible but real, so that shop premises stay empty for months in the upper half while waiting-lists form for those in the lower half.

The total area of the town remained little changed for over 150 years after the publication of the *Ichnography*. The few expansions of the boundary were piecemeal, taking in a few acres here and there on a completely *ad hoc* basis. But with the increase of residential building on the outskirts in the latter half of the nineteenth century, the Corporation was forced to consider an over-all plan. The current casual system was obviously unsatisfactory: how unsatisfactory was made abundantly clear in 1891 when the Corporation clashed with Onslow of Clandon, the major neighbouring landowner. Some twenty acres of land were required for a sewage farm and Onslow's agents, instead of selling at the price of farmland, insisted on £200 per acre, the current price for building-land – with the additional clause that, should the Corporation resell any of the land over the next twenty years, the Clandon Estate would have first refusal at the same price for which the land had been sold, despite the fact that land prices would have soared in the meantime.

The Onslows of Clandon had been not merely good but generous neighbours of the Borough over many generations, and the uncharacteristic action was probably due to the fact that the current Lord Onslow was then serving in New Zealand as Governor. The *West Surrey Times*, the most forceful and outspoken of the local newspapers, admitted this in putting the case for the Corporation.

> We are loath to believe that Onslow is privy to it. . . . He is reported to be favourably impressing aboriginees who have never before gazed upon the Queen's Representative [but] there is apparently a difference between Onslow as Governor of New Zealand and the same peer as the Lord High Steward of the Borough of Guildford. It is a very hard bargain indeed. We ourselves have the less hesitation in expressing this opinion because we have always refused to join in the hue and cry which some persons strive to raise indiscriminately over all transactions the town may have with Lord Onslow.[20]

The *Times* went on to make the point that the selling-price was based on the argument that the Corporation would itself raise the value of the land by building on and near it. There was no point in attempting compulsory purchase, for the existing system was a two-edged weapon: the town had to have a new sewage-farm.

> We are at Lord Onslow's mercy. . . . And even though the full pound of flesh may not have been exacted, some of us will feel that to Lord Onslow or his advisers we owe a very striking proof of the need for the cheaper and simpler means of compulsory land purchase for public purposes which a Liberal Administration will at no distant date confer upon our local governing bodies.[21]

Land purchase was a perennial problem: more recent and more

pressing was the problem of increased building on the outskirts. In 1901 the Medical Officer noted that the census showed only a small increase of 1618 over the past ten years due, he thought, to the fact that the existing 607 acres of the town were now all built over. Nevertheless, there was a large number of unoccupied houses in the Borough itself, while the building both of large villas and artisans' cottages just outside the Borough limits was continuing apace.[22] The Corporation therefore put forward proposals for an extensive over-all increase, having its eye particularly on the wealthy development that had taken place in the adjoining village of Merrow and on that beautiful section on the southern hills known as Warwick's Bench. Strong objections were promptly registered by residents in the two areas and it may perhaps be only a coincidence that these areas, the homes of influential and predominantly London-based people, were ultimately excluded. Years later a citizen vividly described how a Warwick's Bench magnate sat, contemptuously sucking sweets, at the enquiry, not bothering to put his case, confident that all the work had been done. Whether or not his influence spread to Whitehall, the Local Government Board 'lopped off a considerable district known as Warwick's Bench on the southern side of the town, and it in somewhat arbitrary manner, as far as the ordinary man can judge, trimmed off pieces marked down by the Guildford authorities as ripe for incorporation'.[23] Nevertheless, in 1904 the Corporation quadrupled the area under its control, the Borough leaping from 607 acres to 2815, increasing the population by about a fifth to 21,458.

Over the next thirty years there was again limited piecemeal expansion, but the next great increase in acreage was produced by outside forces, the result of the Review of Local Government Areas which created changes throughout the country. In Surrey, however, Guildford was the only borough where a 'general election' of the entire Council was necessary, so extensive was the enlargement. On 1 April 1933, the town more than doubled its size to 7180 acres – this time including the coveted parts of Merrow and Warwick's Bench – and so established the boundaries which, with minor changes, exist today.

The two great expansions of 1904 and 1933 had one important factor in common: although a very large acreage was added to the town, the proportion of additional population was comparatively small, for much of the new territory consisted of open country that had been only sporadically developed. The citizens therefore enjoyed a very high proportion of open space *per capita*: in 1966, with a total of some 840 acres of open land, the average was 13 acres per thousand. Inevitably, almost from the beginning of the century, heavy and continuing pressure was exerted upon this tempting potential building-land. From 1909 onwards, successive Acts of Parliament began to limit the depredation upon the open country. The measures were feeble enough at first: as late as 1930 a local building society could base a massive advertising campaign on the attractions of building new houses on the 'unspoilt downs', cleverly angling an advertisement necessarily addressed to thousands to imply that each house would enjoy total isolation. But public opinion and parliamentary action gradually stiffened that protection of the still open country which culminated in the Town and Country Planning Acts of 1932.

It was natural, therefore, that would-be builders in Guildford looked towards that open land which, now enclosed within the Borough, seemed destined for 'development'. Particularly vulnerable was the small section of the eastward-running range of hills known as Pewley Down, for not only did it overlook perhaps the most beautiful enclosed valley in Surrey but along its crest ran the continuation of the ancient ridgeway. That part of the ridgeway which descended into the town had long since been adopted as a suburban road and its continuation over the down seemed a logical development. In 1907 the Godwin–Austen Estate, owners of the land, actually began to drive a road across the flank of the hill, and about a hundred yards of the road was constructed before the work was discontinued in the face of strong local and national protest. The scar still exists, a planners' *memento mori*, in the form of a broad flat path. But, though the immediate threat to the virgin land of the down had been halted, 'infilling' continued on the flank above the town, and it was obvious that the threat would be renewed. Intermittent attempts to secure the area for the Borough all foundered on the question of finance until 1919 when, with considerable generosity, the local Friary Brewery bought the hill and presented it to the town as a war memorial, the Godwin–Austen Estate retaining the right to build a road.

The matter seemed to be closed, but eleven years later the threat to Pewley Down was repeated in a curious form. In the autumn of 1931 there circulated rumours that the Trustees of the Poyle Charity were planning to build on the down. The Charity, wealthiest and one of the oldest of Guildford charities, owned much of the land on the eastern and northern faces. The northern section had been built over but the eastern was maintained as allotments and was both divided and screened from the rest of the down by a tall hedge.

The rumours of wholesale building had exaggerated – but only slightly. Initially, the Charity proposed to build a road to facilitate development on their side of the hill and, as the development would be screened both by the hedge and the skyline, it was accepted. Then the Charity proposed a modification: the hedge was to be grubbed up, a forty-foot-wide road built along the line of the ridgeway with houses marching up to it. It was rejected: the Council debated the whole situation and public uproar commenced for, in desiring to build the road, 'it seemed that Poyle Charity desired to make use of rights owned by the Godwin–Austen Trustees'.[24]

By a curious irony, the chairman of the Poyle Trustees was the same Leonard Ellis who, in 1907, had led the opposition to the despoliation of the down at the hand of its owners. Ellis was not only a major public figure of the town but was also a considerable benefactor in his own right: he, too, had purchased land and presented it to the town, following that local practice of private generosity which eased the chronic penury of the Council. Now, owing to the interlocking organisations of a small community, he found himself in the embarrassing position of defending a major vandalism on behalf of an honourable charity. A correspondent in the *Surrey Advertiser* neatly summed up the position, quoting the old squib which, it seemed, remained only too apposite:

> A sin it is in man or woman
> To steal the goose from off the common
> But that man's morals must be loose
> Who steals the common from the goose.[25]

But the Poyle Charity had either handled its private negotiations badly or had overreached itself. On 12 December, two months after the trouble broke out, a cold letter to the local newspapers from the agents of the Godwin–Austen Estate demolished the flimsy legal foundations that the Charity was working upon. 'We are instructed by the Trustees of the Godwin–Austen Estates to inform you . . . that they have so far expressed no opinion in the matter, nor have they given any undertaking to transfer their rights to make a road to the Poyle Charity Trustees.'[26] It had been, altogether, a curious affair.

Throughout the critical expansion period of the twenties and thirties, the Borough Council proved to be a steady champion of restrained development, displaying considerably greater foresight than that substantial body of citizens who equated civic prosperity with an immediate flooding of the open spaces with brick. It displayed, incidentally, an impressive integrity, for many of its members were also in their private capacities citizens who stood to make a good profit from development. Grievously hampered by a lack of money, for the bulk of its rates were still levied on individual househoulders, the Council was hard put even to maintain the open lands in its charge and there was a standing temptation both to relieve itself of some of the burden and add to income by disposing of part of the land. Debates on the subject became acrimonious. In 1927, debate turned yet again to the enduring problem of Stoke Park which had been acquired two years earlier and still remained derelict, its future uncertain, while the loan charges mounted and the citizens grew restive. The Surveyor put up a scheme which would, in effect, carve the Park up with roads, establish a massive estate on the eastern side and fringe the whole with houses. It received strong support in the Council. 'We know that we paid too much for the estate and much of it is not suitable for the purpose for which it was acquired,' one councillor argued. 'We have here a box of bricks that we don't know what to do with: the development of Guildford is not coming on the Stoke Park side, but on the Hog's Back side – the Council would therefore be well advised to cut its losses and sell off the land during the current building boom. Another councillor drew a gloomy picture of the decrepit state of the existing open lands in the town, drawing a protest that it was bad policy to cry 'stinking fish' about Council property. A general free-for-all resulted, which was squashed by the Mayor acidly remarking that stinking fish might be in bad taste but the Council existed precisely to allow expressions of opinion.[27] The conservators won overwhelmingly, only two members eventually voting for the dismemberment of the Park.

But though the Council had high ideals it was faced with the abiding dilemma that, if it could not acquire land, then there was very little it could do to prevent building upon it, as the sprawl of houses over the Hog's Back served to ram home. An extension of the southern boundaries to include the beautiful valley and woodlands leading up to the isolated chapel of St Martha's precipitated a crisis in which the Council was belaboured as the supine representative of a philistine community. In May 1932 the Council met to discuss a 'calumnious letter' which Sir Claude de la Fosse, a resident of St Martha's, had written to the London *Times*, imploring its powerful aid to prevent a threatened development between Guildford and the ancient chapel. 'Those who have seen what has happened and is still happening at the Guildford end of the Hog's Back will not need to be told what the fashion in these times in development can do to obliterate the works of nature.'[28]

The protest invited and received a vigorous rebuttal, delivered by the energetic young Mayor, William Harvey, whose letter to *The Times* gave a vivid picture of a town embattled against a rising flood of brick. 'It should be made clear that the Surrey County Council, who have recently taken wide powers to preserve beauty spots, recommended to the Ministry of Health that the area should be entrusted to the Guildford Borough and nothing was further from their thoughts and ours than "development".'

Guildford, far from building indiscriminately, was doing all in its power to exert a brake.

> The Borough has, during the past few months, purchased at a cost of £15,000 the whole slope of the hillside from the Hog's Back in order to ensure that the greensward which makes such a delightful background to the town shall not be built upon for all time . . . it has recently bought Stoke Park for £42,500 and propositions for building of any kind on it have been severely defeated on the Council.

Harvey rejected the insinuation that a beauty spot in the care of the Borough was less safe than in that of a rural authority, and shrewdly drove the point home by remarking that 'the crest of the hillside immediately facing St Martha's – but outside the Borough – has been allowed to be covered by houses along its entire length. In Guildford, the spoliation of rural beauty would be as hotly resisted as in any area of the country – even to the shedding of money which is, after all, the acid test.'[29]

Initially, the town had been fortunate in that there had been sufficient open ground for the railway to come close to the heart and stimulate prosperity, while remaining distant enough to prevent the physical degradation that seemed inseparable from it. The town was fortunate again in that the great expansion of roads and houses that marked the late twenties and thirties, took place after the bitter lesson of unrestricted growth had been learned elsewhere. The clearest possible evidence of this was proved during the construction of the by-pass. At the official opening in July 1934, Chuter Ede, Chairman of Surrey County Council, frankly admitted the planning failure in the matter of the infamous Kingston By-pass.

> Their earliest efforts in making bypass roads for Kingston and Sutton had resulted in devastating strings of ribbon development. They projected a bypass: they provided a by-word. Thoroughly aroused by this deplorable experience, and in earnest of that repentance, the County Council took energetic steps to prevent the perpetration of further horrors.[30]

The Guildford By-pass was still in process of construction when the Surrey County Council Act of 1931 was passed which not only gave the Council power to limit access to the new road, but to control all new building within 200 feet of it. Public opinion again reinforced parliamentary action. In contrast to the building of the railway, when there had been feverish attempts either to sell land for development or to prevent it being sold, local landowners gave land, or sold it at much reduced prices, to enable a continuous frontage to be created, so renewing the natural scenery through which the great road passed.

The task of control was probably rendered more complex initially by the fact that the bulk of building was still carried out by individuals or small local groups, but ultimately the fragmentation was itself a species of protection. The days of the great development companics, with their national interests and immense funds that enabled them to wage long legal battles, still lay in the unimaginable post-war future. Piratical forays into the open lands was still a commonplace, but normally could be disposed of summarily under the existing planning regulations. Considerable light was thrown upon the technique of these forays, when, in August 1931, an enquiry was conducted regarding the plans of an enterprising builder who proposed to 'add to the general amenities' by building bungalows along Halfpenny Lane. The bungalows 'were the most beautiful thing he could get that were likely to attract people who might have been aristocratic and were now in poor circumstances', he claimed at the enquiry. Pressed to describe this 'most beautiful thing' somewhat more precisely, with some diffidence he stated that they were made of 'asbestos sheeting on a timber frame with an asbestos tiled roof'. The point gained, the authority's counsel turned to highlight a lucrative practice that had gained considerable ground in recent years. 'Would it not be possible for an unscrupulous person who bought a portion of unrestricted land to hold to ransom the adjoining owners by letting it be known to them that he was going to put up something very different from what they had? I make no accusation, but suggest the possibility.' The builder denied the implied accusation of blackmail, but a witness later made that accusation both explicit and well founded. 'His son-in-law acted in the same way, and I was forced on the eve of his completing the deal to buy him out at an exorbitant price.'[31]

The plan of the town as it enters the 1970s preserves the traces of its growth as clearly as the growth rings of a tree. At the centre lies the ancient heart, little changed, but girdling it on the north is the railway containing the nineteenth-century development. On the south that development is contained by the hills themselves, so steep is their rise, and later their natural beauty is itself a defence against expansion. Radiating from the centre to the Borough limits are tongues of developed land, each reaching out to the established locality which initially created a species of gravity and so attracted the tongues towards them. The visual effect of these localities is of a series of gates, approaching very close to the ideal where town and country are sharply delineated. It is shown very clearly on the east where the village of Merrow marks the outer limit. Three roads radiate from this point: the southern road passes through a narrow gap between a church and an ancient inn and almost immediately enters the high and empty downs. The eastern continuation of the main road is held between the same church and the private lands of Clandon Park, in its turn gaining open country immediately. A village lane runs northward, sprinkled with cottages and gardens, a farmhouse and a school whose tiny walled playground gives on to open meadows so that the low wall seems a child's model of a city wall. For the town marches solidly up to the left-hand, western side of the lane, but from the gardens of the houses on the right-hand side open country falls away. This natural eastern boundary of the town is doomed, for the true, legal boundary lies a few hundred yards further on to the east and the Development Plan foresees the land between the lane and the boundary as an 'area for residential growth'.[32]

Even on the north-east, where the A3 careers into the town, and on the north-west, where massive estates bearing rural names have swamped the farmlands that named them, the sudden transition from town to country remains. On the west the by-pass curves following the contours, the topography of the town defending it against this, the most destructive of developments. More houses sprawl up the flank of the Hog's Back, but they are invisible from the high ridge whose natural road has remained basically unchanged from century to century. And on the south the hills and the river impose their own pattern and rhythm.

(iv) THE HOUSES

In 1899 the *West Surrey Times* brought out a guide to *Our County Town*. Its style compared badly with the *Times*'s usual vigorous and lively reportage, being in the excruciating 'hallowed stones' formula of the newly evolved municipal guide. But buried in the soggy rhetoric were some nuggets of hard statistical fact relating to local water-supply, death rate and the like – the pill which was to be swallowed. The whole purpose of the guide was disclosed, unambiguously, by the large folding plan which accompanied it: the plan showed the town in simple outline while dotted in and around it were areas indicated as being available for development. They were disposed completely at random, coinciding with those areas which three major landowners desired to sell at that time. 'In the belief of many Guildfordians the town has not in the past attracted to it so large a residential population as its exceptionally varied and numerous attractions should enable it fairly to gain,' was the publisher's opinion. True, there was now any number of 'neat, prim, attractive-looking dwellings for the working and lower-middle classes...[but] a lack in and around the town of houses of medium size calculated to meet the requirements of such a class as Guildford and its neighbourhood should attract'.[33] The public – particularly that part of the public resident in London – was urged to come and build houses in Guildford on the spots indicated on the plan.

Something over a generation later, the Greater London Plan described the results of this unrestricted freedom in building and pronounced its epitaph. 'A good deal of cheap and sometimes scattered building has taken place on the west and northeast.

There is a particularly bad example of isolated development just east of the Hog's Back flyover ... especially on the north of the town a good deal of inferior building has occurred outside the borough boundary.... It has suffered more than many towns from sporadic development. Very little expansion of the town is proposed and no encouragement should be given to further suburban development as a dormitory for London.'[34] Well within a single lifetime, the brave new world of the dawning century, with its apparently unlimited scope, had produced a cluttered, graceless reality which either had to be cleared away or disguised as best as possible.

Until the second half of the nineteenth century, the town had developed organically, renewing its parts where necessary and budding off new developments from the central stem. The line of houses followed the immemorial pattern of the streets: in the High Street the medieval tradition remained unchanged with the shop below, the shopkeeper and his family above and the garden behind. As the Castle decayed so the houses crept along the site of the ramparts, fashioning their own structure from the bones of the great building. There was no need for the house-holder to seek the country, because the country lapped the town. In the fifties 'Sydenham Road and South Street was a chalky lane.... Great cornfields came sweeping down to the hedges that bordered it on one side. London Road was quiet, with cows crossing over to browse.' There was no need – but also there was no desire – to pioneer in the open country, for unless a man were wealthy enough to maintain a large domestic staff comfort and safety lay only in the proximity of his fellows.

But with the sudden expansion of population from the 1850s onward the provision of houses on a large scale was seen to be not only a social necessity but, more potently, a financial investment that promised handsome returns. There was a limiting factor to the impending wave of speculative building: the more certain returns came from the building of workmen's cottages, for a man wealthy enough to afford a villa invariably required bespoke architecture. There were some casualties among builders who did not take this fact into calculation, and during the first decades of expansion most of the building was undertaken on behalf of wealthy citizens who could afford the capital investment and were prepared to wait some years before they received their return in rents. In the diary of Henry Peak, the architect who more than any other placed the Victorian imprint upon the town, a fairly constant pattern becomes evident in which a man of substance would have his own villa built – at a cost of between £3000 and £5000 – and at the same time erect twenty or thirty artisans' cottages for roughly the same over-all price as his villa cost, the rents of the one neatly subsidising the other over the years.

It was Henry Peak who laid out the first major estate, beginning in 1862, on behalf of a local doctor, Thomas Sells. The size of the venture was audacious, for the total area of virgin land to be developed was almost as great as the entire area of the town itself, an adequate indication of local confidence in the likelihood of growth. Sells appears to have limited his role largely to that of entrepreneur between the original owners of the land and the purchasers of small plots, Peak's task being to lay out the roads, establish the boundaries of the plots and provide sewerage. Certainly the architecture of the estate, which survived intact until 1968 when about a quarter of it was demolished, bears evidence of a wide range of hands. Peak himself was an able if unqualified architect, fortunately free from the exuberant Gothic imagination of his day and whether his influence was exerted formally through his position as controlling architect, or merely through his professional reputation, the result was a modest, pleasing community, village-like in its atmosphere.

Sells named the estate Charlotteville after his wife and, in honour of his own profession, named the roads after medical luminaries – Jenner, Harvey, Bright, Addison. Apart from its size, the scheme was considerably in advance of its day for, deliberately, it was conceived in terms of a mixed development of medium villas and artisans' cottages. The first major essay in planning on a large scale, it was also probably the most successful in its long-term effects. Again the topography of the town helped to mould and contain what might otherwise have been an amorphous development. The heart of the estate lay in a shallow valley of the southern hills and it reached out to link itself naturally with an ancient lane – the 'School House Lane' of the *Ichnography*, renamed Sydenham Road after the seventeenth-century physician – which ran parallel with the High Street. Most of the cottages were concentrated in the more distant valley, but two or three steeply descending streets carried a number of them between the larger villas almost down to the High Street itself. The true centre of the estate lay far enough from the town to encourage the development of its own life, while the links along a wide stretch of the old town prevented the sense of isolation which was to be a dominant problem in similar developments of the next century. Shops, pubs and, eventually, a large school contributed to the social coherence already encouraged by the physical setting. Charlotteville lay in the parish of Holy Trinity and, initially, Sells had intended that a daughter church to Holy Trinity should be erected among the villas. The plan came to nothing but, ultimately, a chapel was erected at the head of the valley among the smaller cottages. It survived until 1967, its demolition marking the final stages of social disintegration, for throughout its life it had been the prime factor of coherence. Locals referred to it affectionately as the 'tin tabernacle' – an engaging structure in green corrugated iron, looking a little like an alpine chapel with its preposterous belfry, bowered in summer among luxuriant grass and flowers.

For over half its life – until the late 1930s – Charlotteville played a considerable part in the life of its mother town, despite – or, possibly, because of – the fact that it was admirably self-contained. Sells's policy of including villas among cottages ensured that a sufficient number of well-to-do citizens resided in the estate, causing it to be therefore socially linked over as wide a range as it was physically connected. Workmen were present on the committees of its social organisations, but so too were, at one time or another, the Provost of the Cathedral, the Member of Parliament, and the Mayor. Its Cycling Club, founded in 1907, achieved a national fame: its flower shows, by-product of the allotments on the neighbouring hill, brought visitors from miles around and were reported at great length in the local newspapers.

It created its own local charity, its own Working Men's Club: it drew its strength from the town but, being distinct, was capable of working out its own salvation in those areas where the Borough Council was unable to operate.

Charlotteville remained as a single, viable community until the Second World War. Thereafter, it broke into two. The villas in the lower half that connected it with the town fell victim to the hunger for office space or were converted into flats: the cottages among them were demolished as part of a major municipal development scheme. Deprived of the social and physical link, the centre turned in on itself. It could, perhaps, have continued to survive as a self-aware, self-helping community had it not been for the startling rise in house values and cost of maintenance. The majority of the cottages had been rented, but, tacitly, it had been expected that each would pass from one generation to the next in the same family, and in some of the cottages continuity extended over three generations. But gradually, as the older tenants die or move out, the properties are being sold off to immigrants. Physically, the village character remains, together with some of the institutions, but the essential heart has gone with the people who made it.

The immediate and obvious success of the Charlotteville venture stimulated other schemes so that by the end of the nineteenth century all available land, both within and just outside the Borough, had been developed. None of the new estates was as satisfying an urban creation as its exemplar but the individual cottages were solid, decent homes. Most of the builders were local men, susceptible to public opinion in the still small community, and the town escaped the worst scourge of jerry-building. The fact, too, that estates were built in small clusters, dictated by the availability of land close to the town centre, ensured that the nightmare vista of endless rows of identical houses – a commonplace of the day – was absent. Charlotteville had been able to develop its identity because of its size: a large element of luck, in the shape of its topography, prevented that very size from defeating its object. When the neighbouring landowners entered the market at the turn of the century the effect of additional development land became immediately obvious in the sprawl castigated by the Greater London Plan.

Ironically, it was in the confident opening months of the new century, when foundations were appearing in acres of virgin land, that the ominous phrase 'housing problem' was first heard. In 1902 the Medical Officer of Health noted down in his report the two-word phrase which was to preoccupy local government throughout the kingdom for the next half-century: the problem, he thought, was caused largely by the high price of building-land and the proliferation of building byelaws which caused high rents and consequent overcrowding. However, Guildford was relatively free of 'slums' – another new word which self-consciously he placed in quotes.

The cottages of Charlotteville and the other new estates were built on the assumption that their tenants could pay up to 8s 6d a week in rent. All were let, and the tenants rarely defaulted – but there was a very large number of workmen for whom 8s 6d a week represented an impossibly high proportion of a weekly wage. What happened to these people was made very clear in a shock report which the local Y.M.C.A. brought out in the same year as the Medical Officer of Health gave his cautious warning.

The pamphlet *No Room to Live in Guildford* was totally free of either political or religious interest: it detailed, simply, a number of cases which had come to the attention of the officers of the organisation during the course of their work. This submerged population was forced to calculate its rents not in fractions of a pound but of a shilling. In one case a good tenant, paying 8s a week, returned home to find that all his possessions had been dumped on the pavement: a fellow workman had offered 8s 6d for the same accommodation. Rents gulped as much as a third or more of the incomes of some men – even though those rents were less than 8s a week. In order to leave enough over for food and clothes entire families doubled up. In a disreputable tenement four families paid 5s 6d each for two rooms. In a two-room cottage the father and a woman slept in one room, six children of the man and a daughter of the woman slept in the other. It was the probable – the certain – results of promiscuity that particularly troubled the writers of the report. 'Details as to the immorality cannot be published . . . but in two cases the sin of incest has been committed in forms too dreadful to tell. Sufficient to say that we have evidence where even parents have been guilty of immoral relations with their children.'[35]

In 1901 the Borough had adopted part of the Housing of the Working Classes Act of 1890 and now the Y.M.C.A. urged it to use these powers and build houses which workmen of lower means could afford to rent. Compared with the terrible problem of the slums in the great cities of the North, Guildford's 'housing problem' was minute. But the town, too, was small: commuters on their way to the station, burghers on their way to their shops, passed through a festering ring of houses, and now that attention had been drawn to the fact that human beings lived in them public opinion joined its voice to that of the Y.M.C.A. In the following year the Medical Officer was able to report, gladly, that the Council had acquired four acres of land on the east side of Charlotteville and planned to erect eighty artisans' dwellings. But in an oblique reply to the Y.M.C.A. report he voiced the bewilderment of well-meaning officialdom faced with the anarchical element in human society. Most of the overcrowding was among the indolent and the vagabonds, he claimed.

> In many cases they seem content with a roof to cover them and filthy boards to lie on and a few rags as clothes for themselves and their oft-time numerous progeny. Yet these same people either earn, or are capable of earning, as good wages as another family of equal size which perhaps lives nearby in a wholesome and clean cottage in comparative luxury.[36]

One of the immediate results of the Housing Act had been to reduce the total amount of accommodation available. Armed with his new powers, the Medical Officer was able to demand that landlords should make good the more gross deficiencies: some landlords, rather than pay out for improvements, merely evicted the tenants and either allowed the house to go derelict or built another house on the site – at a higher rent. Continually prodded by its worried Medical Officer the Borough Council slowly moved ahead with its 'council house' scheme. By 1906 eighteen cottages were erected in the area acquired in Charlotteville and Cline Road, the first council-house estate, came into being. The essence of the scheme was that it should be self-supporting and though the rents – between 6s 3d and 7s per week – were low compared with those in the free market, they were still far too high for that large number of the population whom the Medical Officer bluntly classed as the shiftless. Nevertheless, 'It is a question whether some provision should be made for this class also, possibly in special dwellings constructed in the plainest manner possible',[37] the 'problem family', arriving at last in the wake of the 'housing problem', was to be segregated, incidentally creating a number of blighted spots throughout the town.

More land was acquired by the Council together with more borrowed money but now, acting as a drag, was the heavy increase in costs and house prices. In 1866 one of the smaller villas in Charlotteville had been mortgaged for £200. Ten years later, in January 1876, it was sold for only £310; but twenty-one years after that, in December 1897, it changed hands again for more than double the price, being sold for £650. By the time that the Council moved into the field costs were established on their upward spiral. In 1912 twenty more houses were built in Cline Road for £3360: just two years later twenty similar houses in the newly acquired area of Slyfield cost £4367. There was shortage of accommodation for even the industrious, decently paid worker: there still remained the problem of the underpaid, the 'shiftless', those who could not afford even 6s 3d per week. Once, they might have made do in one of the 'mumping houses' paying 5d a night for a single bed, or 4d if shared. But these had been progressively closed since the beginning of the century. The outbreak of war saw a social situation which had changed little since the Y.M.C.A. report of 1902.

What had been embarrassing before the war threatened to become catastrophic in the post-war years. The hardly won balance between ability to pay and accommodation available was destroyed and the new Medical Officer was almost repeating the words of his predecessor. Condemning sixty houses as totally unfit in 1928, he cited one particular example showing that yet again the ability to pay did not necessarily secure a home: a shed in Castle Street, housing both parents and their five children possessed only one room and had neither stove, nor water, nor light, nor ventilation, nor toilet – and cost ten shillings per week. But council housing, seen as a tentative and morally dubious solution before the war, had emerged as a workable alternative to social chaos. In 1930 the Council commenced a massive Five-year Plan and, three years later, the Medical Officer triumphantly announced that the battle was all but won. 'The Borough has been slumless at any rate all the six years that I have been here': 51 of the 60 houses he had condemned in 1928 had been demolished and overcrowding was virtually eliminated through-out the Borough.[38] Thereafter, the 'housing problem' dropped into the background of his annual reports.

It was back in all its force in 1948, created by the war and exacerbated by the higher standards demanded by the health authorities and the tenants alike. On 31 December 1948 the housing-list was closed with a waiting-list of 5888. When it opened again in January 1950 the list had been reduced to 3210 – but to qualify even for this uncertain privilege would-be tenants had to wait for two years. The immediate social consequence of the lack of housing available in the Borough was a drastic fall in the birth-rate, declining from the 17.3 per 1000 in 1949 to 13.3 in 1951, almost the lowest point of the century and well below the national average, bringing with it again the shadow of a gerontocracy. The Council responded with another massive programme; between the end of the war and 1951 1192 houses were built, almost as many as had been built in the forty years following the birth of the scheme. But where, for example, in 1912 there had been 35 applicants for 20 completed cottages, in 1951 there were 3200 applicants for buildings still in course of erection. Eleven months later the list had increased by 200, despite the fact that 244 houses had been completed in the interim, and to the harassed Housing Committee it seemed as though the town were pouring water into a sieve. But with the gradual easing of controls, and the corresponding increase of building in the private sector, the highest point of the post-war crisis had been passed: in 1954 the Medical Officer noted a 'welcome increase' in the birth-rate.

In January 1969 the Council owned 4472 of the 18,432 houses in the Borough. At a little less than a quarter of the total houses this proportion, too, was below the national average, but it faithfully reflected the social change that had turned an emergency measure into an accepted pattern of urban life, a change that found clear expression in the buildings themselves. The unadorned cubes built during the first decades of the scheme were, in themselves, architecturally preferable to much of the cheaper private housing where a large proportion of the additional money available was spent in the provision of irrelevant trimmings. But the attempt to cut costs to the bone eliminated all possibilities of landscaping, the houses being set down nakedly wherever there was space. In their sum they formed an important part of the town's corpus, but the effect of the policy was to create a series of ghettoes socially and physically separated from the corporate body. The changed policy of the post-war years, which saw the council house as differing essentially from the private house in terms of ownership, not of architecture, resulted in far greater integration, particularly in the attractive Bellfields estate where the skilled integration of a matured landscape with good modern houses created an asset to the town.

But architectural improvements also produced social criticism. In 1925 the Medical Officer, noting that the 'ridiculously small percentage of bad rents from council houses is gratifying from a financial point of view' went on to remark that a major qualification in selection of tenants seemed to be their ability to pay adequate rent. In the post-war years, when the complex but flexible 'points system' allocated houses according to need irrelevant of income, increased general affluence produced a class of tenant whose income was perhaps greater than that of many private householders but who yet paid less for similar, or even better, accommodation. In 1953 the Council began building houses for sale to those tenants who could afford to buy, but though pressure was relieved slightly both official and unofficial

unrest with the existing system continued. In 1969 the Town
Clerk summed up what was probably the majority opinion in the
town in a speech which showed that the sixty-year-old spectre of
the 'housing problem' had still not been laid though it had
changed its form.

> There will be no solution to the housing problem until the
> policy of subsidised housing is changed. The taxpayers (not
> the rate-payers) were paying thirty shillings a week subsidy to the
> rent of each new council house now being built, and it was time
> for a system of fair rents, with subsidies only for those who
> could not afford the rent. Who is going to move out of a good
> three-bedroomed house at under £3 a week rent to make room
> for those in need?[39]

In the first two decades of the century some of the pressure was
taken off the Council by the appearance of private housing
associations. As early as 1907 the Medical Officer had noticed an
'interesting experiment' by the employees of a printing firm who,
with their employer's encouragement, had founded their own
Housing Club. Their loyally named 'Caxton Gardens' was
planned to consist of some thirty-four houses built on a twenty-
year scheme at the end of which period the tenants would become
owners. The war provided a powerful impetus for the movement.
In 1915 Dennis Brothers, the rapidly expanding firm of vehicle
manufacturers, complained that they could not get the vital
war-workers needed because of the lack of houses in the town.
The Borough Council was refused permission by the Local
Government Board to borrow the £10,000 necessary to meet
the demand and, in a remarkable essay in public and private
co-operation, factory and Council together sought a way out of
the impasse. The Council had land but no money: the factory
had money but no land and, in a sensible exchange, some of the
land earmarked for building was sold at a greatly reduced rate to
the firm for the purpose of building houses, the Council even
passing over the detailed plans that had been made.

The return of servicemen after the war increased the pressure,
and in response the most ambitious of the local associations came
into existence, eventually developing an area larger even than

Charlotteville and one which proved more viable in the context of the twentieth century. The Onslow Village Association took as its model the planning concept of Ebenezer Howard which had led to the establishment of Letchworth in 1903 and, in that same year of 1919, of Welwyn Garden City. More specifically it looked to Hampstead Garden Suburb, for Litchfield, the Association's prime mover, had been closely concerned with the Hampstead project and, later, with the similar development in Liverpool. Lowness of cost was a major consideration and the Association passed from idea into reality largely as a result of that local generosity which maintained a balance between private wealth and public penury. The greatest local landowner, Onslow of Clandon, not only sold some 646 acres at a tithe of their market value – receiving £57 per acre against the £200 per acre of its true value – but also invested some £6000 on mortgage. Herbert Powell, the local resident who was Litchfield's associate, invested another £4000 and the Borough Council, gratefully recognising the value of the movement, came forward with a loan of £20,000, charging only five per cent interest although the Council had itself borrowed the money at six per cent. Later, the Association was able to return the gesture with a literally priceless gift to the town – a long narrow strip of land just below the skyline on each side of the Hog's Back, protecting the town's most dominant feature at a time of feverish building activity.

On 1 May 1920, just ten weeks after the formation of the Association, the foundations of the first two houses were laid and the first completed house was ready for occupation six months later. The intention again was that rents should be kept at the lowest possible level and that the houses eventually should become the property of the tenants. The system worked well: fifteen years later over half of the existing 450 houses in the Village belonged to their occupiers.

The original plan had envisaged a self-contained community with its own factories, small-holdings and public buildings. The plan was steadily modified, mostly due to lack of capital, and it is essentially as a residential suburb that the Village survives. Placed on the conspicuous slope of the Hog's Back its siting was, perhaps, aesthetically unfortunate and duly earned the castigation of the planners of the post-war years. But its tree-shaded streets and gardens and its awareness of contours linked it happily enough with the great ridge. It lacked the compactness, the sense of unity, of Charlotteville but, like the Council's own estates, its very openness was a potent attraction for a generation which, with justice, had come to equate urban living with squalor. The Village contributed strongly to the growing tendency to look upon the suburb as the natural home of the citizen.

Throughout the twenties and thirties, while the Council and a handful of private bodies had been grappling with the 'housing problem', the advertising columns of the local newspapers carried ever lengthening lists of 'Houses and Apartments to Let'. The prospective tenant who could afford to pay above £1 per week in rent could live where he chose in the Borough, free to move in and out of a house at the shortest notice. The building societies were only just beginning to create their immense influence in mass ownership: in the twenties, certainly, most of the lower-priced houses were still being erected as a direct means of investment. As late as 1932 the *Surrey Advertiser* could recommend to its readers, 'In these days of reduced or no dividends, small capitalists might do worse than turn once again to house property as a form of investment and by doing so help in the revival of the building trade.'[40] The same factors which led to the success of Onslow Village now contributed to the formation of rivers of small houses along the verges of the outlying roads. By the early thirties the decline of the old town as a living-area was well established, clearly shown by the heavy decrease of parishioners in the major parish of Holy Trinity. 'The Parish continued to shrink as private residences became business premises and tradesfolk no longer lived over their shops. Many cottages had been demolished, and people had moved to better quarters.'[41] The demand for privacy was the keynote, the hunger for a garden no matter how small, the trend receiving official recognition in a legal brief which the Borough Council drew up during a dispute over compensation for property. 'There is no demand for flats in Guildford.' A particular block of 34 flats, with rents of only 20*s* to 25*s* per week, was an economic loss, and the substantial firm of builders who had erected it had gone back to private house-building. Houses converted into flats were losing tenants. 'People do not come to Guildford to live in Flats.'[42]

The Surrey County Act of 1931 had effectively prevented the worst horrors of the Kingston By-pass being repeated locally, but there was little that could be done to prevent a similar effect within the Borough limits. Houses flooded into every area that was not protected by topography or existing ownership. On the west the steep clay slope of Stag Hill defied cheap speculative building and it appeared now like a green island in an ever extending sea. The more attractive areas in the south and in the west were ramparted by villas: elsewhere there was no barrier.

An extreme effect of the unrestricted building occurred in the north around the ancient village of Stoke. It had been included in Guildford, for all practical purposes, for centuries and yet had managed to maintain a curiously independent existence, both physical and social, an independence reinforced when the railway passed between it and the town. Now it was engulfed by that last degenerate phase of the 'Tudor' revival, in which the social badge of half-timbering was reduced to vestigial pieces of wood knocked on to the front of the house. So swift was the onslaught in this area, produced by the prevailing hunger for a new house on untouched land, that many of the original features were preserved as though overtaken by a lava flow. A seventeenth-century farm-house, its genuine half-timbering mocking that of its neighbours, stands on a road that is still identifiable as a village street. On one side of the street a group of early nineteenth-century houses demonstrates, among the extravaganzas, that plainness and uniformity were not necessarily architectural defects. An abandoned churchyard, almost hidden beneath its luxuriant trees and shrubs, survives to demonstrate in its own way that an open space did not necessarily have to be garnished with 'amenities' to be of social value. Stoke-juxta-Guildford, submerged after centuries of independence, yet maintained just sufficient of its identity to act as an ironical comment on the values to which it had succumbed.

By 1920, the age of the great town-villas was passing into history, rendered moribund less by lack of money than by the drift of the well-to-do into the deeper fastnesses of the countryside and, above all, by that national 'servant problem' which provided a staple fare for *Punch* over many years. In the endless letters on the subject to the local papers there was sounded a note of bewilderment, of indignation. 'Six ladies were competing for a very inefficient servant in Guildford only this week.' Girls wasting their talents in industry were the cause of the current economic crisis: 'They should be encouraged to go into pleasant domestic occupation and not to undercut young men in applyng for jobs.' The possession of a servant was the vital factor in a cherished way of life – or so it seemed in a remarkable suggestion, made in all seriousness, that those who could not find servants in Guildford should emigrate to France: 'French servants may still easily be had. They work hard, expect few outings, don't waste and know many delicious ways of serving food.'[43] The problem was less acute than in other areas for there were far fewer opportunities for working-class girls. But as the opportunity presented itself it was grasped eagerly.

Life in the villas had been, in the main, a hard, dispirited and isolated affair for the predominantly female domestic staff. An example of how isolated and vulnerable it could be was reported in the *West Surrey Times* in 1891 when a builder's wife was charged with the manslaughter of her eighteen-year-old servant. The girl was with her for a little over month and in that time had been reduced from a 'nice, fresh, healthy-looking girl' to a bruised, incontinent, underfed creature who at length slipped out of life after a prolonged coma. Witnesses, both sister-servants and neighbours, trooped to the stand to swear that she had been consistently beaten with heavy objects, fed mainly on bread and cheese – 'admittedly not an ideal diet' – and on at least one occasion had been made to stand in the open for hours on a winter's day, clad only in a thin dress, while her mistress's warmly clad daughter was stationed near by to report if she moved. When, in answer to a desperate telegram, the girl's mother arrived, she was told in so many words that people of the like of her daughter had different physical systems to that of ladies. In a ruling that aroused the *Times*'s indignation, the judge found that the woman, though unusually brutal, had not directly contributed to the girl's death and a light sentence of six months' imprisonment was imposed.

Doubtless it was an extreme example, although the passivity of the witnesses and the judge's ruling argue that the elements were not uncommon. But during the period which ended with the outbreak of the First World War infanticide among servant girls was relatively so common that the local papers, which thrived on a diet of exhaustive and dramatic presentation of crime reports, reported the occurrences only briefly, and usually compassionately. The crime invariably arose out of the attempt to conceal an illegitimate birth which would not only result infallibly in the dismissal of the girl, but would bar her from further employment in the field. Few actively desired the life of a domestic, and these desperate attempts to remain one was indication enough of the economic forces which kept the villas staffed.

But, though their lifeblood was being drained away from them by the rise in the over-all standard of living, the villas proved highly tenacious of life. Long after their London counterparts had fallen victim first to multiplicity of ownership, and then to rebuilding of areas, a very high proportion of the Guildford villas remained – and remains – in single occupation although, with increasing frequency, a house intended for a dozen people might be inhabited by a single old man or woman. The rise of service industries in part compensated for the lack of servants – in 1919 a local laundry began life with thirty-three employees and no vehicles: seven years later it employed 113 people and ran six vans. Young girls might eagerly grasp the opportunity to work in office or factory but their mothers, including members of the largest population of widows ever recorded, were glad enough to supplement a meagre income. The maid was metamorphosed into the 'daily' even as the carriage gave place to the hired car, run by a young man eager to turn his war service to some profit. The homes of innately conservative people, linked to the considerable reservoir of private wealth that, despite taxation, characterised the area, the villas survived on into an alien era. The enormous structures, seemingly designed to withstand prolonged siege, survived even the departure of their last owners. In most cases it was cheaper to honeycomb them with offices and flats, rather than demolish and build afresh. It was not until late in the second post-war years that new building-techniques, backed with immense funds and conditioned to think in terms of hundreds of acres and thousands of houses, began to make serious inroads into the ranks of the dinosaurs, eager to get at the ground upon which they squatted.

The primary enemy of the villa was its smaller counterpart and ultimate inheritor, the detached and semi-detached town-house costing between £1000 and £4000 which began to be erected in the mid 1920s. They followed the line of the villas, particularly those in the eastern part of the town, partly because of the social cachet already established by the villa but also because the grounds of the villas provided the largest areas of desirable sites still available. In 1924 a single villa in Boxgrove on the east of the town provided sites for forty-eight houses to be erected at an over-all cost of between £60,000 and £70,000. From now onwards, comparatively vast sums of this order were to be commonplace, betokening the passing of the small-time speculative builder, his place taken by the large, frequently national, organisation. There were now more people wealthy enough to demand a 'house of character in a desirable area' but correspondingly fewer who could indulge personal idiosyncracies through the medium of a personally retained architect. The speculators benefited financially, a single plan now serving as a basis for many houses; but so did the town benefit architecturally. By a curious and fortunate quirk the fashion for the more expensive houses echoed something of the indigenous character – in particular the use of tiles on exterior walls – contrasting strongly and favourably with the ragged 'Tudor' of the cheaper houses lining the established roads.

In the hilly southern district, particularly along the slopes of the river valley, custom-built houses continued to appear. Here the difficulties of building on steep ground, in part honeycombed with chalk quarries, together with the rigorous official control exerted over the beautiful area, resulted in a very low density of expensive houses. Many were merely expanded versions of the smaller houses in the east, but some, too, echoed the panache of the early villas, making of the area a kind of permanent exhibition of architectural fashion from the time of Edward VII onwards.

In 1935, during the controversy regarding the siting of the Cathedral, its architect contributed to the defence by pointing out that, because of the prevailing south-west winds, English towns developed their social side westward, the east becoming industrial. Almost immediately, the town again gave the lie to an expert by developing heavily towards the east as the new houses absorbed the grounds of the old villas. By the 1960s the tide towards the suburbs had, very slightly, started to return. The Council gave it encouragement by erecting tower flats, new prestige-symbol of municipalities, where the Old Road entered the heart of the town, and dotting smaller developments around on the site of obsolescent buildings in the established central areas. The amount of land available remained constant while steadily the population rose and, dictated by that unalterable equation, fashion perforce changed. An ancient style appeared under a new name, the 'terrace house', known now as the 'town house', frugal of space so that a dozen of them could appear where one modest-sized detached house had once stood. At first unobtrusive, by the end of the 1960s the relaxation of density regulations had resulted in a perceptible change in the pattern of the old town itself. It was less beneficial in the favoured area of the southern hills where buildings, once almost hidden among the trees of the large gardens, now became increasingly visible. But in the urban centre the crisp new houses brought back life, restoring part of the function of a town.

CHAPTER THREE

The Catalysts

(i) THE KING'S CASTLE

SOME time at the close of the ninth or the opening of the tenth century, Saxon military engineers descended upon the King's manor of Guildford intent upon creating a defensive fortification that would command the crossing of the routes. The place possessed an outstanding natural feature ready-made for a fortress, for on the eastern side of the river a kind of platform jutted out from the long flank of the down. Viewed from the river, the platform would have appeared as a low cliff perhaps twelve feet high at the centre but dropping to north and south in obedience to the curve of the platform itself. Ascending this cliff, the platform would be seen running back to join the down, rising as it did so but not so steeply as the fall of the down itself. The builders would therefore have the initial advantage of height on three sides – a cliff where the platform faced the river and a slope to north and south.

At the highest point of the platform where it joined the slope of the down, the builders began to excavate an immense ditch. Ideally it would have been circular, but the slope of the platform towards the river meant that the lower segment of the circle shallowed out so that, in effect, a semi-circular ditch was dug. The excavated earth was piled up in the middle so that eventually a truncated cone was formed, with a base of some 200 feet across. Resting as it did upon a slope rising to the east, the western face of the mound was about twenty feet taller than the eastern face, the highest point from summit to ground level being about ninety feet.

Presumably the builders at Guildford would have followed the normal Saxon custom and surrounded the top with a palisade. Certainly there is no known reason why they should have abandoned this sensible and well-tried defence, but whether they or their successors went further and built a full-scale palace and castle of wood cannot even be conjectured. Folk-memory insisted that they did, and John Aubrey picked up the tale when he made his peregrination of Surrey: 'Here are the remains of a strong castle, the residence of Saxon kings.'[1] But folk-memory also claimed that the mound was built by Julius Caesar and added, for good measure, that the castle upon it was destroyed by Danes who set up 'immense battering engines on Berry Hill which is two miles from hence'.[2] Whatever its dimensions might have been, by the year 1036 it could only have provided the most limited accommodation, for when Earl Godwin entered the town in that year with the royal prince Alfred he was obliged to find billets in the town for his soldiers.

It was on this occasion that the town briefly entered recorded history again, bathed in an incongruously lurid light. Except for that passing mention in the will of Alfred the Great over 130 years before, no one had troubled to record its existence. It owed now its notoriety to the same cause that had brought about its existence and continued to nurture it. The town was a staging-post, an immediately accessible place to which Godwin could bring the Atheling Alfred and his bodyguard, *en route* either to Winchester or London.

The story of the massacre of the bodyguard in Guildford is clear in detail, but obscure and confused in context, so contradictory are its chroniclers, urged to partisanship by fear or loyalty. Despite its impressive documentation its very occurrence has been denied, the extreme in silent criticism being provided in the late nineteenth century when an eminent Surrey antiquarian declined to insert even a précis into his history because 'our own faith in monkish records is so small that we do not deem it necessary herein to discuss the matter'.[3] The cavalier act earned its reward some sixty years later when, in 1929, traces of a cemetery were discovered in the garden of one of the newly built houses on the Hog's Back.

Subsequent excavations produced 222 skeletons, less than a third of which had been decently interred at a proper depth and with their gravegoods which served to date them as being from the late sixth century. But the vast majority of the bodies had been buried so casually that in many cases the skeletons were less than eighteen inches below ground and some had suffered damage from ploughshares passing through them. The sixth-century graves had been properly spaced and aligned: the later graves were at all angles. Some of them had been dug across the deeper, older graves: most contained multiple burials – two, three or even four bodies having been pitched into hastily dug pits. A few of the skeletons may have been those of common male-factors, for a gallows stood at Guildown from time immemorial, but the number quite eliminated the possibility that this was exclusively a criminals' burying-ground. Far more conclusive was the manner in which the victims had met their deaths. They had been butchered, some speared with their hands tied behind their backs, others beheaded, and the skeletons of others again bore evidence of a brutal and insensate hacking that could not have been simply the product of a military engagement. The inescapable conclusion is that these men were the victims of a massacre, and the only massacre recorded in the vicinity of the town is that of the wretched bodyguard of the Atheling Alfred in 1036.[4]

The incident arose out of the confusion that had fallen upon the land with the death of Canute. There was a king, Canute's dubiously legitimate son Harold, but there were also two very legitimate pretenders, the Atheling Alfred and his brother Edward, later known as the Confessor. Their mother, the tough-minded Queen Emma, had married Canute, son of the man who had deposed their father; and now, it was said, she was planning to restore her son's fortunes after their long exile in Normandy. Alfred came to England, the chroniclers ascribing to him a wide variety of motives for his journey. The Anglo-Saxon Chronicler

Guildford from the south-west. Watercolour by Henry Prosser, 1865

THE HIGH STREET
Eastern prospect. Lithograph by Henry Prosser, 1870
Western prospect

The Corn Exchange. Engraving by Henry Harling, 1819

Detail of the Guildhall

The Coaching
Inns
The Lion
(*demolished 1957*)

Now
Woolworths

The Angel

The town mill

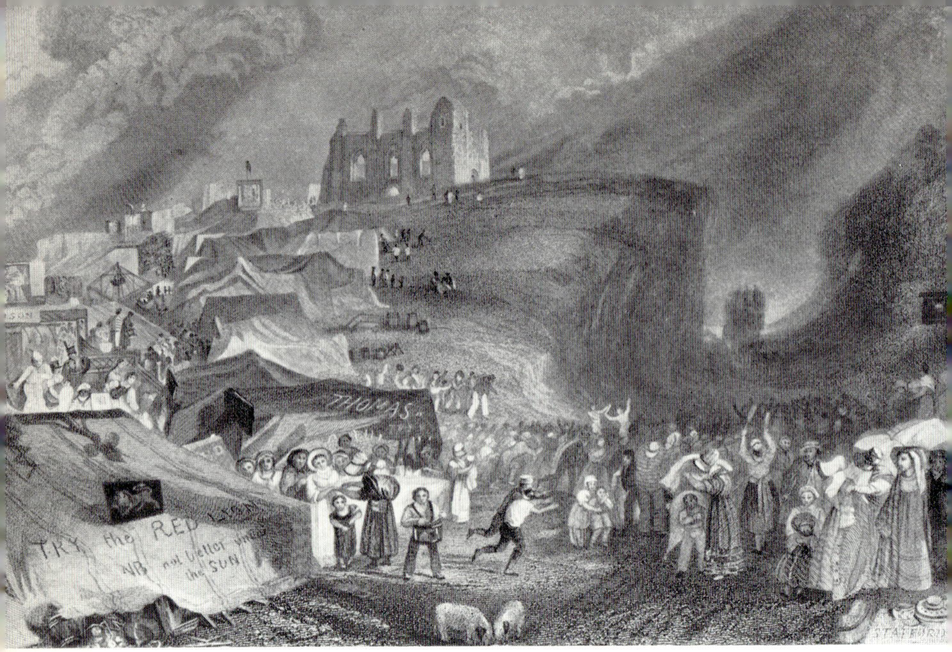

ST CATHERINE'S HILL

St Catherine's Fair. Engraving after J. M. W. Turner, 1832

Aerial view of St Catherine's Hill today

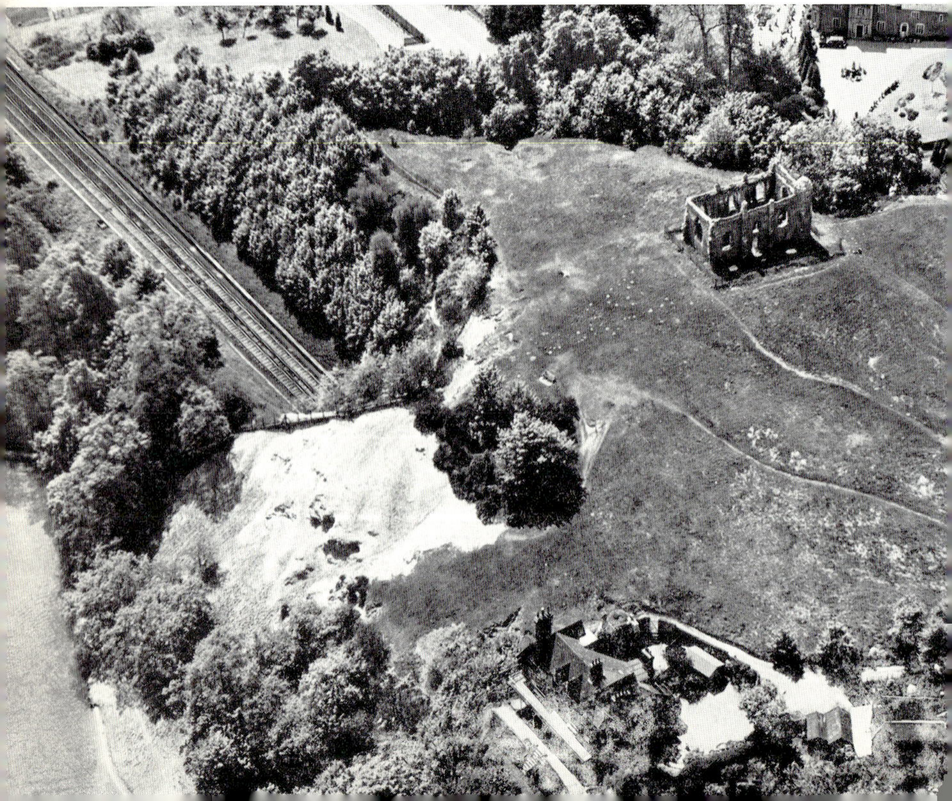

John Russell (1711–1804).
Mayor in 1779, 1789, 1791, 1797

Henry Peak (1832–1914). Mayor 1899

William Bray (1736–1832).
Portrait by John Linnell

George C. Williamson (1858–1942).
Honorary Remembrancer 1933–42

THE CASTLE
The east face
Wey Valley panorama

says simply that he came from abroad to visit his mother at Winchester and that Earl Godwin arrested him. Florence of Worcester gives a more circumspect tale: 'He [Godwin] detained Alfred as he was hastening towards London to a parley with King Harold, and placed him in close confinement, and of his companions ... many he ordered to be sold and he killed by various miserable deaths 600 men at Guildford.'[5]

Florence was writing some years after the event, but a detailed contemporary account was given by the skilled although unknown writer of the *Encomium Emma Reginae*. Propaganda was his avowed purpose, as his title showed, and to achieve it he did not hesitate to invent and distort. In his version it was the king, Harold, not the much maligned Godwin, who was the villain. Godwin merely met the young prince after he had landed at Sandwich and escorted him on the road to Winchester. They broke the journey at Guildford, where both Godwin's and Alfred's men were billeted overnight. During the night, Alfred's bodyguard was attacked, disarmed and manacled by the King's men and then, in a vivid piece of writing, the writer describes the events of the following day whose results fit in only too well with the discoveries of 1929.

> When it was morning, the innocent men were led out and were iniquitously condemned without a hearing. For they were all disarmed and delivered, with their hands bound behind their backs, to most vicious executioners who were ordered, furthermore, to spare no man unless the tenth lot should reprieve him ... following the example of that murderer of the Theban Legion who first decimated guiltless men. But that pagan, though he murdered Christians, nevertheless ordered that they should be beheaded on an open plain, unfettered by bonds, like glorious soldiers. But these ... butchered the innocent heroes with blows from their spears, bound as though they were swine.[6]

The reasons that the writer gives for the massacre are tendentious in the extreme, but he had no motive for giving an inaccurate description of the massacre itself – all chroniclers agreed that it was marked by an unusual degree of bitter hatred. He does, however, raise a curious problem with his implication that the massacre took place within the town. The execution of the prisoners near their places of overnight confinement was a reasonable action from a military point of view. But why did the executioners afterwards go to the trouble of transporting some hundreds of bodies, many of them in pieces, across the river and up the steep hillside to the old pagan cemetery instead of burying them outside the town? It may perhaps have been a last act of malice, the hope that burial in a pagan churchyard would condemn the victims to an eternity of pain. More prosaically, it is probable that the inhabitants, with a lively fear of plague if not of ghosts, insisted on the removal of the bodies well outside the town, and a disused cemetery was the natural place for them.

Buried in the *Encomium* are a handful of valuable, but tantalisingly obscure hints as to the size and importance of the town. If the writer is telling the truth that it was the King's men who were responsible for the massacre, then the Castle must have been strongly garrisoned, for the stop at Guildford was unpremeditated. Somewhat more certain is the indication of the size of the town itself, contained in the statement that soldiers of both groups were billeted in it. The later estimate of 600 men might have been exaggerated: less than 200 relevant skeletons were discovered – although the possibility is that as many more still lie buried, for only part of the cemetery was excavated. But even if this estimate were halved the town must have been large to supply, without warning, lodgings for at least 600 men, for it is unlikely that Godwin's escort would have been smaller than that of Alfred's. The Atheling's bodyguard was overcome by treachery: but they were soldiers on their guard in an alien country, and an overwhelmingly superior force must have been used to overcome them without a struggle in the town. If the King's men did not do the slaying, the Castle garrison being small or non-existent, then the total for Godwin's force would have to be revised upward. On either view, it is likely that anything up to a thousand armed men were lodged in the town that night, some in the Castle, the rest in private dwellings, arguing the existence of a substantial community.

After the massacre, the town sinks back again into documentary obscurity, the next glimmer of light being provided by the Domesday survey of 1086. By then, the Castle had apparently decayed, for the tax assessors, alert to every source of wealth, did not trouble to record even its existence. They were not interested in the fact that their master himself had initiated a new phase of building on the mound, for that was outside their brief. After Senlac, William had marched northwards to London and, finding the city still defiant, wheeled left and followed the Thames as far as Weybridge. There, the army struck southward on to Guildford, the destruction created by its passing causing that fall in post-Conquest values which Domesday later meticulously noted, incidentally providing a means to trace the passage of the army.[7] Guildford escaped damage but the nearby hamlet of Shalford went up in flames: presumably the army crossed the river here, for they next appeared in Farnham which, too, suffered heavy damage.

Guildford was not particularly important in terms of either wealth or politics: strategically, it was obviously of considerable value and it was inevitable that the Normans would place their enormous, ineradicable imprint upon it. With that same energy and skill, Roman in its application and ruthlessness, with which they raised their great buildings in every land that knew them, they set about adapting the simple fortification on the Saxon mound. Habitually, they built in stone, but there was neither time nor desire to seek far afield for impressive material. Prestige was unnecessary: what was required was a military shelter for man, beast and provisions in the shortest possible time. The new race of military engineers therefore sought and found the commonest material to hand – chalk. A few hundred yards to the south of the mound was a deposit which, both by reason of its accessibility and of its substance, was ideal for their immediate purpose, and here they began quarrying.

The Normans were adapting, not building afresh, and the simplest way to turn a roughly conical hill into a castle is to build a wall around it just below the crest. Such a shell-keep has to bear only the weight of its own walls: at once it contains and is supported by the top of the mound and buildings can be erected against it along the interior circumference. Here, the shell-keep rose about twenty feet above the flat surface of the top of the mound: inside, there was an area perhaps ninety feet across – more than sufficient to allow erection of the first vital buildings which would provide protection while work continued on the platform below. Access to the keep was from the east, over a causeway that passed across the deepest part of the ditch that now separated the whole complex from the slope of the down.

This was the heart of the Castle, and so remained essentially unchanged for the better part of a century. At the foot of the mound other buildings were erected – domestic offices for the most part – and the whole protected by a girdling wall which, in time, encircled the whole area of the platform. The Castle was essentially a military establishment: nevertheless, over the next generation the outlying buildings must have been elaborated to a reasonable degree of domestic comfort, for in 1136 Stephen and his queen Matilda were recorded as staying in Guildford. Their residence was brief, a day or so at the most, but it was sufficient to establish the fact that both castle and town were deemed adequate to entertain a royal household.

The original shell-keep was built for a clear-cut military purpose – the control of an intelligent and resentful native people by an occupying foreign power. The next significant stage of the Castle's development was the product of more subtle social reasons. By the twelfth century the foreigners were established and semi-integrated, and inevitably began to fight among themselves. For over a generation the kingdom was torn apart as the reigning king, Stephen, sought to impose his rule on men who enjoyed more real power than he possessed himself. The common people suffered – 'Men said openly that Christ and his saints slept' – and when at length the autocratic, violent but competent Henry II succeeded the wretched Stephen the lesser people, at least, had cause to welcome him. Ultimately, they were to remember and execrate him as the man who murdered a saint, but in his day he gave the nearest to peace that men had known since the time of Alfred.

The essential means of domestic control was the castle and

that at Guildford was naturally included in the widespread programme of construction and renovation, the intention here being to erect a keep. Pinpointing the date of commencement of work is now virtually impossible. The major relevant document[8] alludes simply to the fact that £26 was spent on the Castle at the time of the 'young king's rebellion'. This can only refer to the massive coalition of Henry's enemies in 1173 when a determined effort was made to place his young son on the throne. But £26 seems an extremely low sum to spend on the construction of a keep, particularly when it is compared with the £100 spent on works at the Castle only thirty years later – admittedly extensive works but, for the most part, relating to repairs and decoration. The architecture of the keep itself provides no clue. Although over a century had passed since the Conquest, military architecture had changed but slowly: the great changes were to take place over the next generation when returning crusaders brought back exotic new forms of military engineering, including the stronger but more complex round tower. The keep of Guildford Castle could have been built at almost any time in the twelfth century: work may very well have commenced long before 1173 and then been hastened forward by the political crisis.

But though the builders might have been following a species of blueprint as guide to the shape and function of the keep, they made an almost unprecedented departure when selecting its site. Very rarely indeed did the Norman builders place the enormous masses of their stone keeps on an artificial mound[9] and the fact that they now decided to do so is good evidence that the mound had been in existence for many years before the Conquest, settling to provide now a solid foundation. They were not building wholly on made ground, however, for the eastward-rising slope of the platform made it possible to place the foundations of the east wall of the keep on natural ground. This wall was therefore designed as an immense anchor, nearly twice the thickness of the other walls and, unlike them, solid throughout. Part of the old shell-keep on the east was incorporated within this massive wall, the rest was left standing to provide the wall for the inner courtyard.

Now that there was time to spare and prestige counted, walls of chalk were not considered adequate. Quarrying went on at the same site which had provided material for the first generation of builders and the chalk was used for the heart of the walls. But Bargate stone, transported from a few miles away, was used for the facing. The stone occurs naturally in comparatively small fragments so that the finished appearance of the keep was less impressive than other buildings created out of hewn stone, but it was a considerable advance on the old walls of humble chalk. The ubiquitous Roman tiles found their way into the facing, sometimes used as they came to hand, sometimes arranged in simple patterns, and the Bargate stone itself was here and there worked into herring-bone design. The brown stone keep at length towered over sixty feet above the white wall of the shell and the Castle of Guildford, as it was to survive in its essentials, was complete.

With the exception of its capture by the Dauphin Louis in June 1216, Guildford Castle was involved in no event of sufficiently national importance to warrant even a reference in independent chronicles. Documentary references to it are therefore either oblique, occasioned by the fact that the monarch happened to be in residence there when he signed some document, or are exclusively concerned with the minutiae of bills and estimates for repairs or preparation for the King's arrival. Individually unexciting, though important in their sum, most of even these documents were unknown until the twentieth century so that, as late as 1845, Laurence could firmly give the earliest documentary reference to the Castle as relating to the Dauphin's expedition of 1216, nearly 150 years after its construction. Research for the massive *Victoria County History* uncovered a sparse handful of documents which pushed the first mentioned date back to 1173, and in 1926 the local antiquarian George Williamson, after indefatigably plundering the treasure house of the Public Record Office, was able to take the date back even further to 1130. The actual document was, like the rest, unexciting – a reference to work spent in Guildford on behalf of Henry I for the sum of £4 4s.

In the absence of documentation legend flourished, finding particularly rich soil in the bizarre career of King John. Statistically, Williamson was able to show that it was Henry III, not John, who was Guildford's patron king, residing in the Castle on over a hundred occasions as opposed to John's nineteen. But though the ever-memorable John might be dethroned mathematically, he was safe in folk-lore. It was in Guildford Castle that there occurred the event that perhaps gave rise to the ballad, *King John and the Abbot*, which mocked the clergy but showed the King in a generous light. John had kept the Christmas of 1199 in Guildford in considerable splendour, tricking out his household in new and sumptuous clothes, and was enraged to learn that a prelate – the Bishop of Canterbury in some versions – had outshone him. In the ballad the prelate is summoned to account for his presumptuousness, presented with the three unanswerable riddles and saves his head only by the quick wit of a humble shepherd.

Thomas Heywood used Guildford Castle as the setting for a play in which John appears, not as the spontaneously generous king of the ballad, but the ravening monster of later legendry. But it was the Victorian poetaster, Martin Tupper, who made of John a three-dimensional figure and at the same time allowed his exuberant imagination to play on the Castle itself. He claimed that his historical romance *Stephan Langdon* 'might be depended upon for archaeological accuracy in every detail' – though somewhat weakening that claim with the subsequent boast that the massive work 'was finished in exactly eight weeks, reading for the work included'.[10] Nevertheless, such was his capacity for narrative and evocation of atmosphere that much of his details of John in Guildford percolated into local folk-lore as fact.

Guildford was merely one out of eighty-odd castles that John possessed and the frequency of his appearances in the town was testimony to its enduring role as a staging-post. During his brief and tempestuous reign John achieved prodigies of marching and counter-marching over England, and Guildford was a pivot in the south. In the last few months of his reign he passed twice through the town, at the beginning and end of that incredible

march through rebel territories which took him from the Channel
to the Scottish border and back in seven months. His last visit
to Guildford, in April 1216, occurred just before the French
invasion when the barons, leaguing themselves with King Louis
of France, invited the Dauphin into the country. The nearby
chronicler of Waverley Abbey recorded the brief inglorious
epilogue for Guildford Castle. 'Louis, the eldest son of the King
of the French, came in the summer to England and took the
castle of Reigate on . . . the 8th of June and on the morrow
(which was Thursday) the castle of Guildford and the castle of
Farnham the day after'.[11] The barons in the Dauphin's following
did a considerable amount of damage and that concluded the
Castle's military activity in history.

But the potential still remained, and over the next fifty years
considerable work was carried out upon the complex. Military
defence still remained important, but the maintenance bills show
the gradual evolution of a domestic building from the purely
military structure during the reign of Henry III. The locality
took his fancy, and during his long reign of over fifty years he
returned again and again to it. The town benefited incidentally,
particularly through the employment of masons, but the Castle
was transformed to reflect his love of luxury and genuine, though
undeveloped, culture. His master of works in Guildford in the
latter part of his reign was an Italian, the result of that partiality
of his for foreigners which caused no little part of his endless
troubles. William the Florentine appeared in Guildford during
the first spate of work between 1245–67 when he received a
commission for decorating the walls, and thereafter more and
more of the control of the work fell into his hands. The actual
buildings for which he was responsible, together with his own
murals in the Castle, have long since passed into rubble, but some
of his work may have survived into the twentieth century for
there is a strong possibility that the murals in the nearby church
of St Mary's were also by his hand.

In the building accounts the usual bald estimates are developed
at some length, arguing that Henry knew precisely what he
wanted and was determined to get it. The royal family was at

last to be decently housed on their visits to the town. There was to be a special chamber for the young prince, Edward, 'with proper windows well-barred'. The Queen was to have an entire new wardrobe 'with a chimney and private chamber and window equal in width to the two existing windows . . . with two marble pillars and close it with glass windows between the pillars'.[12] Elsewhere, the luxury of glass, both plain and coloured made its appearance: the great hall was to be 'fitted up with white glass lights with the picture of a certain king sitting on a throne and a certain queen likewise sitting on a throne'.[13] It was also to be 'whitewashed both inside and out, and the story of Dives and Lazarus [painted] in the hall', opposite the King's throne, which was itself to be decorated with 'a certain figure with beasts'.[14] A garden was to be constructed for his queen, Eleanor, porches and cloisters built, the chapel repaired and decorated. On its high platform with the beautiful valley of the Wey before it and a small but thriving township behind it, the Castle probably represented as high a level of domestic comfort as anywhere in in England in the thirteenth century.

But with the death of Henry the Castle began again to return to obscurity. His son, Edward I, spent part of his childhood there and joined King John in local folk-history when, in single combat, he defeated the outlaw Adam Gordon and brought him back to Guildford to be presented to the Queen. But, as King, Edward was preoccupied with graver matters than the proper alignment of a window or the provision of a cloister, and the condition of the Castle rapidly deteriorated. In 1332 a lengthy list of defects which went back over three generations was compiled, and by the 1340s royal interest had shifted from the Castle to the Park, a great area reserved for the royal chase upon the other side of the river. A high State official still resided in the Castle but even that link was broken in 1382, the last resident official being the statesman Simon Burley, executed for alleged treachery and embezzlement three years later. 'I was exceedingly vexed thereat and personally much grieved for in my youth I found him a gentle knight and of good sense,' Froissart recorded indignantly.[15] Burley certainly had reason to regret abandoning the backwater of Guildford for the dangerous honours of higher office, the accusations being largely the product of courtier warfare.

After Burley, the Castle became entirely a prison, for in an increasingly stable society its defensive value no longer compensated for cramped conditions. The roles of prison and castle had naturally long overlapped. As early as 1306 the Constable, on receipt of an influx of prisoners from Sussex, had protested that the keep was not adequate and suggested that a proper prison be built. He received a short answer: the King had no intention of going to the expense of erecting another prison and the Constable must do the best with what he had – an open invitation to manacle the wretched men. Pressure became so great that the chapel in the western wall was turned into a cell: ironically, the carvings desultorily executed there by prisoners whiling away the hours became the only decorative piece of work in the entire complex to survive into the twentieth century. Complaints of the keep's unsuitability as a prison were made regularly over the next two centuries that it discharged this exclusive function, finding frequent echoes in the reports of escaped prisoners. In 1381 the Peasants' Revolt resulted in such gross overcrowding that the people of Sussex were permitted to house their own prisoners in Arundel and Lewes, creating a precedent which led to the establishment of their own prison. Guildford Castle was thereafter the prison for Surrey alone until the building of the Marshalsea in the mid-sixteenth century ended its ignoble role and heralded its final severance from royal interest. In 1612 a certain Francis Carter obtained the entire complex on payment of twenty-six shillings a year to the royal exchequer.

By the time that the Castle came into Carter's hands most of the ancillary buildings were probably already in a ruinous condition, for Carter attempted to make his home in the keep, as evidenced by the crude windows of the period still existing in the structure. A Parliamentary Commission, surveying the possessions of 'Charles Stuart, late king of England', in 1650 gave an inaccurate, confusing but, by reason of its rarity, invaluable account of the Castle when it still retained buildings other than the keep. It consisted then of 'one handsome building with a large parler. A kitchen and Buttry beelow stayres, three chambers and two garrets above stayres. And also of one tall stone building about twenty foot square a part of the castle and late used as a cockpit.'[16] Such was the ignoble end of the great keep, so unimportant now that the Commissioners did not trouble even to measure it accurately, its dimensions, in fact, being twice the figure they gave. The gaunt comfortless building proved quite unsuitable for domestic purposes and the family built a handsome house on the site of the western section of the encircling wall. The family possessed the estate for over 150 years and one of them, at least, seems to have been affected by something of the Norman arrogance of the place, the town records bearing a tantalisingly brief account of what was evidently a first-class row between the parvenu lord and the townsmen. 'Mr Carter, dwelling in the Castle, for being altogether averse and refractory to the good government of this towne, denying to do and observe and of the orders and constitutions of this towne is, by general consent disfranchised and dismissed from the freedom and societies of this corporation.'[17]

By the nineteenth century the keep was a roofless ruin and the ancillary buildings reduced to scattered amorphous piles of stone. The entire estate, including the Carter's town house, was now a private school whose prospectus of about 1880 showed an idyllic picture of boys playing where kings walked – and incidentally reducing yet more of the Castle to irretrievable ruin. The school must have been one of the very few in the country that could boast of a medieval castle in its grounds, but the principal laid far less stress on this than on the croquet lawns, bath and lavatory that were lavishly provided. The ruins, indeed, seemed more of an encumbrance than an attraction to potential buyers. In 1885 the Borough Council paid only £2200 for the Castle complex, including some attractive houses, but the adjacent bowling-green with a single decrepit inn cost them £2050, and one of the tenders for laying out the Castle grounds as a public park actually proposed to remove the keep and erect a tasteful bandstand in its stead.

After nearly 300 years in private hands the Castle fortunately had passed into public keeping at a time when antiquarian interest was reviving. The preliminary task of survey and restoration was entrusted to Henry Peak, the first Surveyor of the town, an unqualified but competent architect with a lively awareness of the historical importance of his responsibility. As a by-product of his activities, Peak was concerned to prove or disprove the presence of dungeons under the keep. Over the years fantastic legends had built up, the lack of documentation and visible architectural details serving to heighten imaginative fever. 'If ever there was a place which might excite idle curiosity to search for hidden treasures Guildford Castle is surely one. The walled-up cavities, the unaccountable circumstances of there being no little closets or small chambers in the walls of the state apartments above, and the large dungeon beneath all, with its entrance so carefully walled up as almost to escape sight and yet so originally well guarded [tempts] a sanguine imagination to search.'[18] The unimaginative but practical Peak set about tracking down these treasures. 'Several excavations were therefore made in depth from seven to ten feet, and proving beyond all doubt that no vault or chamber has ever existed beneath the present chamber.' Nothing of interest was found, apart from a large quantity of bones and a religious token.[19]

The Castle was undoubtedly the most impressive piece of property that the town had acquired in centuries and Peak's proposals for the layout of the grounds and general restoration sparked off a lively controversy, in which he defended himself with vigour and asperity. His design for the grounds was unexciting, if adequate, but his restoration of the ravaged keep earned him high professional praise, not least because he had declined to add the almost mandatory Gothic touches of his day. The *Builder* was unrestrainedly enthusiastic. 'He has resisted the temptation to tamper with the dilapidations and such repairs as have been actually obligatory have been done in such a way as to clearly tell their tale.'[20] The Society for the Protection of Ancient Buildings gave slightly more guarded praise. It had been brought in during the local squabble – 'their representative came, we believe, at the institution of a resident in the neighbourhood and without any previous correspondence with anyone' – but though it had some doubts about the appearance of the iron safety-cage which Peak had erected on the top of the north wall 'the Committee wishes to say that, as far as it can judge, you have dealt with the ruins most wisely'.[21] Rather more unnerving to the purist, perhaps, was his intention to turn the ruins into a species of rockery by placing soil in all the crevices and planting 'ivy and other climbing plants', a suggestion which received the surprising approval of the Society.

The topographic distinctiveness of the natural platform, coupled with the fact that comparatively little modern building has taken place in the vicinity, makes it possible to trace out the whole Castle complex with considerable clarity. The entire area enclosed by the girdling walls was a little under six acres, a very high proportion of the total area of the existing town. The area at present in public keeping, and therefore linked visually with the heart of the complex, is perhaps two-thirds of the whole on the northern side. In 1852 the Corporation had the opportunity to purchase the southern section but declined to go above 'one bidding beyond £2500' with the result that the area was sold off and developed privately and a new road, Castle Hill, was constructed which bisected the complex and visually divorced the southern from the northern sections.

The largest and most interesting surviving part of the Castle, apart from the keep, is a long southern section of the encircling wall which still remains in private hands. Here, more than anywhere else, can be seen the original topography of the site, the original reason for placing the Castle where it stands. The wall, running due east for about one hundred feet, acts as a retaining wall for much of its length, marking the extreme southern limit of the original platform. Outside, it is perhaps thirty feet high from ground level – twice the height of the inside measurements. Where it once joined the road known as Quarry Street a postern gate stood, controlling access from the south. At its furthest end it meets the natural cliff of chalk and not far from this point are the enigmatic caverns which have figured constantly in folk-lore as the inescapable secret passages associated with all castles. They were explored in 1871 by a military engineer who came to the prosaic conclusion that the extensive workings were created by the prolonged quarrying for the chalk that was used in building both the Castle and many private houses in the locality.

The side of the platform facing the river has long since been built over, although the steep flight of steps, called Rosemary Alley, that runs up from the riverside road to Quarry Street gives a clear indication of the sudden change in level. The cellars of one of the houses on this side of the street bear the remains of a strong wall, composed of massive blocks of chalk that may have been the retaining wall that clad the original low cliff – an impressive defence in itself for the narrow strip of land between the foot of the cliff and the river was mostly marsh and even today is liable to flood.

From the postern gate on Quarry Street the encircling wall ran straight along the eastern side of the street, broken half-way along its length by a massive gate, probably built at the time of Henry III but incorporating solid Norman work, which today consists simply of an arch though bearing traces of the use of a heavy portcullis. Further on, a public house marks the possible site of another postern and here the line of the wall probably turned east again. But a little further beyond this turning-point the High Street of the future began to develop – probably well before the thirteenth century – and over the ensuing centuries the houses crept back towards the wall: when the Castle declined in importance the process of cannibalisation began so that today no trace of this northern section remains.

(ii) THE MERCHANTS' HALL

A plain white arm, emerging from the white gable, thrusts the great clock out high over the street and almost to its centre. The arm is long, so that it appears slender, almost fragile, its delicate metal supports of black and gold purely ornamental, but it is a massive beam leading deep into the building behind, for the clock is heavy. The black and gold motif, elegant but sombre, is fully developed on the timepiece itself, the hours glinting even on a dull day, the background night-black, lustrous. The street slopes steeply beneath so that the clock, though visible along the entire length of the highway, changes its background with distance, becoming a surrealist symbol of time suspended against the hills or the sky. It is the true badge of the town, far more so than any detail on the official coat of arms, familiar not only to natives but to two centuries of travellers for whom the town is otherwise merely a point on a route.

Beneath that confident, almost arrogant statement, even the splendid façade appears quieter by contrast, product though it is of Renaissance exuberance. In its sum, the public face of the Guildhall of Guildford is a poignant living example of the power of a culture to transmit its essence from race to race, affecting at last the mind of a people far distant in time and manners. Over two centuries before its builders were born, a complex politico-social revolution in the heart of Italy created a new architectural form as a by-product. The idea behind the form travelled slowly up the peninsula, crossed France, entered England, decorated London and, modified but still recognisable, spread throughout the country. The merchants of Guildford, resolving to refurbish their plain guild hall, in their turn naturally expressed themselves in the idiom of the confident new age. The unknown builder who carried out their desire into practice was obliged to translate that idiom into terms of local materials. Glass, fortunately, was plentiful but marble, the common material in which the style naturally expressed itself in its land of origin, was beyond the purses of the local merchants and he had to make do with wood.

The compromise brought about a work of art in its own right. The building he created in 1683 could not have better expressed either its status, its purpose, or its community. Some years later the architects employed by the Duke of Somerset erected a larger and more classically correct building a few hundred yards up the street. There the idiom was translated into expensive brick — creating a building that was physically as aloof from the town as the Duke was socially aloof: Somerset House was a staging-post for a wealthy man, and looked it. The Guildhall was, essentially, a burgher's home – its windows a little grander, its balcony wider and deeper, its turret giving it a touch of civic grandeur – but these were the attributes of its status as the first among equals, a place where the town's merchants met fraternally and not a place whence edicts emanated.

> Edward, by the grace of God, king of England, lord of Ireland and Acquitain, to his archbishops, bishops, abbots, priors, earles, barons, justices, sheriffs, rulers, officers and all baylies, and his faithfull subjects, sendeth greetings. Know yee that we have for the furtherance of our towne of Guldeford and for the tranquillity and quietness of the good men of the same towne, of our special grace granted, and by this our charter confirmed to the same men being tenants of the towne aforesaid, the same towne with the appurtenances TO HAVE AND TO HOLD, to them, their heirs and successors, in fee farm of us and our heirs with all rents, yssues, profitts and emoluments which John Brocas late keeper of the town had . . . yieldinge therefore to us and our heirs at our exchequer every yeare tenn pounds. . . .[22]

So, in October 1366 the thousand or so citizens of Guildford were informed, in a lengthy and curious admixture of noble sentiment and mercantile calculation, that their town had at last come of age after more than four centuries in which it had been considered a part – and the least important part – of the Royal Manor. King Edward III was, in fact, giving very little in hard cash to his faithful subjects in Guildford. John Brocas, the last 'farmer' of the town, had paid exactly double for the privileges of collecting the revenues of the manor – but Brocas had been granted the entire estate for his field of operation, Castle, Park as well as Town, and nevertheless complained that the revenues were hardly worth the £20 a year he was obliged to pay. The Castle and the Park were specifically excluded from the grant to the town: what the townspeople were receiving were the taxes on brewers, tanners and butchers – a third of which went, in any case, to the Earl of Surrey: the profits of the local courts and the goods of criminals.

But, far more important than the actual cash-value of the gift was the theory of autonomy implied in the power the town now possessed to collect its own revenues. By 'fee-farming' the town to its inhabitants the lord of the manor had commuted its total potential into a yearly cash-rental: the gardens, the houses, the markets, shops, streets now belonged, in practice, to the citizens. The lord of the manor here was also the all powerful monarch and there was nothing in theory to prevent him bringing the town again under his direct power. Three hundred years later James II, in the last defence of absolute monarchy, did indeed withdraw the town's charters, together with all others in the United Kingdom and imposed his own nominees to the town governance, but his successor was in some haste to restore them. Charter rights might not possess the theological sanctions that the divine right might possess, but few kings were disposed to test their relative values by arbitrarily abrogating sworn promises and gifts.

Guildford had received not only a limited gift but also a very tardy one. There was little altruism in the royal grants. Throughout Europe the system of feudal tenure was relaxing, responding not only to the spirit of free association but to its products, the subtle changes that were turning the Continent from a land-based economy to one fuelled by specie. In England, Guildford was among the last to receive formal recognition of the fact that, in practice if not in law, it had long possessed a corporate identity. Over a century before the Conquest the Saxon kings had established a mint in the town, sure evidence that it was regarded as a borough – a community which lacked the dignity of a city but was indubitably urban. By the beginning of the thirteenth century its merchants had already organised themselves into that formidable body, the Guild Merchant, which was to rule the town for the next six centuries, for it was specifically used as a model for the Guild Merchant which Kingston-on-Thames established in 1256.

In the January of the following year King Henry III granted the town its first charter and in so doing recognised the growing trade-potential, for the grant was essentially a merchants' charter, freeing the 'good men of Guildford' from the threat of arrest for other people's debts. Eight months later Henry gave an additional and rare honour to the town, decreeing that the County Court and Assize should be held there, turning it thereby into the formal County Town of Surrey – an honour which the citizens' own indolence forfeited seven hundred years later when the Assize, for lack of decent quarters, migrated permanently to Kingston. The fee-farm of 1366, though welcome, was merely the end product of a powerful existing trend. It seems, indeed, to have brought the citizens little immediate value. In 1488 when Henry VIII, tardy in his turn, granted the town its Charter of Incorporation, turning it into a legal entity with the powers of possessing property and of suing and being sued as though it were an individual, he gave as one of his reasons the fact that 'the said towne is soe decayed and impoverished by the payeing of the fee farm, and by other charges hanging daylie upon the said towne . . . we of our special love have graunted to the now mayor and good men of the towne aforesaid and to their successors for ever that the same towne be corporated from henceforth for ever . . .'.[23]

The casual mention of the 'mayor and good men' was again the first formal recognition of a long-established fact: that the title of the first citizen had been changed, responding to the change in the community's status. Even the fee-farm charter of 1366 had used the title 'Seneschal' when referring to the *de facto* governor of the town, but the offices of seneschal and mayor were worlds apart in concept. The Seneschal was an officer of the King's household – his major domestic lieutenant for whom the running of the town was only one of many responsibilities: the Mayor was a merchant, elected by his equals, for whom the prosperity of the town was the prime consideration. In gaining the great freedom of creating its own governor, the town also lost something in status and influence, for in the Seneschal it had automatically possessed a friend both at court and in Parliament. Later, the creation of the office of High Steward for the county enabled the town to restore the direct connection with the court, for the Steward was by custom chosen from among the local nobility, while the parliamentary link was continued through the town's right, as a borough, to return two members.

The Mayor's status as first citizen was a by-product of his other, and far more important role – the head of the local guild of merchants. It was the Guild Merchant, the local development of a continent-wide system, which ultimately inherited the town, running it as a closed society for the benefit of its members, presiding over its own court, governing the lives of the citizens down to the minutest detail. The natural heir of the King, it discharged its functions efficiently enough until the inherent weakness of an inward-looking organisation produced, in Guildford as elsewhere, that deterioration in control which led to the municipal reform of 1835.

The Guild Merchant of Guildford, as a historical subject, is wrapped in considerable obscurity for, additional to the hazards attending the identification of a single organisation in a homogeneous society, an unusual paucity of local records creates a veil which is at times impenetrable. Most of the light shed upon it is provided by a characteristically indirect source. In the late nineteenth century George Gross, an American scholar preparing a thesis on the guild merchant for a doctorate in a German university, included the Guildford archives in his search for sources. He too encountered the lacunae which hampered earlier and later workers, but the design of his book was such that not only did the Guildford material contribute to the understanding of the working of the guild in other communities but the sum of all the material enabled the outline of the Guildford system to be traced in fair detail. Within that outline, the significant records that remain achieve a coherence that would otherwise be denied them.

The concept of exclusion lay at the heart of the Guild Merchant. The smaller craft guilds of the town, whose masters formed the Guild Merchant, were exclusive enough but they could claim legitimately that they were concerned with upholding the standard of workmanship as well as reducing competition. The Guild Merchant existed only to trade and the trading facilities of the town – the town itself – existed only for the benefit of Guild members. 'No forayner of what craft soever shall use the mercate, unless by consent of the mayor and his brethren'[24] was the point hammered home again and again. Consent was granted – but reluctantly and expensively. The time-honoured story of John Aylward and his clock exactly illustrates the point, even though its details are suspect. Aylward, a foreigner, was supposed to have been either unable to pay his fine for admission into the Guild or was refused permission to enter. He thereupon set up a workshop just outside the town limits, made the handsome clock for the Guildhall, and was rewarded with membership as a result, henceforth trading in the town. It seems unlikely that a man who was unable to pay the admission fees was yet able to find the considerable time and money necessary to make the clock or, alternatively, that the merchants who had rejected the unknown John Aylward should have promptly accepted the John Aylward who had proved himself so formidable a competitor. But though documentary confirmation or rejection of the story are alike impossible, due to another gap in the records, its survival as folklore throughout the final two centuries of the Guild Merchant's life argues that as late as 1683, when the clock was supposedly made, the town was still firmly under the control of the medieval system.

The sphere of a guild merchant's influence varied widely from town to town, ranging from an independent body more or less subordinate to the town council to a body indistinguishable from the council itself. In Guildford the Guild had existed, from its earliest days, in so close a symbiosis with the town that 'Guildhall' and 'Town Hall' were virtually interchangeable terms. Even in the eighteenth century Parliament could find that the right of parliamentary election lay 'in the Mayor, Freeman and Freeholders residing in the borough. And it was admitted that one who has served seven years' apprenticeship in the town to a Freeman is, ipso facto, a freeman'.[25]

It was impossible to be totally exclusive, for Guildford merchants, too, desired to trade in other communities and some form of reciprocation was essential. Nevertheless, strangers bore the burden of almost crippling restrictions. They were obliged to bring their wares to a public place for inspection; they could not sell by retail; they were forced to yield first choice of any material in short supply to the native guildsmen – and could not in any case remain in the Borough for more than forty days. But inevitably the earlier rigorous prohibitions were relaxed with time though couched still in the negative. 'Noe craftsman shall sett up his occupation in the towne unless he shall take an house and beare lott and scott'[26] – in other words, if a man were prepared to bear his full share of the general expenses he could trade in the town. Guildford, too, seems to have followed the common guild-custom whereby a widow inherited her husband's status and could transmit it to a second husband: 'no person shall use the trade of fuller nor sheerman . . . unless he hath bene apprentice thereto or by reason of marriage'. In 1596 George Austen could record, in the foreword to his priceless collection of town records, that there was a growing tendency to admit foreigners into the town. Austen was a mayor as well as a scholar, and though he might applaud the decline of the ruder habits of his forebears, he could not but deplore that tendency which, in the eyes of conservatives, was weakening the town. 'As for ther ffeastinge and bull-baytinge they are things worn out of use and not fit to be revived. But for fines paid by foreyners for there freedom and admittance into the liberties, to buy and sell within the said towne, there hath been a contynuall custome and use thereof, although of late years much neglected, which I wish may be renewed and brought into use again.'[27]

It is difficult to reconcile this complaint with the implication that, nearly a century afterwards, John Aylward found it impossible to acquire his freedom without a substantial bribe – unless George Austen saw his wish almost immediately fulfilled with a revival of the earlier exclusiveness. This may well have been the case, for in 1625 it was decreed that even the possession of property in the town did not automatically guarantee civic rights. Altogether, Guildford seems to have applied the exclusion principle with unusual rigidity. It was a natural policy for a town heavily dependent upon trade but it led inexorably to a decline in prosperity. This cause and effect was a national phenomenon, as the commissioners of Henry VIII noted. 'Many and the most partie of all the Cities, Boroughes and Townes corporate wythin this realm be fallen into ruyn and decay'[28] – due entirely, in the commissioners' opinion, to that policy of mutual exclusion of which Guildford was exemplary.

The Guild Merchant, in theory open to all merchants of the town, was in practice run by a handful of some twenty or thirty men – the Mayor and Approved Men of the Borough. The precise circumstances under which the *probi homines* were approved, and by whom, are obscure, the phrase being recorded as a formal title long after it had first appeared as a definition. But the sequence of recruitment to its ranks are clear enough. Annually, a Bailiff was elected for the town, his duties being roughly analogous to a present-day Treasurer – one of his major responsibilities was the collection and payment of the fee-farm rent. On vacation of the office he became eligible for enrolment among the Approved Men and, ultimately, for election as Mayor. The Approved Men formed the Corporation and it was they who elected, at an annual meeting of the Guild Merchant Court, the officials of the Guild.

Parallel with the Court of the Guild Merchant was the Court Leet, the vernacular term for the *Curia Legalis* which had directly inherited the King's powers in the town. The business and powers of the two courts overlapped so that it is almost impossible to make any valid, long-term distinction between them.[29] In general, the Guild Merchant concerned itself with the financial and fraternal business of the town appointing, among other officials, the Bailiff, and the Hall Warden – custodian of the Guildhall and collector of guild fees, while the Court Leet appointed the Constables and the various Tasters – officials responsible for the control of food prices and qualities.

The Mayor enjoyed considerable ceremonial honour: it was not merely customary but decreed that all living ex-mayors should accompany him 'from his house and bringe him to the Courte one the Court daye or ellese to lose for every defalte xiid & that to remayne to the hall'[30] – the decree, incidentally, being made at a Court Leet, clear evidence of the overlapping functions of the courts. In addition, the presiding mayor was granted certain perquisites – including the tolls on the corn-markets and, later, the right to the street sweepings – which continued on into the nineteenth century. But the provision of substantial penalties for any man who, being elected, declined to serve argues convincingly that the office was regarded as an onerous duty rather than a privilege or means of making money. There was a similar reluctance to serve as Bailiff also, for this office, too, carried a penalty for the man who declined the honour. The reluctance obviously stemmed from the heavy expenses connected with the honour of high office. The Guild was not only an organisation of men associated for profit but also a fraternal body and, in accordance with the widespread custom, corporate celebration was as integral a part of its activities as the regulation of trade. The Mayor and the Bailiff were expected, as a matter of course, to feast their brethren both on accepting office and also on different occasions through the year. It was a social custom that proved highly tenacious of life, for though in 1596 Austen had remarked that it was 'worn out of use and not fit to be revived' in the late nineteenth century the sober Henry Peak recorded his disgust at the marathon banquet, followed by a prolonged drinking-bout, that celebrated the Mayor's inauguration. The custom perpetuated and exaggerated the tendency towards a small ruling class, for there was no point in electing a poor man who could neither pay for the feasting nor afford the heavy fine in lieu. It is no accident that the same family names occur again and again in the lists of Approved Men, for the majority of the citizens were virtually disfranchised by lack of means.

The lives of the citizens can be perceived, if only dimly, through the medium of the records of the courts. The picture presented is that of a strongly coherent community with a corresponding lack of individual privacy, and of public control extending over a very wide field. It was to be expected that butchers and shoemakers, brewers and bakers should be under constant surveillance during working-hours and that they should suffer an appropriate penalty if their goods fell below standard. But control extended, too, into the citizen's free time. That leisure was scanty enough on any comparison. In 1664 it was decided that the 'antient and laudable custom' of ringing the bells of St Mary's to call the citizens to work at four in the morning, and again at eight in the evening 'to give their masters notice what tyme it is expedient they should leave off' should be revived.[31] A sixteen-hour day would seemingly have left little time or energy for dissipation but it was still considered necessary to warn innkeepers to be on their guard against carousing workmen: 'If any inholder, taverner, alehouse-keeper or other person or persons whatsoever shall willingly . . . suffer any servant or apprentice dwelling withing this town to continue, remain or abide in his or their houses at any tyme or tymes after nyne of the clock of the night unless it be with the consent of the master, mistress or dame of such servant or apprentice . . . shall forfeit and lose for every such offence iis vid.'[32] Citizens were ordered to church as a matter of course, both before and after the Reformation, more fines being levied on the unfortunate inkeepers if they sold ale during divine service. Criticism of public officials carried penalties amounting even to disfranchisement, and more commonly imprisonment. Private morality was very much a public affair. The ducking-stool on Millmead awaited the whore and the respectable scold alike. George Burges, shoemaker, is fined not only for creating an uproar in his house at night but also for 'keping a woman servant in his house suspected of lewd and evill behaviour'.[33]

Recreation and entertainment again were provided and enjoyed on a communal basis. The tormenting of captive animals, characteristically the English sport, was faithfully adopted locally. Bear- and badger-baiting seem to have been a matter of private enterprise: the more prestigious and expensive sport of bull-baiting was the responsibility of the Guild, groups of citizens being ordered from time to time to provide a bull for the corporate entertainment. The traditional site for these games was in the open space known as the North Town Ditch, a tradition which was continued even after the wasteland became a street – the present North Street – for the more modest sport of cock-fighting was located here and, ultimately, the town theatre found a natural home in the same street.

The pre-Christian rites centred around the Lord of Misrule, known in the town as the Summer King, continued to find vigorous expression. Again, private inclinations were not allowed to interfere with public pleasure. 'Iff eny yong man or yong men schall from hens forthe be chosen . . . to be somer kynges princes and sword berers and iff the sayed yong men reffuse . . . then the [somer] kyng so chosen shall lose vs, the prince to lose iiijs iijd and the Sworde bearer xx[ti]d [20d].'[34] In 1610 the ancient Summer Pole or Maypole outside St Mary's was found to be in such a dangerous condition that an order was made for its removal, the sound parts thriftily being used for the making of ladders. No order was then made for its restoration, but in 1791 the artist John Russell sketched the town Maypole in its new position outside St Thomas's Hospital on the opposite side of the town, his drawing emphasising the remarkable height of the pole. Even after the formal and widespread celebration of May Day had come to an end, the chimney sweeps of the town carried a survival of it into the mid-nineteenth century, perambulating the town in costume on May Day and performing a dance, in groups of five or six, beating out the time with brush, shovel and triangle.

The greater part of the town's trade was naturally concerned with supplying the everyday wants of citizens and travellers – shoes and bread, ale, meat and the like. But the stable balance was upset by the immense expansion of the wool industry during the Tudor period. Throughout the country, town after town abandoned their traditional crafts to pursue the immense riches that the industry could bring. Wool was the universal clothing medium, in demand from nobles and plebs alike. It created a chain of wealth, beginning with the farmer, continuing on to the craft industries, the international merchants and ending with the individual shopkeepers. It made the fortunes not merely of individuals and towns but of entire states. But it carried with it, too, the seeds of destruction for that guild system upon which Guildford was so firmly based, for it was impossible to control it on a narrow local base. The wool gathered on Surrey hills might finish up as cloth made in Florence and sold in Cairo, although

English monarchs from time to time attempted to prohibit the export of wool to favour the production of cloth at home.

Guildford successfully channelled some of the wealth into its own coffers. The town was well placed to undertake the formidable task of transforming raw wool into finished cloth, retaining the profits at all stages until the moment when the bales entered the books of an international merchant. One of the five major European deposits of fuller's earth, used in the vital stage of cleaning the cloth, occurred only a few miles away near Reigate. The River Wey provided clean, fast-moving water both for fulling and for driving the mills. Teasels, the thistle-like plant used in raising the nap, grew locally and were even farmed on a commercial scale for export to other areas. The town specialised in the coarse, narrow cloth known as kersey, producing it in such quantities and with such profit that by the time of Richard III, when the town's arms were granted, it was natural that the Guild Merchant should request that the woolsack should appear as part of the arms. It was not an automatic honour. The great merchant company of the Staple had to give its approval, and its appraisal of the cloth as honest workmanship gives independent evidence of the strict control exercised by the Guild in the town.

The most common dishonesty was to stretch the cloth by various mechanical means, and later John Aubrey was to claim that this was the main reason for the collapse of the industry, citing as an example what happened in Wonersh and Guildford. Their trade 'chiefly consisted in making blue cloth for the Canary Islands: the decay and indeed ruin of their trade was their avaricious method of stretching their cloth from 18 yards to 21 or 22 or 23, which being discovered abroad, they returned their commodity on their hands and it would sell at no market'.[35] But the records of the local Guild Merchant show that the town was well aware of the possibilities of this fraud: the industry's decline was brought about by national, not local, causes and was largely due to the fact that the powerful companies of Merchant Adventurers and the London Drapers eventually exercised a monopoly, by-passing and ruining thousands of small independent men.

It was while the trade was still alive but obviously moribund that in 1614 George Abbot came forward with his ready advice and offer of money to revive it. He was himself the son of a clothworker, born in the town in 1562 though he had long since abandoned it for the perilous path of ecclesiastical politics. He became Archbishop of Canterbury four years earlier but he was quick to point out to the Mayor that 'considering my perpetual expence my means are not great'. Nevertheless, he went on in his prosy but rather touching letter, because the town was so dear to him he had been giving earnest consideration of the best means to succour its inhabitants during the trade decline. He was careful not to offend the susceptibilities of the Guild Merchant. 'If I shall acquaint you with my thoughts you will bear with me, because they all proceed from a good mind towards you, and if I erre in anything upon information I shall quicklie be informed.'[36] Nevertheless, the polymathic author of *A Brief Description of the Whole World*, who was also the son of a cloth-worker, had no hesitation about plunging into the technicalities of the cloth industry. Mistaking completely the causes for the decline, the gist of his advice was that the local industry should switch from the narrow, coarse kersies to broadcloth. The retooling necessary would obviously be expensive, and as a substantial contribution towards that expense he was sending £100 to the town.

Nothing came of the attempt to redirect the wool industry, but in 1627 the Archbishop returned to the problem with an even more drastic suggestion. The citizens should forget all about wool and concentrate on linen. 'The sowinge, of hemp and flax, a matter not used in your part is very considerable for the common good. The sowinge, the pullinge, the pillinge the beatinge of this thing will set many on worke: the spinning and weaving of it is very needful unto the kingdom. . . . If this be liked by you, if we may hier land for this purpose and gett seeds for money I would even at Michaelmass next have some tryall made, that if it soe seem good unto the almighty, I may in my lifetime sett the wheele a goeinge.'[37]

It was not given to the Archbishop to see his plan put into action for he died 1633. But the Guild Merchant honourably executed his intentions, erecting a manufactory near the Arch-bishop's recently built Hospital and a certain amount of cloth – both linen and, later, wool – was produced there, 'But neither of these ways being of that profit to the town as by the said will was intended, because such as were employed there to work, would not work without greater wages than others gave'. The manufactory was abandoned and the money provided for its purpose thereafter distributed annually to 'such honest poor tradesmen and housekeepers of the said town who want stock'.[38] By the end of the century the wool trade was little more than a memory: by 1739 it had passed so completely out of public consciousness that when Richardson surveyed the town in that year he either did not know, or did not think it worth recording, that 'Mr Wilkins's Pit Field' on Quarry Street was once better known as Rack's Close – the place where the town's cloth was racked for drying. Apart from that open space, with its enigmatic humps and ridges, the only tangible relics of a once all-important industry are the wool-packs on the town arms and the plain rectangular building that was Abbot's manufactory, the means whereby the glory was to be restored.

The High Street of Guildford was born of the town's topo-graphy, but it also perfectly exemplified the English dislike of planning, their preference for crowding everything into one main street and adding haphazardly to it, rather than starting logically with the local variant of the forum as was the standard Continental practice. The town records provide ample evidence of the result, for they are punctuated with resolutions or reports on schemes to move this or that obstruction to the traffic-flow. The ordinances irresistibly give the impression of a man in a cluttered room hopelessly moving objects from one place to another in attempting to find room for new acquisitions. A market house, known as the Fish Cross, had stood from time immemorial exactly in the middle of the street opposite the Angel Inn, effectively blocking traffic. In 1592 it was ordered to be removed – 'forthwith. And a convenient place shall be appointed [for the fish market] and built there for the same.' Over two centuries later Russell noted wryly that 'As it appears there never had been a place built and appointed . . . and the fishwives were forced to make use of the wheat market house.'[39]

The poultry market was first jammed between the Tun and the White Hart, then moved across the street to a similar position between the Lion and the George and finally moved, appropriately enough, into the recently vacated cockpit. The unpleasant nature of the butchers' trade did enforce some attempt at long-term planning. Originally it had claimed its share of the High Street, spilling out towards the centre but in the same year that the Fish Cross was removed a complete lane leading off the Street was set aside for the Shambles, a name which it still bears. Sellers of crockery and shoes, leather and cereal each staked their claim to the limited accommodation of the open market. The cattle market dominated all. For year after year and century after century a motley crowd of oxen, pigs, cows, sheep were driven in from the surrounding country into an already overcrowded street. The market survived long enough to figure in a railway guide, whose neat engraving showed the cattle pens extending well into the centre of the street and down its length for a considerable distance. In the early nineteenth century it was moved, not without protest, to North Street where it remained for another generation before being banished to the then outskirts of the town.

The High Street belonged to the natives, except on the occasion of the two annual fairs when foreigners crowded in. But the Guild Merchant was firmly in control even during these periods, for Edward I had granted the town the power of holding the Court of Piepowder, the ancient institution designed precisely to control the sudden invasion of strangers at fairtime. The great fair of St Catherine's lay outside the town limits and therefore outside the control of the citizens. St Catherine's Hill is not the obvious place for a fair: Turner's engraving shows clearly the steep – in places the precipitous – nature of the hill on which the fair booths seem to cling uneasily. But the hill, with its beautiful little chapel, marked the point where the primeval Terrace-way, companion to the Ridgway along the Hog's Back, crossed the river. The chapel upon it, rebuilt in 1317, bears architectural evidence that it played an important religious role in the pilgrim traffic,[40] and the road to Portsmouth runs below the sandy cliff on its western face. It stood upon a natural cross-road, and was reinforced in importance by the pilgrim trade – creating altogether a valuable commercial site. Initially, the tolls fell to the Rector of St Nicholas, one of the three town churches, but they were so lucrative that the Rector was despoiled by the Bishop, who was in turn despoiled by the King.

A pious local tradition for long insisted that either St Catherine's or the nearby fair at Shalford formed the model for Bunyan's Vanity Fair, and out of it arose an elaborate theory seeking to identify the points of Christian's journey with the landmarks from Guildford to Leith Hill. The identification of Vanity Fair is, admittedly, almost as various as that of Camelot, but St Catherine's Fair was large enough, wealthy enough and unruly enough to give colour to the local story. Clashes between citizens and fair people were commonplace and continued into the nineteenth century – at least one citizen was killed in what appears to have been a pitched battle that took place in the early years of the century and even the late-comer Henry Peak, writing at the end of that century, remembered the fair as 'a wild and weird scene forty to fifty years ago as I saw it'.[41]

The public buildings of the town contributed heavily to the overwhelming commercial and social dominance of the High Street for, with the exception of the extra-civic Castle and Friary, all were spaced along its length. The first casual groupings of the houses that ultimately formed the town were stabilised and formalised by the three town churches. They followed each other in time and space along the length of the town, providing a kind of growing skeleton fleshed by the secular buildings. So clear was their influence that, separated from each other by only a matter of yards, each became the nucleus of a community, the Upper, Lower and Middle Towns.

At the bottom of the town, and separated from it by the barrier of the river, was the church of St Nicolas. The records of the church, like those of its sisters, provide no certain date for its foundation, and time has wrought the greatest of the changes upon it so that it appears now almost wholly as a late nineteenth-century building. The riverine barrier is both physical and psychological so that the community in which it stands is essentially different from the rest of the town. A stubborn tradition claims, indeed, that it was here, on the west side of the river, that the first community grew, migrating across the river when the Castle appeared to alter the centre of gravity. The tradition is unsupported even by such scanty documentary materials that support the claim of the eastern bank. There is no reason why it should have developed and survived except, possibly, that it is true, folk memory preserving what the archives have lost.

The church's parish extended deep into the country, including St Catherine's within its bounds. Its historian, indeed, argues cogently that the original church of the parish stood upon this legend-haunted hill and that it was moved by the notorious Randulph Flambard, justiciar of the Conqueror, on to his own lands in Guildford some time after 1086.[42] Writing about 1777 John Russell gives a tantalisingly vague hint as to the possibility of a Saxon structure on the site – '[It] had a new tower about a hundred years since' – and attempted to buttress the claim to antiquity with a footnote: 'It had a round tower, said John Apark, an old inhabitant and formerly beadle of the town.'[43] Apark himself could only have been retailing hearsay, unless he was considerably more than a hundred years old, but there seems to be no reason why he should have remembered that the church once possessed a round, Saxon tower, instead of the later square tower, unless local memory was again better than local records. But less than a century after Russell had recorded even this frail link, the much patched and altered church was demolished and 'a truly atrocious building in churchwarden Gothic' appeared in its place in 1837.[44] In 1875 this, too, was knocked down in favour of another design and the only early coherent architectural evidences that remain are provided by the Losely Chapel, the mortuary chapel for the wealthy family of More-Molyneux that was built in the late fifteenth century and precariously survived the restless changes.

Immediately across the river, and standing slightly out of alignment with the High Street, the church of St Mary's tells an architectural story the exact opposite of that told by St Nicholas. The fabric of St Nicholas has been totally demolished at least twice in its history: the fabric of St Mary's faithfully bears the evidence of the attempts made by succeeding generations to adapt it for current use, creating thereby a three-dimensional textbook of architectural history extending over nine centuries. The changes, coupled with the lack of records, have created a number of enigmatic features as, for example, that 'low side window' which has been variously described as a leper window, a confessional window 'or possibly to shew a light to guide people to the ford'.[45] But the solid, immensely strong structure of the church tells its general story clearly enough. Tradition, again the only source for its early history, asserts that the tower pre-dated the Conquest and it may very well have been erected, about 1050, as a Saxon watchtower, replacing an earlier wood structure. In 1966 an archaeological examination gave some substance to the theory of an original wood-tower, and was able to establish the fact that the stone tower could have been built before the Conquest. The relevant evidence was a sherd of pottery, of a type manufactured between 1050 and 1150 – not sufficient to date the tower finally but enough to give colour to the story that it might have been incorporated as part of the outer works of the Castle.[46]

The church benefited directly from the presence of the monarch, its successive enlargements corresponding closely enough to the rhythm of the building-activities on the Castle mound. The predominantly Norman chancel and transepts had appeared by about 1100, their construction probably begun about the time that the shell keep would have been completed. By 1180, when the immense keep now towered above the town and the church, the body of the church was substantially rebuilt, aisles and chapels appearing to give it dignity in keeping with its status of a church under royal protection. One of these chapels – that of St John's – was decorated with mural paintings, reputed to be executed by William the Florentine, Henry III's resident master of the works. They disappeared under successive coats of whitewash over the centuries, were discovered accidentally in 1825 but by the end of the century had perished, the only remaining traces being a formal design over the arch. The church suffered only one other major depredation after the builders of Henry III had given it a final form: in 1825 the apse projecting into Quarry Street was cut short, supposedly at the request of George IV, who found it difficult to get his coach past the obstruction in the narrow street. It was a brutal truncation, rendered all the more puzzling by the fact that, immediately opposite, was the wall of the town prison, a few feet of which could well have been spared for the purpose of widening the road. Presumably, penal accommodation was measured at a higher value than preservation of the town's most venerable structure.

Despite its antiquity and the indisputable fact that it was the mother church of the town, St Mary's fell under the shadow of the larger church up the hill, that of The Holy and Undivided Trinity. In 1698 the two parishes were combined because 'the revenues and profits of the said churches do not amount to more than £70 per annum together, and they lie convenient to be united'.[47] Henceforward, the same rector was appointed to both churches simultaneously, but it was the younger church which predominated.

Holy Trinity Church echoed the architectural fate of St Nicholas, although here it was not excessive enthusiasm that wrought drastic change but sheer neglect that culminated in bringing the church down about its parishioners' ears. The original church was probably built in the first decade of the fourteenth century – the ubiquitous paucity of town records again wrapping its origins in deep obscurity. In 1734 what seems to have been a remarkably inept attempt to repair dilapidations hastened the day of its ruin – 'as the arches and pillars which supported the steeple were then taken away it was soon after supposed to be in a very ruinous position', are the words in which Russell describes the operation, although whether uttered in irony or naïveté it is difficult to say. Russell possibly witnessed the inevitable result six years later. The churchwardens had belatedly decided to do something about the weakened building when – 'On

Wednesday 23d [April 1740], the steeple of this antient church fell down and beat in the roof with such violence, that by the compression of the air, all the glass windows were blown out as if it had been done by a blast of gunpowder. The workmen had quitted the spot about a quarter of an hour before the accident happened, so that no person received the least injury though a great number were spectators, it being the fair day.'[48]

The churchwardens launched an appeal for funds for rebuilding, but so lukewarm was the response that nine years passed before the foundation stone was laid, in August 1749. The funds collected proved insufficient, work came to a halt, lands belonging to the church were sold to raise more money, work began again and continued sporadically for fourteeen years. In all, over twenty-three years elapsed between the collapse of the tower and the first service celebrated in the new church on 18 September 1763. Little of the old was incorporated in the new. On the south side, a chapel belonging to another wealthy local family, the Westons of Sutton Place, survived to add a relief of sixteenth-century flintwork to the plain red brick of the new building. In the church itself Archbishop Abbott's elaborate tomb, a tumbling confection of marble skulls and books with the Archbishop himself drawn out man-size in marble, was re-erected in a dark corner. The tomb had survived the catastrophe probably because it had been erected under an arch, and it reappeared now to add its Caroline floridity as counterpoint to the sober Georgian of the interior.

'The exterior of the building has something repulsive in its aspect' was the frank opinion of Russell's continuator.[49] The harsh judgement of the nineteenth-century native was considerably modified by the twentieth-century visitor: 'This is Surrey's only big C18 church, handsome and pedestrian at the same time: handsome in the smooth brickwork and the proportions, pedestrian in the details. Nothing deviates from the correct Palladian canon.'[50] The exterior has remained little changed – dominant in both eighteenth-century engraving and twentieth-century photograph is the broad, handsome flight of steps that contribute to its ceremonial nature. But the interior felt the hand of the restorer in 1869 and again in 1888, and at present is in a somewhat shabby condition. Curiously, though this is the major church of the town, local pride seems always to have centred around its elder sister St Mary's. Between 1930 and 1961 Holy Trinity knew the brief honour of cathedral status, but it bears no tangible record of this save for a murky oil-painting hung in a dark corner depicting the enthronement of the first bishop.

> Forasmuch as every Christian man is bounde, according to the measure of grace and mercy which he hath received from God, to render back again to his Eternal Father such tokens of gratefulness and thankfulness as are in his power: and I George Abbot Archbishop of Canterbury . . . having been partaker of some earthly and worldly benefits, more than most of my birth and rank have attayned unto, I have held it agreeable with my dutie to leave behind me to posteritie some monument of my thankfulness to my Creator. . . .'[51]

In these words, with their ring of a more than formal humility and piety, George Abbot began the lengthy and detailed statutes for the governing of his newly completed Hospital of the Blessed Trinity.

There is something peculiarly poignant about Abbot's relationship with his native town, infusing into the recorded details of his character a warmth and an attractiveness lacking in the portraits of the ecclesiastical prince caught up in courtier intrigues. It needed an unusual strength of will to retain both independence and integrity within the orbit of King James I, and Abbot, though certainly no trimmer – twice he defied both King and nobles on a question of principle – owed his career as much to his qualities of courtier as of priest or scholar.

The origins of the town's godfather were undoubtedly humble, though local piety tended to exalt his father's profession. Abbot himself made no secret of the social distance he had travelled, and the legend of his birth and childhood substantiates it. He was born in the parish of St Nicolas in a building which surviving contemporary illustrations make plain was the cottage of a workman rather than the mansion of a merchant. Legend told how his mother dreamt in pregnancy that if she were to eat a pike the child she delivered would become a famous man. Busy at household tasks, she lowered a bucket into the river for water and, on bringing it out, found that a pike had entered it, and she later cooked the fish and ate it. The story was supposed to have gained immediate and widespread fame, and some years later when the boy was playing with his brother on the town bridge, the legend continues, a passing stranger was attracted by their lively appearance and learning that the younger boy was he of whom the pike story had been told thereafter educated the brothers at his own expense.

The legend has neither more nor less value than such legends usually have, but it does give colour to the story of the humble circumstances of the Abbot household. The wives of wealthy merchants do not go down to the river to draw water, neither are their sons educated by passing strangers. In whatever manner George Abbot was launched on his high career, he passed on to Balliol College from the local grammar school and graduated at the age of twenty. Oxford University remained his home and centre of activity for the next twenty-two years. He entered holy orders, was chosen Master of University College in 1597 at the early age of thirty-five and was three times appointed Vice-Chancellor of the University. His greatest claim to national fame is, without doubt, the fact that he was one of the eight Oxford scholars who formed the Oxford Greek Committee of that great translation of the Bible now known as the Authorised Version, unimpeachable testimony to his learning, for the body of translators were chosen on the basis of merit, not of party. Abbot was to produce, with the usual Puritan prolixity, a very large body of secular and sacred writing including that ambitious *Geography, or a Brief Description of the Whole World* but nothing he produced as an individual measured up to his product as a committee member.

In 1608 his effective relationship with Oxford was severed and he began his upward political path, for in that year he went to Scotland to take part in the negotiations for the Union of the Churches of Scotland and England. So favourably did he impress King James that almost immediately he was made

Bishop of Lichfield and Coventry, was appointed Bishop of London a month afterwards and then, within the year, Archbishop of Canterbury. The meteoric rise of an obscure scholar was credited, accurately enough, to Abbot's ability to flatter the pompous little king's rather pathetic yearnings towards scholarship. But, having gained the coveted position, Abbot proved himself an honourable priest. He vigorously resisted the divorce suit of Lady Francis Howard and the Earl of Essex, even though the King himself made it clear that he favoured the divorce. In 1618 he actively prohibited the reading, in Croydon, of the royal proclamation permitting pastimes on the Sabbath. He survived – but a macabre accident gave his numerous enemies a potent weapon against him. While out hunting, he aimed his crossbow at a deer, but the bolt struck and killed a gamekeeper. He suffered immense personal distress – which seemed, indeed, to have affected his mind – but his enemies were able to claim that even involuntary homicide disqualified him from sacred office. King James found a technical answer to the technical accusation but thereafter Abbot's power was spent. The actual cause of his final overthrow was an honourable one. After James's death he refused licence for a sermon designed to extend the prerogative of the new King, Charles I, was deprived of his functions as primate and, though the King afterwards found it necessary to restore him, he thereafter remained in virtual retirement until he died in August 1633.

Abbot founded his own Hospital in Guildford specifically on the model of that founded by his predecessor, Whitgift, at Croydon. Puritan though he was, Abbot could not but be aware of the social loss created by the destruction of the monasteries in the previous generation. Guildford had lost its own friary in 1538, and though it had been small and poor enough it had yet been part of that system which ameliorated the lot of the poor in an essentially ruthless society. The secular charities had not yet arrived to bridge the gap between spontaneous religious care of the unfortunate and the formal systems of the State. In 1612 the Austen family had established the first of the town's charities, but this provided only for the payment of a few shillings a year to selected widows. Abbot had a far more ambitious object, a foundation which would continue the best traditions of the monastery and provide a communal home for both men and women in their declining years.

He had referred to the possibility as early as 1614 when he had made his first suggestion to reviving the woollen trade but – 'my meanes are not great to bring about some such thing as my heart hath desired, as, perhaps, for the erecting of some hospitall, as my worthy predecessour the lord archbishop Whitgift did at Croydon'.[52] But, those means eventually improving, he turned again to the scheme. The logical place for such an establishment was, perhaps, the old Friary but that had fallen into private hands and the Hospital therefore appeared on the prestigious High Street, attracted by and in turn creating a powerful centre of gravity. The foundation stone was laid on April 1619 and the building was finished three years later, a celerity that consisted dramatically with the later tardy building of Holy Trinity across the street. In 1629 the founder turned to a task for which he was particularly suited, the detailing of a system of government for an institution which would probably survive for centuries, doing his work so well that the Hospital could be run on basically the same lines in the late twentieth century as in the early seventeenth. 'On the right side [of the Hospital] I put the poore men, whom I call Brethren, and on the life side the poore women, whom I terme Sisters.' They were to be chosen from among 'suche onely has have ben born in the Towne of Guildford, or have lived there, at the least for Twenty Years before [and] be Threescore years of age before they be chosen'.[53] In the last chapter of his statutes, Abbot underlined the fact that the Hospital was intended for Guildford citizens only, and carefully defined exactly what he meant by Guildford: 'My setled purpose and meaning is . . . the towne of Guildford taken as it was in ye yeare 1620, and not according to any addition that hath ben made since, or may be hereafter. Whereof, if I should be demaunded a reason, it were a sufficient aunswer, to aske as it is in the Gospell, May I not do what I will with mine own?' However, he went on to detail his reasons, based on the argument that it was better to keep a few in reasonable comfort than to dole out a few shillings to a great many.

> It was the good of Guildford, old Guildford as it was when I was borne and my parentes lived in it, that I did seke, which I did know would be the greater to the poore of that place when it was kept restrayned within itself, and not communicated to any other. It is well knowne that I was born in the parishe of St Nicholas in that towne, unto which parishe are belonging many howses in and about Katherine Hill, unto whom notwithstanding I did not enlarge my benevolence, because they were not under the government of the Maior, and my desire was and is to keepe my Charitie within boundes, that after my death things may go quietly and there be no variance or controversie.'[54]

The government of the Maior in the twentieth century extends over a far greater area than in the seventeenth and the 'Guildford' so carefully defined by Abbot is virtually extinct as a residential area. Nevertheless, the basis upon which the residents of the Hospital are currently selected continues to honour the founders' essential intention for they have been born, or have lived for many years, in the community now recognised as composing Guildford. Until 1964 the residents lived, as Abbot had planned, without cost to themselves except in the matter of food. But the operation of the official welfare service, together with a massive programme of modernisation in the Hospital itself at once eliminated the need for some of the archaic provisions – in particular a regular weekly supply of coal to each resident – and made necessary a small weekly contribution from each resident towards the general upkeep. Nevertheless, Abbot's endowment enables the Hospital to remain self-supporting, and it would be an interesting actuarial exercise to calculate how much the seventeenth-century prelate's gift to his native town saves the welfare services of the central government.

Despite its sobriety, the Hospital effortlessly dominates: from a distance the turrets on its great gatehouse identify it among the medley of roofs: close too, the massive, red-brick front at once merges with the line of the street and proclaims its individuality. 'The main feature, the huge gatehouse, is a deliberate anachronism, looking back at least to Hampton Court and possibly to the semi-military gatehouses of the C15. Outside the universities, this is the last great gatehouse in the country and very nearly the best.'[55] The architect of even such a late-built structure as this is unknown, but though he lacked the inventive flair of that other unknown who designed the façade of the Guildhall, yet he had more than skill enough to make individual a standard design, creating a home and not an institution. Within, as within the Guildhall, the overwhelming impression is that of an unselfconscious continuity. Gifts casually made over the centuries have become an integral part of the building so that while they remain the artefacts and the decorations of a home they have also acquired a priceless antiquarian value – the Hospital shelters perhaps the most valuable and certainly the most interesting paintings in the town. The beautiful Common Hall is still used, as intended, by the residents: the Master lives in the same rooms which provided a retreat for Abbot himself during his disgrace. One of the most astonishing aspects of the Hospital is the condition of its structure: the great doors and other woodwork have the patina of age but might have been worked in the present century: the age of the towering, fantastic chimneys – a brick forest when seen from the flat roof of the tower – seemingly measured in decades rather than centuries, tribute at once to the skill of the builders and the clean air of the town. Only in one room is evident the effect of time – the large, naked chamber in the gatehouse in which the wretched Duke of Monmouth was lodged on the Sunday night in July 1685 before his appearance in London. This has escaped the general care but plays a valuable role nevertheless for here, in a kind of informal museum, are the artefacts which, no longer in use, are still preserved: the great chest in which, obedient to the founder's instructions, £100 in specie was kept – too obediently, for the coins were ultimately demonetised and were sold for a trifle of their face value: a set of ancient locks with immense keys: a piously dressed image of Abbot himself: a carpenter's masterpiece – the odds and ends of a home preserved for no other reason that that they belong to that home.

The back of the Hospital looks upon the last intact garden of the High Street – formal, beautifully tended and open to view so that it adds a much-needed green dimension in a rapidly developing area. Linked to it by a now isolated arch is Abbot's manufactory that was to have done so much for the town's trade. But brief though was its life as a workshop, by a curious quirk of history, it was to perpetuate the old man's name in an institution – the school known as Archbishop Abbot's School – that was actually founded by another man.

In 1579 the Mayor and Approved Men entered into a somewhat curious transaction with a certain Thomas Baker, a clothier of the town and evidently of some substance for he was Mayor on three occasions. Baker was granted a piece of open land on the High Street, immediately in front of Holy Trinity Church, on which he contracted to build a market house – a plan only too well in keeping with the other ad hoc decisions affecting the High Street. Baker was to put up the money for the building – about £300 – was to enjoy the receipts during his lifetime but after his death, and that of his wife, the money was to be used for the education of the children of poor parents.

At the time that the town signed the covenant with Baker, the Grammar School a few hundred yards away was entering on the final phase of a major building programme that had lasted for nearly twenty years, commencing shortly after the School had received its royal charter in 1553. The paucity of records makes it impossible to determine why Baker should have decided to found a school at this very period when the Grammar School was demonstrably establishing itself as a permanent institution, catering for up to one hundred students. It may be that the School had already acquired that exclusiveness upon which John Mason remarked in the early nineteenth century. His father, a poor man, had attempted to enter him in the School: 'And I have reason to believe that he was much hurt by the remarks of the Trustees that it was not intended for such men as him.'[56] It is unlikely, however, that Baker intended his school to be a rival in any real sense for he provided for only one master, at £10 per year, as opposed to a master and an usher, at £20 and £10 per year respectively, on the Grammar School establishment. The probability is that Baker's school was a purely charitable institution designed to give the barest rudiments of an education to the children of the very poor, as opposed to the Grammar School's role as a genuine academic institution for the sons of freemen, and whose charitable origins were rapidly becoming irrelevant.

Baker's school probably began life in an attic of his market house but thereafter migrated from room to room in the town, at one period occupying a chamber in the tower of Holy Trinity Church. It actually went out of existence in 1731 but was revived thirty years later under the nationally ubiquitous title of the Blue-Coat School, surviving precariously for another century mostly by means of sporadic gifts.

Archbishop Abbot's endowment for his manufactory had meanwhile resulted in a local scandal. It is probable that his initial decision to provide money for wages did indeed erode what slender chances his scheme possessed, for there is little doubt that workmen, aware of the fund's existence, demanded a far higher rate of payment than the norm existing in the town. In turn, however, the Court of Chancery's own decision to make the fund available to any poor tradesman who required stock merely made the money available to any man who could spin a good hard-luck story. In 1852, nearly two centuries after it had so released the fund, the Court of Chancery began a leisurely consideration of its effects and its future. At some stage in the deliberation it was decided that Baker's Charity and Abbot's manufactory fund, together with the Blue-Coat School assets should be consolidated, and the whole used to endow a school to be established in the old manufactory buildings: in 1856 Archbishop Abbot's School came into being under the shadow of his Hospital. Possessed of a permanent home and well endowed, the revived school very rapidly achieved a high educational level, and so confident in its future were its Trustees that they could turn down in 1884 a proposal to amalgamate with the Grammar School. Financial provisions that were both ample and flexible under nineteenth-century conditions, however, proved inadequate in the twentieth-century context and in 1933 the School came to a final end. The Archbishop's name is nevertheless still perpetuated in the title of the George Abbot School, established in the suburbs in the post-war years.

An architectural characteristic of the town, demonstrated by its surviving historic buildings, was its ability to draw on a pool of highly skilled local labour for over 300 years – from the building of the first burghers' houses in the early sixteenth century to the building of the villas in the late nineteenth century. If the surviving records of the Friary and of the Castle give an accurate indication of their appearance, then that tradition could be extended back to the thirteenth century, lasting in all some 500 years until it was ultimately broken by the onset of mass building and mass financing in the twentieth century. The tradition is characterised by a conservatism – indeed, at times an anachronism – in plan, coupled with a vigour in detail and a high standard of workmanship and may perhaps be due to the community's position in an essentially rural area: the hermaphrodites of the Guildhall and the terra cotta mouldings of the villas alike seem to owe far more to a peasant than to an urban society. The Grammar School, the last westward building of the town that still acts as part of its essential skeleton, perfectly exemplified the tradition. Built less than fifty years before the Hospital it, too, lay beyond the watershed of the Reformation but its architects looked back to the tradition of the cloister, reflecting in stone the innate conservatism of the community. The impression conveyed by its quadrangle is essentially ecclesiastical, totally unlike that conveyed by the quadrangle of the Hospital.

The School had been in formal existence for over seventy years before it acquired a permanent home and, like its feebler neighbour, was destined to survive in history under a name other than its true founder for it was not a king but a merchant who first endowed the modest school in the town. In 1509 Robert Beckingham, a London member of the Grocers' Company, bequeathed part of his estate for a charitable foundation that would both educate the young and pray for his soul, a common enough contemporary piety. Beckingham had no direct links with Guildford and the reasons for his generosity can only be conjectured as probably arising from his friendship with one of the prominent citizens. Eleven years later, in somewhat tardy recognition of the gift, the Mayor and Approved Men gave a house and a small piece of land near the Castle for the School and there it survived, if little more, for the next thirty-three years. Like many similar establishments in other towns it would have probably flickered into extinction had there not arisen, during the brief reign of Edward VI, that movement which successfully diverted some of the confiscated ecclesiastical property back into more appropriate channels and so gained for the boy king a vicarious reputation for piety. In 1553 his advisers, in his name, granted the town's petition both for a charter and an income for its school. The *Schola Regia Grammaticalis Edvardi Sexti* came into formal existence on January 27 of that year and, almost immediately, plans were made for a new building that would match up to its resounding title and new financial standing. In 1555 the Corporation bought a piece of open land just within the town limits and two years later 'didd begynne at there owne costes and charges to build and reare the large Rome now used for the Schole house with the great Chamber and garret over the same, and the same healed with Horsham stone and therein made many verie faier windows of ffree stone, well glased, the walls of which Schole-house are all of brick and stone of a very strong, statelie, and faire building, the charges thereof didd amount to above ffower hundred marks'.[57]

In 1596, some ten years after the final completion of the School, George Austen began compiling for it his *Monument* or history. In both the lucidity of its style and the beauty of its physical execution, his work is outstanding and virtually unique among the town records, not only throwing a light of rare clarity on the society of his day but providing a precise genealogy for at least one of the town's major buildings. The story he has to tell in the late sixteenth century was to be repeated again and again over the succeeding centuries: the ambitious beginning of a project: the discovery that corporate funds were unequal to the strain: the ebbing away of endeavour and the final rescue operation by a group of wealthy private citizens. The schoolhouse was successfully completed but provided insufficient accommodation and in 1569 John Austen, George Austen's father, 'findinge a want of the Romes intended to be buylded for the Scholemaster and ussher ... and seeinge noe likelyhode that the Townesmen could performe the same' energetically set about raising the capital for an additional wing. The example encouraged another wealthy citizen, William Hamond, to lauch an ambitious building programme that would provide a second wing and a connecting gallery: work was started on this in 1571. Fifteen years later George Austen was himself a witness to the existing condition of the school. 'After the death of the said John Austen the same [the west wing] lay many yeeres unfynished ... whereupon knowing what travell and paynes the said John Austen my father had taken to buyld the same, and seeinge howe likely it was to fall to utter decay, I did consider what course might be taken to bring the same to perfection.'[58] Like his father before him, he set about raising the capital, enlisting a number of local gentry in the cause, and in 1586, thirty years after work had begun, the Grammar School was completed in the form it would thenceforward retain.

Two surviving buildings of the town demonstrate, as clearly as any documentary sequence, the ultimate realignment of the town's trade following the collapse of the wool industry. Abbot's manufactory, intended to revive an indigenous industry, is tucked away on what was a back street: the Corn Exchange, intended to facilitate the trade of the middleman, stands on the High Street. The manufactory is a plain, almost humble building: the Exchange, too, is plain, for its builders returned to the classic mode then fashionable, but it dominates its surroundings, the stark Tuscan columns and massive entablature overpowering the humbler merchants houses on either side. Built by public subscription in 1818, it was intended to perform the function of an Assize court as well as a corn exchange, but its primary purpose was also now the primary purpose of the town – to act as a trading-depot. By the beginning of the nineteenth century Guildford had returned almost wholly to its original function.

Over two centuries before the railway arrived to strengthen the town's resumed role, a major new communication with the outside world had been established. In 1635 Sir Richard Weston of Sutton Place obtained a commission from the King for improving the navigation of the River Wey. Weston belonged to a later generation – specifically, to that class of eighteenth-century aristocrat who, dabbling in science, contributed to an economic revolution as by-product of their interest. He had a strong personal interest in canals, for his low-lying lands at Sutton Place were continually being flooded and it was probably with the limited interest of flood control that he erected the first lock on the river at Stoke, a mile or so upstream from his home. His later elaborate plan to make the river navigable to the Thames received a check during the Civil War but, despite his strong royalist sympathies, he was able to get an Act passed in 1651 which provided for the building of the Navigation with the Mayor and Approved Men of Guildford as one of the authorities.

The Weston family gained only trouble from Richard Weston's inventive genius. The Navigation was finished swiftly, the twelve locks between Guildford and the Thames being completed by 1653 but almost immediately inefficient administration plunged the Navigation into financial difficulties. Luckily, perhaps, Richard Weston himself died before the work was completed and it was his unfortunate son, George, who found himself involved in the bitter accusations and counter-accusations not merely of inefficiency but also of actual dishonesty. George Weston was first obliged to sell the family shares in the business and then found himself in prison for the debts contracted by his father. The disputes dragged on for nearly twenty years, the Navigation inevitably suffering as a result. In 1671 a second Act was obtained which put affairs in order, two judges and the Exchequer Baron being appointed together with a body of Trustees as the governing authority, and on this new basis the Navigation entered upon its period of prosperity. The great canal boom of the following century resulted in the expansion of the modest link between Guildford and Weybridge into a county-wide system, beginning in 1760 with the extension of the Navigation upstream to

Godalming, and followed, in 1813, with the cross-country link between the Wey and the Arun systems.[59]

Guildford had appeared something less than lukewarm during the establishment of a system that was to put considerable money into local pockets, both public and private. 'So great was the public prejudice against the project in those days that, as tradition informs us, the work of the day was destroyed in the night by the labouring classes till at length it became necessary to have night guards.'[60] Tradition doubtless exaggerated but Guildford Corporation was able to make a profit from the local dislike by obtaining a rare privilege in 1671 – the right to a toll of one penny per ton of merchandise. The Guild Merchant's argument was somewhat specious: it claimed that not only should the town be recompensed for the use of its roads and bridges by carters but that there should also be some form of insurance against the numbers of poverty-stricken bargemen and their families that were expected to descend upon the town. This may perhaps have been true in the early days but the nineteenth-century memoir of John Mason contains a nostalgic picture of the bargemen: they actually looked a different race from the townsmen, he thought – trim and sailor-like in dress and self-respecting in their habits.

The concession gained was nevertheless valuable: even in 1776, when the Navigation extended only four miles upstream, some 17,000 tons of merchandise passed through Guildford on the way to London. By the early nineteenth century this 'River Pence' was contributing over £200 a year to the upkeep of the town's streets.

But the direct gain brought to the public purse was overshadowed by the diffused profit brought to the community as a whole. The Navigation was ideally suited to the transportation of those bulk agricultural products for which, increasingly, the town was acting as a market. The nineteenth-century building boom, too, relied heavily on cheap water-transport for building-materials. The town and the Navigation contributed substantially to each other's prosperity, leaving as evidence the large wharfage along the eastern bank of the river. By a natural process the few industries of the nineteenth-century town established themselves within reaching-distance of the wharf, creating in turn a natural point of development for those of the twentieth century. Even the coming of the railway did not immediately affect the Navigation, for there was more profit in passengers than in freight. But the appearance of Guildford's first railway station in 1845 did mark the beginning of decline. The great treadmill crane on Guildford Wharf, capable of lifting three tons at a time under the combined force of eight men, was probably last used in 1908 after being in use for more than a century. The world wars brought back a transient prosperity – the gunpowder mills at Chilworth alone created a heavy demand for barges in the First World War – and even as late as January 1969 a cargo of wheat was transported commercially. But its transference to the National Trust is indicative of its present role, and it is essentially as a pleasure-ground that the Wey Navigation survives today after acting as a prop to the town's prosperity over three centuries.

In 1905 the venerable White Lion Inn put out an advertisement that could not have better summed up the transitional period in the town. Its claim to be the 'most unique in Surrey' was adequately borne out by the remarkable range of services available. It had eighty rooms to discharge its traditional function, together with stabling for sixty horses – but it also boasted a motor garage and inspection pit, as well as extensive bicycle-accommodation – altogether a brave attempt to be all things to all men. Further up the hill the smaller and less fashionable Angel made a bid for the new trade with the statement that it was the 'Headquarters of the Automobile Club of Great Britain and Ireland'. The wheel had almost come full circle, the road challenging the dominance of the railway but, under new conditions, impressing a new pattern upon the community.

The realignment of the town's trade in the eighteenth century found natural expression in the late nineteenth century with the development of purely retail outlets. Agricultural exchange of produce still formed the basis of prosperity but the wives and daughters of the first waves of wealthy immigrants required their local haberdasheries to supplement their shopping expeditions to

Town: the running of the large villas demanded local grocers as well as local servants. Demand rapidly created supply, and attracted a new class of immigrant – the vigorous imaginative man who divined the trend in the town and arrived to profit from it. Characteristically, the majority of the large Guildford shops and factories were the products of these men, for the same initiative that brought them to the town served to take them ahead of the natives.

A clear-cut chain of cause and effect is provided by the development of an enterprise created by one of these immigrants. In 1895 two brothers, John and Raymond Dennis, arrived from Devon to establish their Universal Athletic Store in the town. Founded firmly on that widespread craze for cycling that gripped Britain at the turn of the century, it was brought to the public eye by the brothers' well-developed sense of publicity. John was the businessman; Raymond, as a crack cyclist, took the family name around the country and both pushed the firm at home. In 1898 John Dennis attracted considerable attention when he was fined for driving a motorised tricycle up the High Street 'at a furious speed'. The escapade cost him £1, but the publicity was worth a hundred times the fine.

The brothers had turned to building motorised vehicles before the end of the century – so successfully that at the Crystal Palace show in 1903 their sales figures topped all others. Two years later they moved out of their cramped quarters to Woodbridge Hill and there went into full-scale production. Cars still predominated but simultaneously they were experimenting with public-service-vehicles in particular with fire-engines. Again, a simple but effective piece of publicity brought their product into the public eye. The London Fire Brigade was in process of acquiring its motorised fleet and there was some doubt as to the power of the Dennis engine. Two of them were coupled together, and a jet of water was projected over the dome of St Paul's, to the delight of the newspapers and subsequent profit to the brothers.

The fire-engine contract altered the course of the firm's development: in 1913 the construction of private cars was abandoned in favour of heavy public vehicles. The decision profoundly affected the future development of the town. The firm became the major heavy industry located within the borough, and had it turned towards the space-consuming production of motor cars it would either have found itself crippled by the planning restrictions of the mid-century or, more likely, it would have continued to develop and so would have swamped an immense area. In either event, the town would have been the loser to a marked degree.

Industry added its vital corrective but the twentieth-century prosperity of the town is linked to retail trade particularly in view of that fact that, since 1968, further industrial development is not intended to take place. The pattern of trade established in the post-war years foreshadows commercially the political regional-isation of the area. The town lies at the centre of a 'catchment area' whose population in 1966 was some 238,500. A little over half of the town's retail trade is generated locally, the rest being created by shoppers coming in from the catchment, the greater part of them from the semi-rural areas that are characteristic of Surrey. The pattern is made explicit by the unusually high number of estate agents there are in the town – thirty-three for a popu-lation of some 56,000 as against, for example, eighteen in Woking with its far greater population. Despite the planning intention to limit the use of the upper High Street to shops, building societies have pushed out the small family-shops that once provided both variation and a social service for the upper part of the town: every major building society is represented in the few hundred yards of the street. The turnover of houses in the Borough is high – the same house changing hands on average once in seven years – but the number of agents and societies can be explained only by reference to the fact that each covers a very wide area outside the town. The national trend towards the chain store and the supermarket, coupled with the local pressure exerted by the catchment area, has made an inevitable mark upon the owner-ship of the shops in the High Street. Poetic justice and commercial economics are both served by the swallowing of the enterprises created by the vigorous immigrants. Nevertheless, the curious physical resilience that the town has displayed finds a social expression in the survival of small local firms dotted down the length of the Street, overshadowed by Marks and Woolworths and Debenhams but with the same names on the fasciae that were there a century ago. The records of the Guild Merchant and the current telephone directory contain some of the same names, frequently with the same mispelling now sanctified by centuries of usage.

(iii) THE FRIARY

Socially, the loss of the Friary had a minimal effect upon the town, for at the Dissolution Guildford's major religious institution consisted of only seven brothers and such was its poverty and 'the great clamour of debts' that its despoilers were obliged to sell some of its possessions to satisfy legitimate creditors. Architecturally, the loss proved to be disastrous for, by a series of accidents, its open grounds remained almost intact in the heart of the town until the mid-nineteenth century and into the vacuum flooded the worst possible kind of commercial and industrial development.

The Friary existed for at least three hundred years but its written history is brief, the archival malaise of the town rendered lethal in this case by the act of physical dissolution. Some of its records found an ultimate haven in the library of Cambridge University but these consist in the main of purely formal records – scriptoria regulations, the Constitution, which followed the usual Dominican regulations, and a lengthy obituary calendar. That it could not have been founded before 1236 is made clear by a petition of the friars in which they referred to Eleanor of Provence as their first foundress, and Eleanor did not marry Henry III until that year. Purely negative evidence for a late foundation is provided by the apparent fact that the friars were not among those who prayed for the soul of young Prince Henry, grandson of Eleanor who died in Guildford. The Friary may then perhaps have been founded in his memory, for his heart was contained in a reliquary in the Friary church for some years afterwards.

The community seems never to have been very large – even in 1336 there were only twenty brothers – but it enjoyed a steady largesse from the Crown during the period that the town was a royal residence. The friars evidently turned the Dominican horticultural skill to profit by laying out and tending the royal gardens of the Castle and Park: in a pathetic appeal to Henry VIII for alms they were described as being unable to carry out their usual tasks of 'seeking out, trimming, and fashioning grounds and gardens about the Kings place'[61] – presumably being too weak from hunger.

But during the days of its prosperity, pious gifts from the local nobility followed the fashion set by the monarch. There remain only the vaguest hints of the physical appearance and size of the buildings, the few indications being contained, ironically, in the inventory drawn up at the time of its dissolution. It consisted of a fair-sized church with a central tower, a great and a small kitchen, a main hall and a dormitory. A part of the stained glass used was reputed to have found its way into the chapel of Abbot's hospital, and if this is true the Friary must have maintained the normal standard of Dominican culture, for the glass is the most beautiful thing of its kind in the town. John Leland thought it worth while to refer to the community's library, an expected possession of a friary of the intellectual Dominican order and some evidence of the community's role in the town.

Behind the main complex, and stretching northward along the river bank as far as the wooden bridge over the river, were its gardens and pastures. The land on the other side of the river was part of the King's Park, and in 1274 the Dominicans were granted limited access to it. They planted walnut trees there, and the name of that area, Walnut Tree Close, endured by a quirk of history although the present road could not more belie the name and its associations.

Altogether, the Friary seems to have been a small but comfortable community, honestly pursuing its particular vocation of preaching and teaching, modestly endowed but secure in royal favour until the monarch abandoned the town. Thereafter it declined, and the Dissolution probably only just forestalled its financial collapse. There was a peculiar irony in the fact that it was unable to give hospitality to its destroyer in 1537, when

Henry and his Chancellor Thomas Cromwell were in the town, for the royal entourage were housed in the nearby rectory of St Nicholas. On 10 October of the following year 'the prior and convent of the Black Friars of Guildford, with one assent and consent, without any manner of coercion'[62] freely gave their lands and house up to the royal use – one of the results of that brief royal stay in the rectory of St Nicholas, for it was then that a further series of dissolutions was put into effect.

Nothing much was done with the vacant building for many years afterwards. It fell under the control of the keeper of the Royal Park and was occasionally used as a temporary residence during the increasingly rare royal visits to the town. In 1606 it suffered the common fate of an unwanted but substantial building and was cannibalised, and the land probably lay vacant for more than fifteen years afterwards until 1630 when Lord Annandale, the King's keeper, purchased the entire Park, including the Friary grounds, for £5000 and built himself a substantial house on the site of the Friary.

Annandale's house, supposedly designed by Inigo Jones, survived until 1818, and there are accordingly both pictorial and documentary records of it. Local memory, certainly as reflected by John Russell in 1801, seems to have confused the aristocrat's mansion with the original religious structure, for Russell could describe the existing building as 'an antient structure of the gothic order, but much injured in its appearance by the removal of the pinnacles etc and also by the insertion of modern windows'.[63] The windows were probably contemporary with the structure, for its general appearance was that of an Elizabethan manor-house with the later addition of a massive Palladian porch. It was a handsome building of chalk and flint, set back from the curve of the North Town Ditch, facing the town but screened from it by a line of elm trees.

Annandale died some ten years after building his house and it passed through a number of hands, coming into the possession of the Onslows of Clandon in 1736. But throughout the eighteenth century it continued to discharge its natural social function as the largest mansion within the town limits: the judges were lodged here during the Assizes, balls and public breakfasts given, royalty entertained even after it had been converted into the officers' quarters of the newly established barracks, the third phase of the Friary's existence.

The establishment of a barracks in the town in 1794 was alike the result of Guildford's strategic position and the disturbances spreading outward from France. Hitherto, the quartering of soldiers in the town had been done on a completely casual arrangement – mostly at the expense of the local innkeepers. During the War of American Independence their burden became so great that they addressed a petition to Parliament, earnestly begging relief and, incidentally, giving a vivid picture of the troop movements created by the town's position. 'Guildford is the central or halfway Quarters between the Metropolis and Portsmouth and also between Chatham and Portsmouth and consequently can seldom if ever be free from being the settled quarters of some troops. At the same time it is the constant Halting Place of all Troops going to and returning from Foreign Parts . . . of all sick and wounded Soldiers and Seamen their wives and children . . . of at least Nine out of Ten of the recruiting parties going out of or coming into this island which from the vast increase of the Army and Navy has made the burthen almost tenfold upon this Town. . . . The vast numbers of troops that have been quartered in Guildford within three years has produced such fatal effects that more Publicans have failed within that small period than for Thirty years before.'[64]

Nothing was done, for even the sympathy of the local Members of Parliament could not overcome the deep national dislike and suspicion of a standing army. But the ominous harbingers of the Napoleonic Wars forced a national change and in 1794 the central government initiated a systematic policy for the permanent quartering of soldiers, and Guildford was inevitably included in the plan. Pleased though the publicans might have been, the town as a whole disliked the prospect exceedingly, for ill-paid soldiers brought only trouble instead of trade. But their formal protest had as little effect as the early protest of the innkeepers and from 1794 onwards the Annandale mansion formed the officers' quarters of a cavalry regiment, the troopers being quartered in what were evidently temporary hutments. The War Office acquired the Friary lands as well as the mansion and a large open space behind and to the east of the Friary appears labelled simply as the Barrack Field in the 1835 survey of the town.

But the barracks had disappeared before the survey was made for, with the ending of the Napoleonic Wars in 1815, the demand for troops and the barracks to house them had eased considerably. In 1818, Annandale's house was demolished, together with the temporary hutments, and the entire site leased to a brewer. No major buildings yet appeared upon it and the ancient Friary gardens, under their new name of Barrack Field, remained green and empty until 1840 when the greater part of it was broken up and sold to private buyers.

Within a decade of this official indication of settled peace, the international situation again grew threatening, a turbulent era heralded by the French revolution of 1848, followed by the Crimean War five years later and brought to a head by the Franco-Prussian War of 1870. The English response was to call out the long-forgotten Militia, a characteristic compromise between hated military efficiency and total unpreparedness. The local response was either to dodge the Militia, or treat the whole thing as an entertainment. 'Most of us boys belonged to a club to which we paid a weekly sum for providing a substitute for us if our names were drawn in the ballot for the militia,' John Mason remembered.[65] But an anonymous correspondent in the *West Surrey Times* presented an idyllic picture of the life of a militia-man during his summer camp: 'Location very beautiful. Think camp life very jolly. . . . Played quoits and cricket. Make more enquiries from an instructor about the reg'lars. He tells me that the real thing is not so rosy as our camp. Think him very straight for being so candid, as by his honesty he may be losing his "com" on me. *Monday August 6.* Last day, very sorry. Left Dorking for Guildford which I reached (per cattle truck) at 9.30. Never spent a happier week in my life.'[66]

The new wave of citizen-soldiers required more barracks in the town, and about 1852 a completely new complex appeared on part of the Friary site. Sufficient of it survived until 1970 to give a clear picture of the whole – a structure resembling a toy fort complete with Norman windows, arrow slits and decorated with an attractive frieze of terracotta ornaments. Access to the parade ground was gained through a low arch, embellished with the somewhat ambiguous motto 'Salvam Domine Fac Victoriam' ('O Lord Save Victoria'). The parade ground itself, faced with rows of neat houses that were the envy of many a poor, ill-housed townsman, occupied the site of what was probably the ancient friary yard.

In 1854, according to a report made many years later, 'the Government went to Surrey's County Town with £100,000 in its hands and politely asked to be accorded facilities for constructing, on the downs overlooking its sleepy High Street, a permanent military camp for 20,000 soldiers. But Guildford would not hear of such a thing . . . and the Government went away to a little village called Aldershot . . . who welcomed them warmly.'[67] The fear of the presence of thousands of soldiers effectively cancelled what attraction the £100,000 might have had and thirty years later when the War Office was seeking permission to build two of its chain of forts in the town, at Henley Grove and Pewley Hill, it went out of its way to explain that they were intended purely as supply dumps. It seems to be more than a coincidence, and hardly consonant with the official explanation for their construction, that they should have been placed on the Old Road at the ancient entrance and exit to the town. But their military life was brief and harmless: Henley Grove rapidly reverted to wild life and Pewley Hill provided an ideal building-site in the next century.

The Friary was not so fortunate: after it had been locked away from commercial development for more than six centuries its lands were thrown on the open market at the nadir of English architecture. The first blow was delivered by the railway passing through the open lands of the Royal Park to establish its terminus in the place 'formerly called Walnut Close, there being for many years a fine grove of walnut trees down to the river bank – and was usually a playground for the humbler ranks in St Nicholas.

It is unfortunate', the contemporary writer continued, 'that as the population of the town has gradually increased, these places of resort for out of door recreation have as rapidly decreased. Within a few years Bury Fields, the Walnut Close and latterly the Barrack Field have ceased to resound with the cheerful voice of the working class at play.'[68] Worse – considerably worse – was to follow.

The area immediately surrounding the Barracks had disappeared under brick by 1845. There were still islands of gardens in the area and the Lees extended, green and empty, along the riverside, part of them devoted to a cricket pitch. But the proximity of river and rail ensured that this flat strip so close to the town, so conveniently vacant, would suffer the full onslaught of industrial development. The gasworks shifted across the river and squatted among the dwindling remains of the gardens: the brewery, too, moved from the west bank to a site which allowed expansion and grew monstrously. Houses and shops and small factories flooded into the Town Ditch, creating the North Street of the nineteenth and twentieth centuries.

The process was accelerated in 1882 with the construction of a bridge leading from the railway station into the heart of the area. Originally, it had been planned to extend the line of the High Street in a great curve through the dilapidated properties on the west bank, and so make a grand approach to the station. But, word getting out prematurely, speculators moved in, prices soared and the scheme came to nothing. The next move came from the Earl of Onslow. Much of the vacant land belonged to him and the construction of a bridge would obviously increase its value. He therefore proposed to make himself responsible for building the bridge and its approaches if the town would contribute £6500 towards the cost.

It was a reasonable suggestion for the lack of a second bridge was proving increasingly embarrassing. In 1848 the ancient wooden bridge that gave its name to the downstream crossing had been rebuilt in brick but it lay outside the local traffic flow. The vast quantity of traffic generated by the station was all funnelled across the already inadequate Town Bridge, and for the community to acquire a new bridge for a comparatively small contribution seemed good business to the Corporation. But the traders of the town – in particular the High Street traders – thought otherwise. They lost their case and Onslow Bridge was duly opened in July 1882 but the poster that appeared throughout the town on that day of official rejoicing adequately summed up their opinion.

OPENING OF THE NEW BRIDGE

Rejoice O ye ratepayers
That £6,500 of your money has gone to oblige a Noble Lord
Rejoice O ye tradesmen
That it is not spent in the town, but at the Civil Service Stores.
Therefore shut up your shops and be merry, saith the Mayor.[69]

The squib marked the beginning of a long tussle between the rival trading-communities of the High Street and the upstart North Street. There is, admittedly, something ineradicably raffish about this street, at once the oldest and the newest of the town's secondary thoroughfares. Originally, it marked, as the North Town Ditch, the northern limit of the unfortified town, and as late as the end of the eighteenth century its northern side ran beside gardens. Under the ugly but vigorous stimulus of the industrial development in the Friary gardens it mushroomed in the mid-nineteenth century, and with the establishment of the cattle market in it the street moved into direct competition with its venerable neighbour – exactly as the High Street traders had feared. It became the refuge for the true descendants of the early merchants of the town – people who pursued their trade under the flimsy protection of a stall, or with nothing save the open street upon which to display their stock. The established tradesmen of the High Street had no liking for this humble band of traders who impeded the passage of wealthy customers, and gradually they found their way to the more hospitable North Street. The shopkeepers reluctantly agreed that an open produce-market was justified, but protested vehemently at any other kind of trade being carried on from open stalls whose owners paid no rates. They found a strong champion in the editor of the *Outlook*, who launched a blistering attack on 'the Jews from London and elsewhere who, with the approval of the Town Council, descend upon Guildford on Fridays and Saturdays, leave on Saturday night with scores if not hundreds of pounds of residents' money, and who contribute not a cent to the town's rates beyond the few shillings they pay for their "pitches" and not a sou to the cost of clearing North Street of the muck they leave'.[70]

The continual objections had their effect and it is as a fruit and vegetable market that the last open market of the town survives. But that long history of ungentility, beginning with bull-baiting in the thirteenth century and ending with the occasional drunken brawl in the twentieth, has left its mark upon the street. Its proportions are broad and handsome, the vista of townscape and downs at the lower end variegated and satisfying, and from time to time well-meaning attempts are made to realise the potential. But despite the handsome new library and glib office-buildings North Street resists respectability and remains an ugly, unlovable, vital element of its own. Commercial interests have recognised this and a type of shop-trade quite different to that of the High Street has developed along it. During the lengthy negotiations to establish the site of the new Woolworths and the immense new branch of Debenhams, an attempt was made to persuade them to adopt the area. Both refused. Socially, the refusals were unfortunate for it would have both relieved congestion in a dense part of the town and brought trade to a relatively unpopular area. Commercially, the refusals were justified, as was testified by the fate of a large building, erected speculatively on the site of the old Dolphin Inn. It remained empty for years after its completion and was at length adapted to office accommodation. North Street, like Upper High Street, creates its own pattern of life, regardless of planners.

(iv) CATHEDRAL AND UNIVERSITY

THE CATHEDRAL

The impact of the Reformation upon England left the ancient ecclesiastical structure of the country largely unchanged. There was no particular reason why the religious crisis should affect an administrative organisation that worked efficiently. The diocese, legacy of the classic world, had been tested for over a thousand years: the Christian world, inheriting at last the Roman, had itself merely adapted an existing system by substituting the bishop for the *propraetor* and the bishop administered his territory simultaneously as a priest and a very powerful, very earthly lord. As a natural division of land and people, the diocesan system was indestructible, adapting itself to the most alien of requirements.

In England, the physical changes wrought by the Norman administrative genius upon the ancient Saxon divisions proved endurable – in particular that which affected the great diocese of Winchester. Originally, it had run in a great belt across southern England from Devon to Kent, but the Normans limited it to Hampshire and Surrey though still retaining the bishopric in the ancient capital of England. The Commissioners of Henry VIII proposed few other changes. Their recommendation that five new dioceses should be created in the kingdom was adopted and, with a far-sighted awareness of the growth and shift of population, they also made provision for the creation of suffragan bishops – a peculiarly English measure which enabled any bishop to nominate 'two honest and discreet spiritual persons', one of whom the Crown would choose as his assistant, with the style and dignity of bishop. Guildford was chosen as title for a suffragan, but the slow growth of population in Hampshire and Surrey made it long unnecessary for the bishop actually to appoint an assistant. The development of London, too, reduced the total population of the diocese for, in 1846, Winchester lost control of the south London parishes and, later, the parishes of East Surrey. Population increased steadily during the nineteenth century but, even so, it was not until 1874 that the long dormant provision of Henry VIII was activated and a Bishop of Guildford was at last appointed as suffragan to Winchester.

The suffragan status lasted for fifty years and would probably have continued for even longer had it not been for the phenomenon of the 'population explosion' of the south-east. Surrey's population, static for centuries, suddenly began to move towards the half-million mark as the development of the railway brought new blood into the county. A condition that had lasted for 800 years was drastically altered within half a century and in 1923 came the proposals to divide the ancient Diocese of Winchester into three parts, still retaining Winchester as the heart of the mother diocese, but erecting Portsmouth and Guildford into the dignity of full bishoprics. There was strong opposition to the fragmentation and the Bishop of Gloucester made the proposal that was in the minds of many people – the logical development was to divide the diocese into only two parts and combine Surrey, the northern division, with Southwark. Winchester and his suffragan Guildford fought back as strongly: not only would this course perpetuate the system of suffragan but, more important, it would accelerate the already alarming dominance of London over Surrey. It was a telling argument and, ultimately, the threefold division came into effect as originally planned. In July 1927 Harold Greig was installed as the first Bishop of Guildford in the parish church of Holy Trinity, now automatically the Bishop's cathedral.

Holy Trinity was the largest church in the town but, almost certainly, it would prove to be too small to fulfil the manifold functions of a cathedral and, from the first, the new Bishop made it clear that he regarded it as one of his primary duties to bring about the erection of a cathedral. It was a formidable task almost without precedent for centuries. All the recently created dioceses had found to hand town churches large enough to be adapted as the headquarters of a diocese – Portsmouth, Guildford's twin, was an excellent case in point. Guildford would be forced to prove, in the middle of the twentieth century, that the forces which had created the medieval cathedrals were dormant, not dead. And those forces found expression not only in design but in the humdrum but vital ability to provide the money to execute the design. The age of princely gifts was past: the bulk of the money would have to come from an anonymous laity increasingly described as indifferent, if not actively hostile, to established religion. In May 1928 the Diocesan Conference courageously decided that the age of faith did not necessarily lay in the past and resolved to build a new cathedral. In November of the same year Lord Onslow's gift of six acres on the crest of Stag Hill, with an option to purchase more, was accepted and a permanent committee was set up to supervise and raise funds. The estimated cost of the Cathedral was £250,000 – a figure which was to be more than trebled by the time the last brick was in place a generation later.

Lord Onslow's generosity had the effect of creating a *fait accompli* as far as the choice of site was concerned – which in turn created the massive local opposition that continued throughout the first years of the project. A few weeks after the gift was formally accepted, the *Outlook* – the local periodical which specialised in the tormenting of Authority – launched a determined attack on the choice of the site with a letter from an expert who pointed out that 'The whole of Stag Hill is a mass of clay [with] the danger that the whole building may move.'[71] The warning proved perspicuous for a year later the Conference was informed that boring showed the need for massive underpinning at a cost of some £25,000.

But it was the location of the site, not its geology, which aroused opposition in the town that had given a title to the new Bishop, and whose good will was essential to the project. The objectors had good argument on their side for, physically the green mass of Stag Hill was not merely outside the town but divorced from it by river, railway and suburb. Strong claims were advanced on behalf of Holy Trinity Church: it was pointed out that sufficient land around the old church could be acquired for the cost of the underpinning alone of the new cathedral and that a fraction of the over-all estimated sum would serve to adapt Holy Trinity and so establish the Cathedral in its natural place – the heart of the town. If it should prove impossible to acquire land in the built-up centre then, it was claimed, the newly acquired Stoke Park was an ideal alternative site: it was accessible to the main centre of population and there was more than sufficient space both to develop a dignified complex and yet leave a green space in the Borough's heart.

The controversy over the site long continued as a grumbling

undertone, but it faded into insignificance compared with the loud objections to the idea of a cathedral at all. The appeal for funds could not have come at a worse time. Barely six months after the Committee had come into existence in November 1928, the collapse of a complex economic system 4000 miles away heralded the European crisis of the Depression. In England, the numbers of unemployed climbed into their tens of thousands and then in their millions: in Guildford itself, a massive rescue operation for the local unemployed was launched in 1931. The economic powers of those who would be called upon to contribute to the new cathedral declined sharply: simultaneously, the growth of population in Surrey placed an impossible pressure upon existing ecclesiastical facilities. What money was available should be devoted to building new parish churches, it was argued, and not squandered on grandiose, outdated concepts.

The most telling aspect of this attack was that it came from the heart of the Church itself, launched by practising Christians who were as dedicated to the Church as the defenders of the Cathedral concept. In June 1935 – after the appeal had been launched, the architect chosen and the first work on the site begun – the *Surrey Advertiser* published a long letter from a correspondent who signed himself simply as 'An Observer' but whom the leader described as 'written by one actively engaged in Church life in the diocese'. Citing his experience in other cathedral cities, 'Observer' described the average cathedral congregation as being composed of people who came for the music and roundly attacked cathedral clergy as 'a snobbish race apart. The Bishop foresaw crowds of nice, decent people coming into the diocese. Do they frequent the present cathedral now? No!' Finance was one of the barriers between clergy and laity. 'The minds of the clergy seems to be so saturated with thoughts of how they were going to meet parish expenses that they seemed incapable of speaking with enthusiasm on any other subject. . . . Now, in addition, they are urged in pious language to find money and more money for a cathedral.'[72]

The letter triggered off a massive reaction, the heavy correspondence that followed being almost equally divided between opponents and defenders of the Cathedral. The Archdeacon joined the defenders with a sermon, preached in Holy Trinity, based on the text 'Woe unto you when all men speak well of you'. *Vox populi* was not inevitably *vox dei*: the clergy had a duty to the wider concepts of Christianity as well as to the parochial. A month later the Bishop himself refuted the charge that a kind of palace was to be erected at the cost of parish work. 'No one proposed to erect at Stag Hill a cathedral with a dean and chapter and full staff. What was contemplated was a new cathedral of a new kind ... with a provost and one or two clergy ... The idea of a complete cathedral establishment was wholly misleading.'[73] The statement was uttered in good faith but time was to make it as inaccurate as the early optimistic estimates of cost.

The effect of controversy was to slow down the initial impulse. In 1928 Lord Onslow had offered the site on only one condition – that the offer should be taken up within three years: nearly four years later the site was still virtually untouched. In 1932 he wrote to the Diocesan Conference a letter which betrayed 'impatience at the slow progress and a suspicion that there are influences operating to delay any forward movement'. Despite the fact that his three-year option had expired, he wrote, he was willing to renew it but he had no intention of doing so year after year. 'I am a dealer in real estate, just as much as beef and mutton constitute the stock in trade of a butcher or physic the stock in trade of a grocer.' So far there had been no demand for the land under discussion, but it could come about and he could not wait for ever. Did the diocese want a new cathedral or did it not?[74]

Did Guildford itself want a cathedral, or did it not was the direct question which Lord Midleton, chairman of the Appeal Committee put in a letter to William Harvey, ex-mayor and probably the most influential citizen of the town. The Diocese had arrived at a compromise: there was to be a dual fund for the erection of both the Cathedral and the required new churches – but Guildford still seemed lukewarm. It had been expected that the town would cordially welcome the prestige. Midleton went on,

But this has not been the case. . . . So far as any general expression of opinion has been given we have rather met with discouragement. I quite realise that the question of *site* has influenced opinion . . . but in the case of older cities which owe their prominence to their cathedrals in several – notably Lincoln and Durham – the cathedral is as far distant from the business portion of the town as Stag Hill from the incomparable High Street of Guildford. The question will be fully decided at the coming Diocesan Conference on December 6 [1932]. The want of interest in Guildford may prove to be a deciding factor. . . . Please tell me whether you think we can assure the Diocesan Conference that the indifference which appears on the surface is not a genuine expression of Guildford's feeling as to the establishment of a cathedral.

Harvey had gained considerable national, and immense local, prestige during his mayoralty of the previous year when he had launched his fund for the unemployed and he, if any person in the Borough, was in touch with public opinion. He could give only a negative assurance at best. 'The idea has never been present in the minds of Guildford people that we should NOT have a cathedral.' As Midleton had pointed out, the main objection was the siting. 'The ideal cathedral in their mind is one whose doors open as nearly as possible on the main centre of the town's life.' However, once the work was well and truly started he had little doubt that the townsfolk would become wholehearted in their support.[75] It is doubtful if the Conference was finally persuaded by this heavily qualified local support, but in December 1933 it was formally decided to launch a dual appeal and begin work on the Cathedral when £50,000 had been raised. In earnest of that decision a teak cross, made from the wood of the battleship *Ganges*, was set up on the naked hill-top. Edward Maufe's cathedral was, after all, to come into being.

Two years earlier, the Cathedral Council had announced an open competition. The spirit of the cathedral builders was undoubtedly not dead, for 183 architects submitted designs, of whom five were invited, for a retainer of 500 guineas each, to prepare detailed plans over the next year. The Council was still groping for a precedent: an unabashedly traditional Gothic seemed out of keeping but there was a reluctance, too, to countenance any drastic departure from tradition. A generation later, and the changes of thought produced by a global war opened the path for Coventry: in 1930 continuity still seemed both logical and desirable. Maufe's design neatly bridged the gap between the equally uncertain traditionalists and innovators. In his own words it was a 'design definitely of our time and yet in line with the great English cathedrals: to build anew on tradition: to rely on proportion of mass, volume, and lines rather than elaborate ornament'. The Cathedral itself was literally to grow out of the hill for it was to be built of bricks which were themselves to be made of the clay actually on the site.[76]

In the post-war years the design was, almost inevitably, criticised by a generation which again believed that tradition provided a shackle rather than an impulse. 'It was conservative when it was designed – even by English standards – and without any of the genuine fervour of Liverpool. The outside looks as though it will never be more than a well-mannered postscript to the Gothic Revival.'[77] But contemporary opinion was enthusiastic. Charles Reilly, himself Professor of Architecture in the same city where the other great Anglican cathedral was arising, compared Guildford's favourably with Liverpool's.

> Mr Maufe's building [is] monolithic in its appearance compared to that of the old Gothic structures. The rectangular masses will at Guildford be much plainer and more solid looking even than they are at Liverpool. This is not only in consonance with the growing taste for simplicity, which this penitential age calls for but it will make this particular building – isolated from its town on a low hill, with bigger hills in the background – seem to belong to its site in a way which all good buildings should do.[78]

Edward Maufe was inevitably involved in the local controversy regarding the cost and the site. As far as the cost was concerned, he pointed out that the tower alone of Liverpool Cathedral was equal in cost to the whole of Guildford's – which could, moreover, be built within three years if sufficient funds were forthcoming. He, too, defended the site on the basis that it would form the centre of the natural development of the town westward. Thirty years later, at the time of the consecration of the Cathedral, he described how the site itself dictated the form of the building.

> Stag Hill seems almost providentially made for a cathedral. It's a long spine of a hill with a steep slope above the town to the east and an easy approach on the bypass from the west. A building on such a site must be simple in outline and serene: it must grow inevitably out of its site, riding upon the long curve of the hill. We chose the highest point of the hill for the position of the central tower: all the parts of the cathedral build up to this tower.[79]

By 1936 some £36,000 was in hand and, though this was still far short of the £50,000 earlier decided as being the minimum figure necessary to ensure continuity of work, the Diocesan Conference decided that work should start immediately, confident that sufficient funds would come in regularly from now onward. On 2 July 1936 Cosmo Gordon Lang, Archbishop of Canterbury, laid the foundation stone of the Cathedral of the Holy Spirit in the presence of some 10,000 people. Work, once started, went forward smoothly and swiftly. In the following year the last of 778 piles had been driven into the heart of the hill and in 1938 the Mayor of Guilford laid the first facing-brick.

The architect's estimate of three to five years for building would almost certainly have been justified under normal conditions. But, even as the launching of the Cathedral project had coincided with a world-wide economic disaster, so the projected date of its consecration coincided with a world-wide war. By 1939 the choir was complete, the great walls rising high but still roofless – but throughout the country building projects were being slowed and then halted as the demands of war removed both men and materials. Special licence was obtained to roof the choir and provide a temporary cover over the vaulting of the transepts, but after that the great building stood a gaunt shell during the war years. The austerity years followed the period of actual conflict, and by 1947 the only additional work accomplished was the furnishing and consecration of the crypt. Over the next seven years work went slowly and haltingly – at one period there were only half a dozen men working on the site. It seemed likely that Guildford's Cathedral would suffer the same fate as Liverpool's – if, indeed, it were ever completed – but now it was lack of money, not of men and materials that delayed completion.

The fact that the Cathedral was completed within a lifetime provided clear evidence that its creation had touched a genuine popular spring, local as well as national. The Cathedral, by definition, was brought into being by and for a diocese, its role was conceived in regional and national rather than local terms and it is therefore impossible to measure the extent of Guildford's contribution to the building that popularly bore its name. But it is more than a coincidence that the last spurt of energy that brought the Cathedral to completion originated within the town. In 1954 Walter Boulton, the outspoken Provost of Holy Trinity Cathedral, vigorously attacked the Town Council – and, by implication, the citizens of Guildford, for their apathy regarding the unfinished structure on Stag Hill. The Mayor, Leslie Codd, reacted as vigorously. He specifically disclaimed any interest in church affairs, his motivation was civic pride rather than religious emotion but it proved to be more than adequate to act as a catalyst, turning the diffused goodwill into organised support. Again an appeal was launched, a massive pilgrimage initiated, some £42,000 collected, and building gathered impetus again. The original estimate of £250,000 had long been overtaken by the soaring costs of the post-war years: by 1961 a total of £540,000 had been collected, most of it in small sums, yet an additional £300,000 was still needed. But by that year the tower alone remained uncompleted and the building was deemed fit for consecration and launching upon its centuries-long voyage. And with the announcement of the date of consecration – May 1961 – a second controversy burst over Stag Hill.

The first controversy had been largely academic: the second was personal, at times bitterly so, and beginning as a local quarrel ended as a national issue. The Church of Holy Trinity had discharged its double role of parish church and pro-cathedral for over thirty years and its rectors, too, had played a double role of parish priest and Provost of the Cathedral. In the opinion of at least one newspaper the double function was an impossible task and had broken the men who had attempted it. 'The job of raising the money for the Cathedral and at the same time running a responsible parish was too much for any one man. The Very Reverend Eric Southam [first Provost] left Guildford a very sick man. "You tried to kill me in Guildford," he told the writer and there was no doubt that his life was shortened.'[80] Walter Boulton, destined to be the last Provost, had wished to resign but was persuaded to carry on, adding to the existing onerous tasks of Provost the complex responsibilities of preparing the transference of the Bishop's seat from Holy Trinity to the completed Cathedral.

Boulton was an immensely able and vigorous man with a preference for blunt speech and a belief that Christianity should infuse all sections of society even at cost of mixing politics with religion. In a sermon in Calcutta before Indian independence, he had warned European commercial interests that their rapacity was digging their own graves and was unmoved by the resulting storm. In Guildford, he had opened his rectorship in 1952 with a public debate with the secretary of the local Communist Party, followed it up with a spirited attack on Whitehall for its tyranny in local affairs and then, lest Guildford Borough Council be thereby rendered complacent, attacked it for the wanton destruction of the town during the slum-clearance programme. And in 1961 he became the centre of a national controversy with a book on marriage that was first attacked in the *Church Times* and subsequently withdrawn.

Legally, the Provost had to resign when the Constitution of the Cathedral came into force and it was confidently expected that Boulton's resignation would merely be a formality preceding his appointment as Dean. A month before the consecration rumours began to circulate that he was not, in fact, being considered and the Master of Trinity Hospital spoke up for that very large section of the community for whom the Provost was the natural and obvious choice.

> If [the rumour] is true it should not be allowed to become a fait accompli without some protest being registered. It has been fully expected that he would continue his great work after the

consecration of the new Cathedral and to fail to allow this would be detrimental to the best interests of the diocese and a flagrant injustice to one who has proved himself a tower of strength to its Christian life.[81]

It was true, and a deputation that waited upon the Archbishop of Canterbury received only the reply that, despite his manifold gifts, Walter Boulton was not suitable for the post. No reason was given.

It was this aspect which exacerbated both local and national opinion and, inevitably, dark rumours arose. At Convocation a speaker arose, declaring that he wanted to draw attention to the bereavement they had suffered through the 'peculiar ecclesiastical death of the Provost of Guildford'. He was ruled out of order but the Press could not be silenced. The national papers were concerned with the wider constitutional issues involved, the local essentially with the personal injustice. The *Guildford and Godalming Times*, in a skilful and honest piece of reporting, published the results of a survey it had conducted, in which it departed from its usual custom of anonymity and named the reporter. 'I was forced slowly and very reluctantly towards the opinion that someone whose name carries almost overwhelming weight is opposed to the present Provost as Dean of Guildford. I found later that others shared it.' Replying to the official criticism that the Provost should have resigned earlier and so saved the hierarchy an embarrassment, the writer touched on that point which particularly incensed local opinion. 'Considering that he has to think of his family's weekly rent and bills among other things, a hesitation to commit professional hari-kari is under-standable.' No alternative employment had been offered to the Provost of Holy Trinity Cathedral after working seven years for the establishment of the Cathedral of the Holy Spirit: as from 18 May he would be unemployed and without professional income, the report concluded.[82]

The most vocal defenders of the Provost were drawn largely from the ranks of his fellow-churchmen, but the most effective apologia for him was made by a man outside the ranks of the Church – Leslie Codd, the ex-mayor who had responded to Boulton's appeal six years earlier and so contributed to the resumption of building. 'This I should not have done but for the fact that the Provost on Mayoral Sunday vigorously and courageously attacked from the pulpit the Town Council, including myself as the new Mayor for its lack of interest in, and general apathy towards the cathedral project.' As a direct result of another of the Provost's 'indiscretions', the writer claimed, the Cathedral was at last brought to the point of consecration. The Provost had never been informed of the reason for his exclusion – he had, in effect, been judged by a descendant of the Star Chamber.[83]

The consecration was to take place with Elizabeth II as witness. A week before the ceremony a local petition with a formidable sponsorship was drawn up for presentation to Her Majesty. The sponsors emphasised that there was neither desire nor intention to challenge a crown decision but that, owing to an unawareness of the extent of local indignation, the Queen's advisers could well place her in an embarrassing situation during the forthcoming royal visit. The petition never reached the Queen. It was despatched by post but 'according to constitutional practice', it was diverted to the Prime Minister who stated that the appointment of Dean had already been made, he saw no reason to recommend withdrawal of approval and therefore the petition would not be forwarded, revealing 'with certainty what had long been tacitly accepted – that the Queen has no ultimate responsibility for church appointments'.[84]

The *Surrey Advertiser*, most influential of the local newspapers, had declined either to enter the controversy or open its correspondence columns to it, arguing that to do so would be to add fuel to an inflammable situation. The *Advertiser* was on good grounds in declaring that the original issue, conducted on grounds of personal loyalty, had become almost totally obscured by the later attacks that ranged over the whole political spectrum. 'The image of a spiteful and reactionary hierarchy governing the Church has been imposed on the public mind.' One injustice had been compounded by another and 'The new Bishop has been exposed to a torrent of spiteful and abusive letters'.[85]

The new bishop was George Reindorp whom an unhappy chance had thrown into a situation that was none of his making. It had naturally been expected that the reigning fourth Bishop of Guildford, Ivor Watkins, would be the bishop of the transition but he had died suddenly in 1960 and on 12 April 1961 – just a month before the consecration – George Reindorp was enthroned as the last bishop of the short-lived cathedral of Holy Trinity, the ceremony being the first episcopal enthronement ever to be televised in England. It was peculiarly ironical that the new bishop should have been a victim of an almost medieval secrecy on the part of the hierarchy, for as a vigorous advocate of a Church in harmony with its century he had, the previous year, accepted an appointment to the Church Information Board. Despite the obvious fact that, enthroned as he was during the controversy regarding the Provost, he could have had no part in the decision, and despite a public statement to that effect by the Archbishop of Canterbury he, too, came in for obloquy.

The following month the Bishop performed the first major act of his episcopate with the consecration of the Cathedral in the presence of the Queen. It was an overcast day with a cold wind but the steep, unsheltered slopes of the hill were thickly crowded, among the thousands of people being many who, as children, had been present when the foundation stone had been laid a generation earlier. Among the hundreds inside were two men with widely differing emotions: Edward Maufe, come to taste the rarest triumph known to an architect and stand in the completed cathedral of his design and the Very Reverend Walter Boulton, Provost of Holy Trinity Cathedral, in the last moments of his charge. The Biblical parallel of Moses on Pisgah occurred to many and at least one ecclesiastical lawyer was of the opinion that if the Provost did not resign then the church on Stag Hill could have been consecrated but the Cathedral would have remained in the town, in Holy Trinity.[86] But the Provost, who had taken no part in the controversy, acted as those who knew him expected he would act, resigning the following day, and was later appointed to a rural rectorship.

But there was one last pinprick to be administered to local

pride. The Queen's advisers planned a route which would have taken the royal party direct to the Cathedral, thereby negating the ancient ceremony in which the first citizen of the community welcomed its monarch. Protest brought about a change in the planned route so that the Queen was formally welcomed by the Mayor but the *Advertiser* was undoubtedly speaking for the town when it remarked, with some bitterness, 'The fact that the Cathedral could be officially regarded as in, but not of, the town, is a disturbing one.'[87]

'In but not of the town.' Stag Hill forms a curiously balanced physical counterpart on the north side of the Hog's Back to the hill of St Catherine's on the south; but where, through many centuries, some form of shrine had always stood on St Catherine's, Stag Hill remained green and empty, although it was the natural site for a ceremonial structure. It lay, perhaps, too far away from the natural route of the Old Road, and when, as the town grew, covetous eyes might have been cast upon it the powers of the monarch reinforced its natural protection, for some time in 1155 King Henry II enclosed this area and made of it a royal park. But even after royal protection was removed, the town grew so slowly that the comparatively remote spur was of little interest. The railway came as close as possible, sweeping round the base in a great curve, but within that curve the unstable soil, outer rim of the great bed of clay that runs to the north-east, made casual building uneconomic. Topography had preserved a superb site for the creation of a building that was to mark the beginning of a major period of growth in the town's history.

The Cathedral stands with its back to the town, for the great west door, with the embracing porches that give to the plan the appearance of a key, opens to the by-pass and the open country beyond. The orientation was dictated by three widely differing factors: the ancient Christian tradition that the altar should face the place of Crucifixion: the narrowness of the site and the social revolution expressed by the possession of private transport. For the motorist, the siting is ideal for a vehicle may sweep along the by-pass and up to the very door with barely the necessity of slackening speed: the long and dignified avenue connecting the Cathedral with the road is an attractive by-product of this fact.

The pedestrian is less fortunate and it is the pedestrian, casually passing or entering and leaving without prearrangement, who ties a building to a community. In terms of measured distance, Stag Hill is little more than half a mile from the heart of the town: psychologically, it is much further. The river that runs between the hill and the town is still an attraction, not a barrier but immediately beyond lies the massive railway-complex and beyond that again a featureless residential area, neither concentrated enough to be urban nor open enough to be suburb but the dispirited compromise of the 1920s. Again, so swift was the development here that some of the original features were preserved. The road that runs along the base of the hill is still essentially rural on the side nearest the Cathedral, with waist-high grass and flowers in high summer, and the ruins of an ancient farmhouse survived until 1968. The lodge gates of the Cathedral that open on to this road have taken on the colouring of the area, for they have the gentility of a municipal park-gate rather than the pride of an episcopate. But the steps that run up through the still rough grass of the hill are dignified, tempting the imagination to speculate on how this newest of closes will look in centuries' time. The houses of the close form an enclave, half-hidden among trees, on the lowest slope of the hill, leaving the great platform bare around the Cathedral itself, save for the stark teak cross that marked the moment when it came into being.

The controversy regarding the siting of the Cathedral was posed largely in local terms, defenders and objectors alike adopting the traditional habit of identifying a cathedral with its host community and arguing from thence that the Stag Hill site either would, or would not, become integrated with the town. The strict irrelevancy of the argument became evident during the decade following the consecration as the Cathedral of the Holy Spirit embarked on its role of mother church of an independent diocese – and found itself immensely aided by the fact that it was in the physical centre of the territory in its charge. Given that the suffragan had borne the sixteenth-century title of 'Guildford' it was perhaps inevitable that the Bishop would place his seat in that town, but the same factors that led to Guildford's rapid development in the twentieth century served also rapidly to integrate the Cathedral with its diocese. The fact that it was built during a period of high population-growth provided its creators, in addition, with a clear indication of the elements that made an ideal site – in the foreseeable future, it is inconceivable that the diocesan population will ebb from the mother church as has been the fate with many an old cathedral. Placed at the centre of an excellent road and rail system, so that its most distant parish lay within easy reach: surrounded by a population that was urban in its habits if rural in its habitants the Cathedral was immediately enabled to provide a cultural catalyst that was to be equalled only by the University. The great pilgrimages at Easter, when thousands of young people make their way on foot to the Cathedral from all parts of the diocese, provide a powerful demonstration of its religious life. But parallel to its overt Christianity are those activities which, arising from its natural and traditional role of teaching, contribute to the cultural life of its host town. The Guildford Lectures, held every winter since 1963, attract on average 1,000 people on each of the four nights that they are given, and throughout the year the Cathedral provides a setting for activities – dramatic, recitative, orchestral and the like – which would be circumscribed or, indeed, non-existent but for the hospitality so granted. It is in the field of music, however, that the Cathedral has made its most distinctive mark. This, the youngest of the cathedrals of Britain and without a Choir School, has obtained a national reputation for its choral work both through broadcasting and, more remarkably, through the sale of its own records some of which have achieved 'best-seller' status.

THE UNIVERSITY

On 20 November 1961 Guildford Rotary Club met, as was its custom, to listen to a talk delivered by an expert in his field. The speaker was the Principal of the Technical College and he took as his theme the possible effects upon the town of the establishment of a technological university. Three months later, on 1 January 1962, Dr Robert Williams, an expert in electronics, addressed the same club, developing his theme of a 'televarsity' which had aroused considerable national interest. Almost as an afterthought he, too, referred to the possibility of the town acting as host to a new technological university. During the questions that followed it became obvious that a subject of considerable local interest had been touched upon and he was asked to return and speak at greater length and detail upon it. He did so and gave some indication of the requirements and procedure. The Government had not yet allocated a site for one of the new universities envisaged in the far-reaching programme of techno-logical education: an area of up to 200 acres, preferably near the town centre, would be required and if Guildford were really interested then an approach to the University Grants Commission should be made immediately, despite the current uncertainty regarding the establishment of the Greater London Council and the fact that the long-expected Robbins Report would not be published for some months. The Club agreed to form a committee which would sound local opinion and take the matter a stage further.

In that same month of January 1962 the Governors of Battersea College of Advanced Technology had come to the inescapable conclusion that they would have to abandon their sixty-year-old home. The College was a perfect example of the results of the unprecedented technological expansion of the post-war years. Founded – essentially as a charitable institution – in 1894, it had emerged as a College of Advanced Technology in 1956 and by 1960 had some 1500 full-time students. But now it was an idea rather than a place as the wave of students swamped the existing facilities. It expanded physically where it could and, to the normal problems of running a growing institution was the additional hazard of keeping contact with its disparate parts which included, bizarrely, a disused indoor swimming-pool, a church hall and a warehouse. The situation was obviously impossible and, obeying the influence of that slow but perceptible drift of major organi-sations from London, the Governors decided to seek another home outside the capital. A number of localities were considered, but gradually the concept of Guildford as the seat of the College emerged to the front, aided by the fact that the Principal – later, Vice-Chancellor of the University – knew the town well and liked it. The four major reasons that substantiated the choice provided a thumbnail sketch of the factors that had led to the growth of the town. It lay, in beautiful country, at the centre of an excellent system of road and rail communication: it was in close proximity to a number of scientific research establishments: it was a growing cultural centre with a cathedral, theatre and a young but impressive musical culture. The reference to the Cathedral and theatre was an excellent example of the power of institutions to create institutions: the new theatre was not yet out of its scaffolding and the Cathedral had yet fully to enter upon its corporate life but their existence was enough to help attract another body.

Meanwhile, in Guildford, the steering committee of the Rotary Club had done its work well. It is, perhaps, impossible to establish the exact time and the exact factors which create a massive social change in either a national or a local community and other groups were to claim the considerable honour of initiating the movement which led to the establishment of the University. A Council official indeed denied that any local body was responsible, claiming that the proposal came as 'something out of the blue',[88] but later the Vice-Chancellor made the town's debt specific: 'If it had not been for Guildford Rotary Club it is extremely unlikely that there would be a prospect of this university.'[89] The very nature of the Club's constitution, which ensured that the greatest number of trades and professions were represented in its body, meant that its sympathy towards the idea of the University could be diffused throughout the community.

The only real opposition encountered in the initial stages stemmed from the concern felt that the existing facilities of the town might not prove adequate for the support of a large social organisation. In June 1962, shortly after it was made known that Guildford was indeed likely to be the site of a university, the *Guildford and Godalming Times* formulated the problem in a feature which neatly balanced the advantages and disadvantages. Prominence was given to a letter from a Research Fellow at Sheffield University, who had been engaged in an immediately relevant study of the effect of a new university upon an established community. 'The results of recent research . . . revealed that every student place creates employment for some 2.5 persons at least. A college at Guildford of some 2000 students by 1970 will give us some 5000 extra posts. A new pressure on garage services has taken the place of Oxford's demand in the last century for wig-makers!' A shortage of garage services was, at most, an irritation but the shortage of houses could prove a disaster. In emphasis of that fact the same feature published a brief survey of the current housing problem: families faced with eviction still had no place to go. Where would the thousands of students be housed? Was there, too, the chance that as the University developed it might, in time, come to exert an overwhelming influence on the town, the tail wagging the dog?[90]

The growing body of favourable opinion recognised the fact that the town was committed to a very high rate of growth, and that the choice lay between a future as a commercial and residential appendage to London or the acceptance of an organic development which would encourage social autonomy. Admittedly, the town was within the area in which future office-building was rigorously controlled under the 1965 Act – but it was only just within the area and controls had a habit of becoming modified under pressure. It was altogether preferable to work for the establishment of a university rather than maintain a vacuum that might later be filled with office blocks.

In March 1963 the Borough Council gave official encouragement to the project, despite warnings that it might be better to wait until the publication of the Robbins Report on education before committing itself: the college might not necessarily be designated a university. The Council had a clear-cut reason to welcome the establishment of a university. The town possessed comparatively little in the way of industry and the burden of rates therefore bore proportionately heavier upon the private householder, a fact which had hampered much of its activities in the past. The Cathedral had brought immense social prestige but very little money. The University would not only become the largest ratepayer but its estimated population of over 5000 would spend money, as well as generate employment, in the town. A decision which would both spread the burden of rates and stimuate local trade could not fail to be popular. In October the Robbins Report made a fact of what had only been a hope, designating Battersea College of Technology as one of six new universities, and in the following May the Secretary of State for Education and Science was able to tell the House that the University of Surrey would be established in Guildford 'on a site to be provided from a fund to which both the governing body and the County Council will contribute'.[91]

There was little doubt where that site would be. The new university was able to benefit from the lessons learned by its immediate predecessors. In the first phase of university-building in the post-war years little attempt had been made to integrate the academic with the urban communities. The universities tended to be built in the most obvious place – on the outskirts of the town, perhaps three miles or more from the centre. Architecturally acceptable, it was a social error, for the institutions, already naturally self-sufficient, inevitably developed independent of their host communities so that it was not merely possible but probable that the majority of their undergraduates would remain alien throughout their three years' residence. At best, it was loss of a potential: at worst it exaggerated the traditional town–gown hostility.

Despite its austerely technological nature, one of the formative concepts of the University of Surrey was that it should be integrated as closely as possible with its host, creating opportunities for a fruitful cross-fertilisation. Location was the obvious primary need of such a concept and Stag Hill was an equally obvious choice. Not only was it in physical proximity to the town but the Cathedral on its crest was the natural partner of an academic organisation. The impulses that led to the creation of the new university could not have been further in spirit from those which had brought about the separation of the first universities from their parent cathedrals in the twelfth century, but sufficient affinity of purpose and organisation remained to make logical a social partnership. The northern slope of the hill was the property of the town and this was selected as the heart of the complex, while negotiations were set in motion for the acquisition of a large area of land, the old centre of the royal park which still bore its ancient name of Manor Farm, on the far side of the by-pass. As earnest of its sympathy and encouragement, the Borough Council sold its land at far below market value, in effect making a gift of £250,000 to the University. It was purely a notional sum, for planning controls limited the use of the land to agricultural purposes and only a project like the University could have brought about the waiving of the restriction, but it was an index of the strength of the official desire to establish the University.

But what seemed both logical and desirable to the Council and the more distant citizens bore a different colour to the citizens immediately affected. The most disgruntled were the share-holders of Onslow Village, to whom Manor Farm belonged. Ten years earlier the Village had applied for permission to build houses on the land and, despite the acute shortage, permission had been refused. Admittedly, the Village had received adequate compensation but it seemed decidedly unjust that an immigrant organisation should now occupy land that could be used to provide much needed homes for citizens. In persuading the Village to part with its land, considerable emphasis was given to the fact that the land was to be used for playing-fields, not for buildings, and that it could easily be restored to farmland should the need arise. By the time the University was actually estab-lished, however, it was made plain that should the need arise the land would be used for building-purposes, a warning sub-stantiated by the announcement, in 1968, that a £10 million hospital would ultimately appear on part of the site.

In March 1964 Onslow Village grudgingly agreed to sell: it had little choice for compulsory purchase would have followed. But the residents of the area, in particular the tenant of Manor Farm, were not disposed to accept the disruption of their lives without protest. The tenant farmer had strong popular support.

Despite its overwhelming trade and residential bias, Guildford still maintained curiously strong physical and social links with the elemental craft that provided a buffer in times of trade depression – it was no accident that one of the most dominant buildings on the High Street was a corn exchange. Tongues of agricultural land penetrated deep into the heart of the Borough, intermingling farmland with suburbia so that the sight and sound of farm animals and machinery were as familiar as their domestic counterparts. Economics and aesthetics combined in support of the protest against the loss of a traditional farming region – a loss, moreover, exacerbated by the cavalier manner in which the decision was made known. 'The first they [the tenants] knew of it was through the newspapers,' the National Farmer's Union declared in promising its support. 'We will do all we can to keep their livelihood. As you can imagine it would come as a shock to anyone to hear that a university was to be built on their farm.'[92] But urban as well as rural sensibilities were offended – in particular by the proposal to connect the two halves of the University by building a massive bridge over the by-pass, an operation which could not fail to destroy the amenities of the houses in the vicinity. In April 1965 a large protest meeting provided a means whereby the increasing local unease at the speed in which the University project was being implemented 'and the casual, haphazard manner in which the whole matter is being handled'[93] was made widely known. More protest meetings followed and it became obvious that only a public inquiry under ministerial control could do justice to the conflicting interests, and restore the goodwill towards the University concept.

The decision to have recourse to an inquiry carried with it the very real danger that the University, under pressure of its own domestic problems, might not be able to await the decision and would seek a site elsewhere – other communities were as eager as Guildford to give it a home. But the terms of the inquiry dealt not only with the controversial siting but with the basic question as to whether or no the University should be in Guildford at all. The ministerial decision made in January 1966 was therefore able to place on permanent and formal record the reasons why the town had been chosen, and why Stag Hill was the site selected. The Minister took sympathetic notice of the strong local objections to the site, but considered that it offered 'imaginative possibilities for the future of the town which only the most compelling objections could override'.[94] The Borough Council had proposed that an underpass should take the place of the controversial flyover and this the Minister accepted, his inspector pointing out that the residents would actually benefit by the provision of a safe crossing at a notoriously dangerous junction. Before work had even begun on the site, the University had contributed something to its host, for proposals to create a safe crossing of the by-pass at that junction had again and again been negated by financial reasons.

The Cathedral on Stag Hill was essentially the expression of one man's intellect, conceived in the belief that its form and its idea should be consubstantial so long as the physical structure endured. The University was the expression of a group, conceived in the awareness that change was of its essence and that its form must be capable of adaptation to unknowable future functions, and subject throughout to public opinion. In addition to their purely technical problems the architects had the delicate diplomatic task of gaining, at each major stage of development, the approval of the laymen who formed the governing body of the town. The Council was itself acutely aware of its dilemma and the debate of 26 September 1967, which ended in the rejection of a substantial proposed section, faithfully reflected on a local scale the national factors that steadily modified architectural originality. The architects had planned a dormitory section that had some of the qualities of a village, a praiseworthy attempt to break away from the current fashionable cubes that had earned the approval both of the Council's professional staff and of the Royal Fine Arts Commission. The plan just scraped through the committee stage on the casting vote of the chairman, and came under heavy and sustained attack in the Council itself. But though speaker after speaker arose to condemn the project, describing the dormitories variously as 'Noddy house ... pig houses ... too modern for so old a town ... too sharp and angular . . . restless. . . .' each speaker was anxious to make it clear that the opinions were personal, born doubtless of formal architectural ignorance but for that very reason representative of local opinion. There was a universal awareness that the decision made that night would affect the appearance of the town over decades or even centuries, and a corresponding attempt to project the plan into the future. The Mayor was doubtless correct in pointing out that the Council would look decidedly foolish if, at this stage, it were to reject the professional advice it had been at such pains to obtain, but the rejection, when it came, did establish the fact that a lay Council could still exert control over professionals. In the immediate context the decision was unfortunate but it augured well for a period in which the Council was being continually belaboured with expert advice on environment. The same reluctance that served to check architectural originality also served to check some of the more destructive suggestions for adapting an ancient town to modern conditions.

Work began on the Stag Hill site in January 1966. The architects had two clear-cut goals: the exploiting of the 'imaginative possibilities' of the Hill and the social integration of the University with the town. They envisaged 'a compact hill town. . . not conceived as a military camp with fences and gatehouses but as an open, free, welcoming community, open to the town's people and nearer to the centre than any other postwar college or university'.[95] By the time the first students had moved in eighteen months later, the town was able to see that rising out of the churned clay of Stag Hill was a building that reflected its age as authentically as the Renaissance flourish of the town hall or the Jacobean dignity of Trinity Hospital. Seen from a distance, the buildings of the University do indeed seem to form a hill town rising up to its natural apex, the Cathedral on its high platform. Within the complex, as within a town, the sense of being within a single unit disappears, passages and courtyards taking the place of roads and squares. The steep slope of the hill and the footbridges connecting the major blocks create different levels so that the viewpoint changes constantly, creating variety within a limited compass. The sense of a hill town occurs again at the exits for they are at the end of rather narrow passages and passing through them the open hill is immediately gained with the bulk of the University towering behind like a city wall pierced with narrow gates. The very instability of the slope has been levied to create variety, for the humdrum function of drainage has produced a lake that lies, triangular and placid, high up on the hill.

The University of Surrey came formally into existence in September 1966 when it received its Royal Charter: a month later its first Chancellor was installed in a combined civic and academic ceremony that took place, significantly, in the town's recently completed Civic Hall. The lack of such a hall had, over the past generation and more, weakened the town's position in its perennial battle to be recognised as a major community – substantially contributing, indeed, to the loss of its ancient privilege of Assize in 1930. The fact that the new hall was completed in time for the ceremony was coincidental but indicative of the town's sudden growth. Before the ceremony, the Vice-Chancellor had emphasised the somewhat remote functions of the institution about to be grafted on to the body of the community: 'Let there be no doubt that it is, and that it will continue to be, a technologically orientated university. This is explicit in our charter and inherent in our plans.'[96] It was made further explicit by the choice of the first Chancellor – Lord Robens, Chairman of the National Coal Board – and by the recipients of the first honorary degrees, five of whom were technologists. But the choice of the sixth, Dame Sybil Thorndike, was a graceful gesture on the part of the University not only to a person but to its host community for the Dame had been instrumental in the founding of the town's new theatre. The University had declared its intention and desire to be reckoned as part of the corporate body and both were faithfully honoured in the months immediately following the effective establishment of the University in the autumn of 1968. The slope of Stag Hill still resembled a combination of builder's yard and battlefield as the feverish pace of building was maintained in a year of heavy rains. But it was not only the first body of students who picked their way through the heavy clay: townspeople, too, trudged up the hill, some exploring the sudden community, others visiting the public art exhibitions which were staged almost from the first. The University might be heavily technological in bias, but the existence of a Faculty of Human Studies gave evidence of its intention to bridge the 'two cultures' gap so far as it was possible in an increasingly fragmented academic universe. In November 1968 – less than a month after it had arrived on Stag Hill – the University provided a natural home for a teaching centre for the area: the need for such a forum for the exchange of educational ideas was spectacularly demonstrated by the fact that over 1000 visitors attended the official opening on 23 November. In the following spring the Students' Union launched the Guildford Festival, a development of Battersea College's own festival but the first that the town had ever known on such a scale. The Festival was a financial loss but abruptly it expanded the town's cultural horizon, giving substance to the earlier optimism that the establishment of a university in Guildford would be mutually beneficial over a very wide field.

The University of Surrey was new in status but long-established in form: its officers, indeed, were fond of referring to its establishment in Guildford as similar to that migration from Oxford that had produced Cambridge University in the thirteenth century. The pressing need to take advantage of the new facilities as they were completed meant that, for over a year, the University existed simultaneously in two places – at Guildford and at Battersea. The plan for transference provided for the establishment of 1000 students in Guildford by October 1968, the remainder being transferred in the following October, bringing the total strength up to 2450 by the autumn of 1969. The long-term plans were rather more vague. In the initial stages it was assumed that the total student body would be in the region of 5000 some time after 1980, although it was emphasised that, because of the 'sandwich course' in which each student would spend a year in industry, one-eighth of the students would be continually absent. In January 1969, however, representatives of the local authorities involved were invited to a meeting at the University to discuss the implications of an experimental study envisaging a theoretical maximum of 10,000 students. Such a population would obviously be too great for the facilities on Stag Hill and the meeting had been called to consider where, if necessary, additional buildings could be raised. There was, in fact, only one possible site – the 200-odd acres of Manor Farm which were supposedly to be devoted to playing-fields. The architect went to considerable lengths to reassure his audience that the study was purely experimental, that no decision to expand the University had been, or could be, taken without a major public enquiry. The knowledge that Manor Farm was not necessarily protected, and that the town might be called upon to support a student population double the original estimate did, however, create some unease, and the opinion of the meeting was probably accurately summed up by the councillor who remarked shortly that it seemed to have been convened 'to break the news gently to the locals'.[97]

Official and group opinion in the town had been consistently in favour of the University from its conception. General public opinion, of its nature, was more difficult to obtain. The idea of a university had played no particular part in the Borough election campaigns for there was no particular aspect of it that irritated or attracted the bulk of individual electors. Despite the fact that the University had been established in the town at the height of the widespread 'student revolt' when, throughout the country, an older generation was watching with bewilderment the seemingly incoherent protests of a favoured younger generation, an innately conservative town's people had nevertheless seen no cause to object. The 'revolt' had indeed entered the town with a long-drawn-out dispute that threatened to destroy the Guildford Art School but here, in fact, the bulk of interested opinion had been firmly on the side of the 'rebels' if for no better reason than that the clumsy official handling alienated its potential support. The invasion of the town by the first wave of 1000 students in the autumn of 1968 made no appreciable difference to opinion, for the level of undergraduate discipline was conspicuously higher than in many a more mature university. The University's branch of the National Union of Students claimed that it was the structure of its constitution which eliminated the self-destructive unrest:

> At a time when students are rioting in Germany and France, and sitting outside the Vice-Chancellor's office of a British university, the name of Surrey University is missing from the headlines. This is because the Union effectively represents the student viewpoint to all levels of the University Administration ... primarily through the President who attends all meetings of Senate.[98]

Altogether, diffused public opinion was probably indifferent with a mild bias towards approval.

It was not until January 1969 that the diffused opinion found a focus in the Town Council's decision to contribute £18,000 a year for ten years towards the University. In the previous May an appeal for funds had been launched which clearly indicated the financial position of the institution. The over-all cost of establishing the University was estimated at £18,280,000 spread over ten years. Government grants would cover the greater cost, leaving some £5 million to be raised by private and commercial subscriptions and local-authority grants.

Guildford Borough Council was therefore behaving neither unconstitutionally nor hastily in deciding, nearly a year later, to contribute to the University. But a public which had been indifferent while general principles were being enunciated, reacted vigorously when it became obvious that actual local money was involved. Much of the opposition came from that extreme fringe which had earned for itself nationally the title of 'Disgusted Ratepayer' and for whom 'idle, unwashed' were the natural adjectives to 'students', arising from the sense of genuine affront that an extended education should be provided at the public expense. But much, too, compared like with like, arguing that if the town had any money to spare it should be spent on the town's own decrepit facilities and institutions – its library, hamstrung by a remarkably low financial allowance; its battered pavements; its barrack-like schools, some still with the uncompromising nineteenth-century legend 'Board School' emblazoned upon them; its limited provisions for recreation for the very old and the very young; its dangerous roads. The *Surrey Advertiser*, which had throughout proved itself a staunch ally of the University, replied to the protests in a special leader.[99] It had already pointed out that the gift was virtually a paper transaction – the University in effect being excused that proportion of rates for the first ten years of its life – and now it disclosed that the voting in the Council had cut across all political and personal divisions to create a heavy majority in favour. 'In the voting 22 were for the grant, three against and five canny or slow-thinking councillors abstained: two were absent.' In the opinion of the *Advertiser* the councillors, risking unpopularity, had made a wholly correct decision. 'They see the question of a university grant in a longer perspective than most of their critics.' Guildford benefited substantially from the University, not only from the millions of pounds that would flow into it from students' grants and staff salaries but also by the infusion of new life into the town's own institutions. In return, the town was voluntarily contributing a tiny fraction of the £18 million total in order to enable 'this major asset to become firmly established'. There were some attempts to create an organised protest but they came to nothing, the town accepting the logic of the situation. But the episode had served to show that that spirit in which the citizens of Erfurt, faced with a rather similar situation in the fifteenth century, dragged up a cannon and bombarded their University was by no means wholly dead.

Guildford in 1739, from the *Ichnography* of Matthew Richardson of Guildford

CHAPTER FOUR

The Corporate Memory

It must be admitted regretfully that, though Guildford Corporation has now provided for the safe custody and repair of its
archives, it has in the past been very careless of them. It is
remarkable that the surviving records very rarely mention the
town Charters and other documents and contain no reference
to their regular transference from one Mayor to the next. . . .
The documents have enjoyed, if that is the correct word, very
varied accessibility in the past.[1]

I find a very auncient booke of this towne called the Black Booke
written in the tymes of Edward III, Richard II, Henry IV,
Henry V, Henry VI, Edward IV, Henry VII, sometymes kings
of England, wherein are written and recorded the choice
of divers officers within the said towne yerelie, with divers
accoumpts of money . . . which booke is so ragged, torne, and
rent one piece from another, yea almost every leaf one from
the other that I could hardly bring them into order again. . . .
It hath fared with that booke as with a common hackney
horse, being hired by many and often journeyed, cometh by
the neglect or yll usage of some of his riders to a galled back,
or to some incurable disease.[2]

OVER 350 years separate these two quotations, for the first is taken
from the introduction to the authoritative text of some of the
surviving records published in 1958, and the second is from
George Austen's melancholy preface to the selections he made
from that maltreated Black Book in 1596. The substance of the
complaints regarding the town's indifference to its recorded
past could have been written at any time in the intervening or
preceding period. In 1383 the townsmen were able to use the

convenient and probably untrue excuse that their records had all been destroyed in the Peasants' Revolt two years earlier, and received a renewal of their charters from a complaisant king. But these, too, disappeared. During the long controversy in the 1930s regarding the propriety of establishing a public library a leading scholar of the town made the urgent point that valuable private archives were melting away for lack of a depository. In 1899 the cataloguer of the once valuable library of the Grammar School painted a picture of recent neglect that would not have been out of place in the Dark Ages. '[The books] were at one time stored between the joists of the big schoolroom. At another time legend describes them as packed away in some cellar, where they were invaded by leakage from the town sewer. There is yet another tale of a bonfire of books some thirty or forty years ago.'[3] In 1629 Abbot complained that one of the difficulties he was meeting in running his Hospital was that 'there hath not been commended unto me anie person that cann soe much as write or reade, whereby I may have some helpe to give assistance to the maister for the good government of that foundation'.[4] The records of the Guild Merchant bear unwitting testimony to a level of near illiteracy remarkable in a small town that possessed a good grammar school. Much of the handwriting defies all but the most expert analysis, and the orthography displayed in the printed version is eccentric even by Tudor standards, well meriting the editor's advice that 'it is easier to read by ear than by the eye. If read aloud without attention to the spelling one finds that, e.g. . . . "John Raus late mak and naxsyon of det a gans Tomass Bottune of Waltetune" is "John Raus lately makes an action of debt against Thomas Bottume of Walton".'[5] The man who compiled that highly personal interpretation of spoken English made a powerful argument against the supposed simplicity of its phonetic spelling.

It is difficult to account for the continuing history of illiteracy and indifference to the preservation of records. The town was not only a merchant community, presumably with a lively awareness of the necessity of recording transactions, but it also possessed three institutions – the Friary, the School and the Hospital –

which overlapped in time and which could reasonably have been expected to act as a depository, at least. The fact that the library of the Friary had attracted the attention of John Leland argues that it was unusually well furnished, and though its books and records were scattered after 1538 it possessed a natural heir in the Grammar School There was already a formal link, for friars taught at the School, but if local results were to be taken as test they proved singularly incapable of transmitting the Dominican reverence for learning and the written word. The School, in fact, produced a large number of scholars of national reputation, particularly in the sixteenth and seventeenth centuries. One of these, George Parkhurst, Bishop of Norwich, later made a return to his old school and native town by bequeathing his valuable library to it in 1573. It was intended to serve the town as well as the School, though remaining under the control of the School governors, and successive gifts made of it a potentially priceless asset to the community. Ironically, it retains a high antiquarian value in the present century, for many of its now cherished volumes are still chained, making the collection one of the seven rare libraries of this nature in the country.

But its value as an instrument of learning and as a nucleus for a common foundation had vanished long before the nineteenth century, victim of the neglect of its custodians. The School did indeed act as an involuntary host for some of the town documents. In 1929 the first coherent catalogue of the town's archives listed among the School records a document of prime historic importance to the Borough – the indenture relating to the outright purchase of the fee-farm in 1610 when the town commuted the annual payment of £10 for a lump sum of £200. In 1968 the errant document was returned to its parent body, Guildford Corporation, after an absence of some 350 years.

Abbot's Hospital may have been inhibited from acting as a corporate repository by its founder's explicit prohibition of the entertainment of outsiders. He had a good and clear-cut reason for doing so: 'experience in other places hath taught me that ffathers and Mothers are not unwilling to draw their Children and Kinsfolk unto them, which will be both a burthen to the

House and so will the receaving of other strangers be, besides the disorders yt cannot be foreseene'.[6] His prohibition related, strictly, only to the literal entertaining of visitors, in particular to their lodging at night, and he allowed some liberties to the Master 'provided always that none of these bring any detriment or expence to the Hospital'. But, from whatever cause, the Hospital followed the lead of the School and protected its own records reasonably well but gave scant shelter to anything not connected with the foundation.

A possible explanation for the lack of any coherent system for preserving and administering both books and archives lies in the town's proximity to London. Technically the county town, Guildford nevertheless possessed formidable rivals in the northern communities which were absorbed into London. Camberwell and Croydon, Kingston, Lambeth and Southwark might have lost their separate identities but they gained wealth in return. Their ever increasing pressure of population forced them to gain, too, an awareness of social services, including the immense social value of libraries. In Guildford, the nineteenth-century concept of a public library as being a charitable foundation for the deserving poor continued to flourish strongly in the mid-twentieth century. Books were a private luxury, libraries irrelevant to the common good. 'Today's "free libraries" are unnecessary. Libraries abound where any book can be borrowed for twopence, so the proposition to spend £15,000 to £20,000 to establish a "free library" must be to lend books to those who cannot afford the twopence to borrow one from the existing libraries'[7] was the substance of a letter written in 1935 and even when the town at last acquired a library, it was officially proposed that its book stock should be supplied by charity.

In 1777 John Russell, bookseller, issued the first history of the town from his shop in the High Street. He was well equipped for the compiling of such a work, for his family was not only one of those whose names had occurred regularly in the town records over the past centuries – he himself was four times Mayor – but over the ensuing half-century the Russells produced a number of scholars and artists, including the John Russell who gained national fame and considerable fortune as a portrait painter. As a result, there appeared under the Russell imprint three books which not only preserved some of the fast-vanishing records but gave a reasonably coherent history of the town from the mid-eighteenth to the mid-nineteenth century.

The first history was merely a pamphlet both in its first and its second edition of 1800. But during the years between the editions the Russells had obviously been compiling material for a far more ambitious work which appeared simultaneously in London and Guildford in 1801. *The History of Guildford, the County Town of Surrey* is without doubt the most valuable and the most exasperating of the local printed compilations. If Russell intended it to serve in part as an advertisement of his trade, he did himself an ill service, for though the typography is good its eccentric pagination and vile paper make it simultaneously difficult and unpleasant to use. There is no index, no lengthy chapter-summary fashionable at the time, little discernible order so that it is necessary to hunt backwards and forwards, with increasing frustration, to find any desired fact. It is the work of a printer, not a publisher, for the material bears every evidence of having being composed as it came in rather than of being worked into a meaningful whole beforehand.

But the book not only presents material in an accessible form: it has also preserved much that has since been lost in its original form so that some of its entries assume the status of archives. Russell drew heavily upon the extracts that George Austen had taken from the old Black Book. Austen himself was selecting, for his extracts were intended as part of a history of the Grammar School so that the material relating to earlier centuries that Russell presents is a selection from a selection. Again, there is no formal indication of the basis upon which his selection is made, but internal evidence makes it apparent that what he has done is to select those entries which are either exemplary or important – in effect, plotting the course of the town's development by a series of points. The scholarly production in 1958 of the Borough records for the years 1514–46 has considerably reduced the value of Russell's extracts for this period, but until such time as the publication is extended Russell still remains the main accessible source for the later period.

In describing contemporary or recent times Russell is, if anything, even more eccentric. He seems quite unable to detach himself from his own day and place his material in historical perspective, his work abounding with private references which were obviously common contemporary knowledge but are now as enigmatic as an Assyrian record. Speaking of the construction of the Guild Hall in 1683 he remarks that 'the old market house which stood across the street' was taken down at the same time. 'This was related by a very old woman of the name of Watts, who remembered the pulling down of the market-house. She died in the hospital about thirty years since.'[8] This is on a par with the reference to the old beadle who remembered that St Nicholas had a round tower 'about a hundred years since'. On the other hand, he will sometimes give the most precise information about unimportant subjects which, presumably, caused a stir at the time, as with his detailed description of a funerary urn found near Henley Grove 'On the 29th of May 1781'.

In 1845 another history of the town appeared under the Russell imprint. No author is given on the title page, although the illustrator is credited, and for long the book was simply described as being the third edition of the Russell history, an injustice corrected by George Williamson in 1904. 'The book . . . was written for Messrs Russell by a Mr F. Laurence in 1842. This fact, not hitherto known, is rendered certain by the autograph inscription in the copy of the book given in 1852 by the author to his friend Mr Parry, in which he has recorded the fact of his authorship and the date when he wrote the book. This volume is now in the writer's possession.'[9] Laurence's book is different in kind from that of Russell's. It is smaller, contains less detail and draws upon Russell for much of the earlier history – but it is a connected, ordered story, lucidly written, accurately reflecting its period but disengaged from it. It is decorated with exquisite vignettes of the contemporary town, testimony to the existing standard of the Grammar School, for the artist

C. C. Pyne was afterwards appointed drawing-master to the School.

Laurence had the considerable advantage over his predecessor in that he had access to a monumental work of scholarship, *The History and Antiquities of the County of Surrey*, whose first massive folio volume appeared in 1804. The work was that of a clergyman and of a lawyer, Owen Manning and William Bray, and in the opinion of the conservative *Dictionary of National Biography* 'It still remains one of the best county histories that England can boast of'.[10] Manning was born in Northamptonshire but became Rector of Peperharow in 1769 and, in the best tradition of the rural clergy, utilised the leisure and the learning of his office in laying the groundwork for the first true history of the county. He died in 1801 before the work was completed, and his collaborator Bray, in a characteristically modest preface, gave him the major credit for the work. But the work bears throughout the imprint of Bray's orderly mind, backed up by his wide and deep learning. Whatever the proportion of Bray's contribution to the actual compilation of material – and he himself stated that he had visited almost every parish and church in Surrey – the county was fortunate in that it was he who saw the work through the press.

Bray was born in the village of Shere, some five miles from Guildford, in 1736. His family was substantial, and on the death of his elder brother in 1803 he inherited considerable property in the locality. He entered Rugby at the age of ten, was later articled to a solicitor in Guildford and ultimately practised in London with chambers in the New Inn. Prosperity naturally followed competence and family connections, but it was his appointment to the Board of Green Cloth, the archaic court responsible for the accounts of the royal household, that allowed him both the leisure and the social contacts that enabled him to pursue his major interests, the study of local antiquities.

In 1756 Bray commenced a diary that he continued over many years. Potentially of priceless local value, it is as tantalising in its brevity of style as Russell's work is irritating in its diffuseness. The reader is just able to discern behind the laconic entries the

SOUTHERN AND WESTERN
EXITS
*Quarry Street: southern
prospect*

*The Mount: eastern
prospect*

ARCHBISHOP GEORGE
ABBOT
*Detail from
the sepulchral
monument by Gerard
Christmas*

*An illustration of
his birthplace and the
'pike' legend (p. 89)*

The Grammar School

Abbot's Hospital: garden front

NORTH STREET *Western prospect, showing the last cattle-market in 1895*
A photograph of North Street taken in 1970

M&S

Charlotteville *Villas, Harvey Road*
Cottages, Addison Road

Stag Hill
University and
Cathedral

Detail of the
University campus

Guildford House (Childe House)

Yvonne Arnaud Theatre

Town panorama

steady rise of a cool, self-sufficient young man into the highest ranks both of society and of scholarship. The opening pages depict a calm, enclosed world of little walks and tea-drinkings and balls. 'Drank tea at Mrs Westbrooks. Mr and Mrs Fortery there: they played at Quadrille. I went home for an hour, and went again. Played and supped there. Home a little before 12.' National events receive the same dispassionate treatment from the pen of this rather elderly young man. 'May 22 1756. War with France. Went to see wire dancers (in Guildford). On the whole quite silly.' The unfortunate Admiral Byng receives almost a full biography by contrast. 'December 22 1756. Admiral Byng went through the town this morning on his way to Portsmouth to attend his trial. They tolled the bell and burnt his effigy on the churchyard steps [of Holy Trinity].' The names of men who were even then household words, among them Horace Walpole and Joshua Reynolds, are mentioned casually in passing, although Bray was on intimate terms with them. He found nothing particular to say regarding his first meeting with Manning in 1781. He was staying at the house of a mutual friend at the time and noted simply, 'Mr Manning supped and lay here.'[11]

But the restraint, though regrettable from the point of view of a historian seeking a view into local society in the late eighteenth century, creates confidence in Bray's major work. Bray was already a scholar of national reputation when he began his collaboration with the older Manning. His first publication, *Sketch of a Tour into Derbyshire and Yorkshire*, was published with cautious anonymity in 1777, but it attracted such great and favourable atttention that he put his name on the second edition of 1783 and thereafter it was frequently reprinted. He was a Fellow of the Society of Arts, becoming its Treasurer in 1803, became a member of the Council of the Society of Antiquaries and later a Trustee of the British Museum. Manning must have been as pleased to receive the collaboration of Bray as Bray was honoured to give it.

Although published only three years after Russell's work, the *History* might have belonged to another century. Bray was able to make use of his widespread professional and social contacts to gain access to archives still in private custody, and as a result both depth and breadth are added to the county history and, specifically, to that of Guildford. The standard contemporary practice of painstakingly transcribing epitaphs occupies a considerable body of space, as do the meticulous genealogies and records of transference of property rights. But they are linked together in a narrative which, though dry and legalistic in style, effectively illuminates and interprets. Legend is carefully disentangled from fact and the copious footnotes not only substantiate but act as a guide to valuable but frequently obscure and remote sources. The value of the work as a reference book varied according to the locality of which it treated, but in Guildford, with its lamentable history of non-history, it must have come as a revelation of the possibilities of scholarship.

The coming of the railway to the town in 1845 initiated a demand for popular guides and during the second half of the nineteenth century a number of them duly appeared. Few of these 'Rambles' and 'Tours' are of much value. Embedded in them here and there are some nuggets of contemporary information, but the majority consist of standard descriptions of the town's set pieces – the Guildhall, the Castle, Abbot's Hospital, the Grammar School – culled from the established histories and garnished with more or less turgid topographical rhapsodies. The relatively high number of printers in the town made possible the private publication of a few skimpy memoirs, or inept attempts at local history running to a score of pages or so.

John Mason's odd little book is outstanding in this class of vanity publications, not least because it presents a remarkable attempt at a topographical poem in praise of the town, cast in approximately the heroic style. Mason the son of poor parents, became a prosperous builder and, ultimately, Mayor in 1884, the attractively common local story of individual success that followed the decline of the Guild Merchant. The preface to his book is pleasantly self-deprecating but it contains some valuable, and presumably first-hand, vignettes of life in the town at the mid-century: the squealing of pigs on an autumn morning when the animals were slaughtered for winter and the boys of the town would gather round the fires used for swaling; the fish-carts drawn by sturdy dogs; the bustle and ceremony of the Assize processions when the County would turn up in its carriages to welcome the judges; the endless succession of farm carts bringing wheat into the town and taking back chalk from the quarries to be burnt into lime – 'the large disused pits will perhaps give the best idea of the extent of this industry'; the battle of St Catherine's; the uproar of parliamentary elections. But though the little book makes pleasant reading its value as a record is undermined by an almost total lack of chronology – and by a suspicion, too, that he was not above telling a good story merely because it was a good story. He claimed that his mother knew the boy who owned the famous Guildford jackdaw: the *Guildford Jackdaw* was a moral tale concocted by John Russell decades before Mason was born.

But it was during this barren period of local historiography that what might fairly be described as the town's chronicle was being compiled in the form of the diary of Henry Peak. The absence of the chronicler is a characteristic of English urban history which contrasts unfavourably with that of almost any Continental country, and is one of the strongest indications of the rural idealism of English society. In France, Germany, the Low Countries and, in particular, Italy, communities little larger than Guildford and with markedly similar mercantile interests could point to some merchant who, inspired by no other reason than civic patriotism, kept a form of private diary recording the current activities of his community. The chronicles might vary immensely from bald entries made at irregular periods to copious running narratives: their compilers might be barely able to write, or could be possessed of a superb literary ability. But whatever their defects or pretensions they provided a framework for the history of their community denied to the majority of their English equivalents. The lack of the chronicle is at once a cause and symbol of the long English indifference to civic history: the official records might be present but the enlivening mind of the contemporary commenting, questioning, judging is absent. Guildford's lack is therefore by no means unique: it is, however, curious that after centuries of an indifference unusual even by English standards the town should have acquired, at such a late period a chronicler outstanding even by Continental standards. The fact that Peak was an immigrant is, perhaps, more than a coincidence.

Peak was born in London in 1832, the son of a gilder who practised in a small way. Plain living and high thinking characterised the household, for the elder Peak clung stubbornly to the traditional methods of his craft and money was tight though the home was a happy and, indeed, lively one. The works of Cobbett and the Bible were the twin poles of the household but, as leaven, there was a constant coming and going of the artists who were the elder Peak's customers. At the age of seven young Peak sat for Benjamin Robert Haydon and was much impressed by his enormous studio. The eternally curious, restless Henry Bessemer was another frequent visitor: he was deeply interested in Peak's method of silvering glass, wondering if it had commercial possibilities. Altogether, it seems to have been an innocent little world, radical in political intent, intensely conservative in personal habits, characteristics which Peak himself was to bear all his life.

Lack of money prevented the young Henry from being formally apprenticed to any trade or profession. He picked up the rudiments of architecture in the offices of two fashionable architects in London, but it was a frustrating and unsatisfactory experience. All his life he was aware of his lack of formal education and qualifications, and was justifiably proud of his attainments despite them. 'I have had to gain my own livelihood from an early age [but] I have sought self-culture and, feeling my deficiencies, have constantly longed for more knowledge and wisdom and it seems wonderful to me that, in pursuing the profession of an Architect and Surveyor . . . I should have been able to acquire sufficient knowledge to practise the same with at least *some* measure of success.'[12]

London proved a dead end for him, and in 1851 at the age of nineteen he took advantage of a local contact to come to Guildford as assistant to a prosperous builder, Moss, 'a short, fat, bald, bespectacled man aged about 58. He was *not* a man of much education but quick and determined of purpose – a terror to builders. Neither was he a draughtsman or architect in the proper acceptation of the term, but he possessed great practical knowledge.'[13] Moss was doing very well out of the railway boom, as well as the building boom that it precipitated, and there was more than enough practical work for Peak. He kept up his studies, sticking rigidly to a curriculum that covered an immense field, living frugally ,'I made my bed-room my study where I constantly employed myself for an hour or so every evening and for this purpose added to my expenditure by purchasing a spring lamp for composite candles. . . . I rarely expended more upon my supper than the sum of one penny which supplied me with a biscuit and apple or the like and for drink I was contented with a glass of water.'[14]

But again misfortune struck the industrious apprentice, for his employer Moss burnt his fingers badly in an ill-timed essay in speculative building. Peak noted disapprovingly as his employer got into ever greater difficulties: it was obvious that the business was going to fail and in 1858 Peak was faced with the choice of seeking another master, or striking out on his own.

The ancient spirit of association and exclusion was still strong in the town, and Peak's problem was that which all immigrants faced – that of breaking into a close-knit circle. 'The practice of tradesmen and others of Guildford and Godalming of meeting in a social way at hotels and discussing business was much more prevalent and more potent too . . . than at the present day. I was not without friends. Some, on their part, invited me to their circle at the White Hart promising to introduce me to those who would put work in my way, others sought my presence at convivial gatherings at the White Lion for the same purpose.'[15] He declined all such invitations. It was a bold decision for an unknown young immigrant to make, but it was of a piece with his tough though courteous independence, and ultimately proved a wise one for he stood free of political faction during the early hazardous years of setting up on his own.

He succeeded, for he was an honest man and a thoroughly competent if uninspired architect – and his lack of inspiration was, if anything, fortunate at a period when the worse the architect the more fanciful his designs. He never lacked commissions: plans for churches, halls, cottages, villas, roads, cemeteries flowed from his office, and he, more than any man, was responsible for the Victorian town. Civic honours came his way inevitably for he had acquitted himself well in the onerous post as the town's first Surveyor: he held it for more than twenty-eight years during a vital period of the town's development, and more often than not he was out of pocket. Somewhat reluctantly he entered local politics and eventually crowned an honourable career by accepting the office of Mayor of his adopted town.

Peak's 'Recollections and Activities as Mayor of Guildford' remains still in manuscript. Strictly, it is not a diary, for it was compiled in the latter years of his life and its range is far greater than its tentative title indicates. It is personal, in the sense that Peak made no attempt to prospect back into the past history of the town as well as in the sense that it tells the story of one man's path through life. But he had a well-stocked mind and wide-ranging interests so that, unselfconsciously, he could put his story and that of the town in the larger context of national and international affairs, making of it a kind of barometer which accurately recorded the pressures of contemporary life in England. Above all, he had a genuine if unpolished talent for writing, an ability to record with lucidity and precision; and the same honesty and competence that made him a prosperous architect makes his written work an invaluable document for though he displays strong opinions and even prejudices they are rarely allowed to cloud the issue he is presenting.

In decided contrast to Henry Peak, both in personal nature and range of work, was George Williamson, the last local representative of the great race of English antiquaries. Williamson was a native of the town, being born there of a prosperous merchant family in 1858: in 1902, however, he moved to London for professional reasons and remained there for some twenty years, a period which enabled him to widen his already impressive range of social contacts. The nature he displayed in his numerous historical controversies was one of considerable irascibility and pugnacity, but he obviously had a gift for making friends in all classes of society. His non-local books are freely spattered with the names of the great, among them Gladstone and Roseberry, Queen Alexandra, Jenny Lind, Sarah Bernhardt, David Livingstone, many of whom he met in the course of his professional work as an art historian, Lewis Carrol gave him a copy of *Alice in Wonderland*: he saw Queen Victoria pour her 'tea or coffee' into a saucer: the legendary millionaire Pierrepont Morgan commmissioned him to reproduce a sumptuous catalogue of the Morgan miniatures. He specialised professionally in the study of miniatures, but he had a very wide background knowledge of general art history, editing the prestigious *Bryan's Dictionary of Painters and Engravers* as well as writing and editing a series of monographs on individual painters. He had a liking for the lame dog, the obscure painter about whom little or nothing was known. His monograph on John Russell arose naturally out of his local interests but his book on Bernadino Luini, who even Vasari virtually ignored, seems to have been written only because it presented a challenge and is a small masterpiece in the art of historical resurrection.

In his local work Williamson displayed, in full measure, the strength and weakness of the antiquary – on the one hand the devoted amassing and preservation of unglamorous but vital detail, on the other the determination to include, in his published work, every discovered fact no matter how irrelevant in its immediate context. It is this unselectiveness which mars his *Guildford in the Olden Time*, a book which his immense local knowledge could otherwise have made into the definitive history of the town. Its detailed description of, for example, the town plate is a legitimate if highly technical record, rendered all the more valuable by his professional knowledge. But one can only regret the perversity of the devotion of an entire chapter to Guilford, Connecticut, particularly after the author has been at some pains to point out that it is extremely unlikely to have any connection with Guildford, Surrey.

But, although the editorial standard of his local books might fall below that of his professional work, their very existence extended the depth and range of the town's historiography in a manner unknown since the time of Bray. The sheer mass of Williamson's work, coupled with his fiery enthusiasm, led to certain inaccuracies for which he has been posthumously criticised; but his critics, to a large degree, have been forced to use his work as starting-point for their own investigations and critical conclusions.

Williamson's published work is important, but his role as the town's historical conscience has had an equally valuable long-term effect. From the end of the nineteenth century almost until his death in 1942 he maintained a steady barrage of criticism directed against official and private indifferences to the town's archival and architectural heritage, combining it with positive attempts to remedy the situation. He founded the first Guildford Society, for the protection of the town's amenities, in 1896 and brought in a number of influential people, including a rising young architect, Edwin Lutyens. The Society was immediately effective in modifying the wave of demolition that accompanied the building boom, but dwindled away after Williamson left for London, sure evidence of his role. He was largely responsible for bringing the Surrey Archaeological Society to the town, thereby indirectly opening the way to a rational system of archive and museum preservation. He lent his local influence to the long movement to bring about the establishment of a public library. And in 1933 the Town Council recognised his efforts by appointing him to the post of Remembrancer or official chronicler, an office which he himself resurrected and for which, at his own expense, he designed a robe and chain. His official title of the 'Honorary Remembrancer' comprehensively sums up George Williamson's contribution to the history of his native town.

In 1855 Parliament withdrew the stamp duty on newspapers and on 29 September of that same year the town's first newspaper came into being. Its ultimate title reads like a local gazeteer for, as it stated in its first editorial, 'We seek to remove the reproach from Surrey of being the only county in England which has no newspaper of its own.' The *West Surrey Times and County Express, Surrey Mail, Guildford Gazette, Godalming Chronicle,*

Chertsey Mail, Dorking Herald, Farnham Herald, Epsom and Leatherhead Record and Horsham Star did not long retain its unique position. Between 1860 and 1870, ten new journals appeared locally, seven of them in four years. Some lasted only a matter of weeks – the *Guildford Chronicle* put out five numbers in February and March 1963 before its owner's editorial enthusiasm succumbed to commercial reality: the *West Surrey Express* survived for three months in 1862. They changed names and owners with bewildering frequency, creating an almost inextricable historical tangle,[16] but out of the welter there rose in 1864 another viable paper, the *Surrey Advertiser*, destined to be the *Times*'s major competitor and its ultimate survivor over a century later.

The *Times* and the *Advertiser* almost immediately took on the political colouring that had entered the town with the Municipal Reform Act of 1835 and their sparring is irresistibly reminiscent of the Eatanswill journals. The *Times* was aggressively Liberal, the *Advertiser* cautiously Tory. Its restraint was perhaps due to the primary function embodied in its title, for it was founded simply as an advertising medium and, though rapidly achieving all the full status of a newspaper, it never wholly shook off the early caution engendered by a natural reluctance to offend potential clients.

One of the results was to make the *Advertiser* less attractive than the *Times* which was not only prepared to attack over a wide range but also acted as the forum for an articulate radical element. The *Times* established thereby a tradition of largely unpaid contributions which both broadened its scope in national terms and gave it considerable depth in local historical reportage. It published a valuable local Notes and Queries column so that in the same issue could be found a vivid first-hand description of the building of the Forth Bridge and a disquisition in minute detail regarding the local growing of teazels. Some of the material was reprinted in pamphlet form, a particularly valuable series being the monographs of J. K. Green, published in the 1950s under the general title of *Sidelights on Guildford History*.

Both newspapers were excellent examples of the vigorous

local newspaper that flourished before the emergence first of the national daily and then of electronic media limited its topical value. Crime, reported in luscious detail, was their staple in the first decades but so, too, was literature, the *Times* in particular specialising in immensely long serialised novels. Long after they had lost ground to the nationals they continued to reflect what was probably a more accurate picture of English life than that presented by the London-based papers, with their necessary formulae and simplifications.

The *Advertiser*'s reactions to the outbreak of the two world wars are vignettes of English social history that concentrate the feeling of an entire epoch in a headline. On 18 July 1914 it published a grim leader entitled 'Peace or War' – referring to the troubles in Ireland. On 25 July it mentioned briefly Sir Edward Grey's interview with the German ambassador regarding Serbia, but like the overwhelming majority of his countrymen the editor saw nothing particularly important about events in an obscure Balkan country. The War was three days old before the *Advertiser*, publishing weekly, was editorially aware of it. Its reaction was the reaction of the country. 'Surrey's Splendid Patriotism. Ready response from every town and village. Stirring Scenes. Splendid Send-off to men.' Twenty-five years later, it spoke again in precisely the national accents – wearied, disillusioned, dogged – its headline reading, accurately, as though the intervening quarter of a century had merely been a temporary and uncertain truce. 'Wartime Conditions Again.' There were no stirring scenes of splendid patriotism to report, merely the picture of a community reluctantly turning to an unpleasant task. 'Protective Action at Guildford. More Evacuees received.'

After a number of changes in form and control, the *Times* finally disappeared in August 1968, leaving the field clear to its one-time rival. The *Advertiser* retains something of its traditional caution, preferring to reflect local events rather than comment upon them, prepared indeed to close its columns to any acutely controversial topic as when it declined either to discuss or report the controversy regarding the appointment of the Dean of the Cathedral. Overtly Conservative in politics in an overwhelmingly Conservative town, it nevertheless provides a free forum of generous dimensions in the shape of its 'Letters to the Editor'. This has grown immensely from a few sporadic letters scattered about the paper, to the present feature occupying two full pages and sometimes spilling over into others. The feature discharges locally the identical function that the London *Times* discharges nationally in its correspondence columns – the introduction and development of subjects of public interest that might not otherwise be brought to public attention. An excellent example of this was the heated correspondence that followed a cavalier proposal to turn the ancient Rack's Close into a car-park – a correspondence which culminated in an indignant letter from the son of the man who had given the Close to the town many years before. On some occasions indeed, it seems that the first intimation authority receives of some pressing local problem is the appearance of a critical letter in the *Advertiser*.

The letters fall into a clearly discernible pattern. Politics and religion dominate both in proportion and in sheer mass of words. The generous allowance of space allows correspondents to develop their theme in minute detail and, in religion, the whole range of theological doctrine is paraded from time to time in a manner reminiscent of eighteenth- and nineteenth-century controversy, for not only are the fundamentals brought out again for airing – the Apostolic succession, the identity of Christ, Darwinism, among them – but the contestants indulge in a species of personal vituperation long since departed from the national papers. Politics tend to be conducted on strictly party lines mostly in the form of a three-cornered fight between the younger representatives of the three major political parties. Towards the end of the year charity appeals take up considerable space, the *Advertiser* indirectly contributing to them for the saving in advertising costs must be considerable. National events find champions and opponents of predictable colour, but the emphasis is on local personalities and events – in particular, events as they affect the physical well-being of the town.

In 1923 there appeared the last independent journal to establish itself in the town. The *Outlook* began life, like the *Advertiser*, purely as an advertising medium, but when it, too, achieved independent status the form it adopted was that of a modestly illustrated magazine. Throughout the years of its direct association with the town, it bore the powerful imprint of its editor, G. H. Brierly, a professional journalist who had received his training on the nationals, successfully edited newspapers in Cornwall and Wales and come to Guildford now to entertain, castigate, inform, nag and in general galvanise a still leisurely small town. His particular victim was the Borough Council, and week after week his readers were entertained with accounts of the unfortunate Council's procrastination, its miserly habits and spendthrift ways, its addiction to red tape. A favourite gambit was to analyse its expenses, comparing them unfavourably with the corporate expenses in the nineteenth century. He attacked vigorously and continuously the closed circle of power whereby mayors invariably came from the body of the Council itself, arguing that much needed new blood would be infused by occasionally taking a mayor from outside the Council. Attacked, in his turn, on the reasonable grounds that so vociferous a critic should himself join the Council and work reform from within, he retorted unanswerably that he preferred the freedom of the outsider.

If the Council was his predestined victim, the merchants of the town were his favourite protégés, and he happily combined both preferences by attacking the Council on behalf of the merchants, particularly in the matter of municipal trading and the Council's system of hair's-breadth tenders. He was continually bringing bizarre instances of these to light. Caps for three water-inspectors, total value about thirty shillings, were put out for tender – and the contract went outside the town. A Berkshire firm's tender for painting a school was accepted – at 2s 4d less than that tendered by a local firm. 'In order that the Corporation might save that 2s 4d hundreds of 2s 4d's were lost to Guildford in wages for work by its men.'[17] His campaign seems to have been effective for, at its height, the Council accepted a large local tender for sewage-pumping which was, in fact, more than £200 greater than that of an outside firm.

A singular aspect of the *Outlook* under Brierly's editorship was the apparently inexhaustible vein of local history that he was able to tap. Month after month and for years on end he was able to present some new aspect of the town's history, drawn in part from the personal memoirs of living older citizens, in part from unpublished material in private hands. The little magazine circulated over a wide area – a regular feature was the triumphant list of its subscribers from India to Canada via Battersea and Hawaii – and many of these scattered ex-citizens contributed their quota to the sum of a living memory. Editorially shortened though it was, the material gives some idea of what the town has lost through lack of institutional preservation. Brierly particularly urged the need for a pictorial collection and was prepared to lodge the *Outlook*'s collection with the embryonic reference library. 'It would have been well if many years ago the Corporation or other body had initiated a plan for the preservation of old Guildford. Such a step ought not to have been left to the *Outlook* although in a sense we are proud it has been.'

Brierly's remark was rendered all the more pointed by the fact that there did exist three institutions which could, in theory, have initiated such a plan: the Museum, born of the Surrey Archaelogical Society, the Guildford Institute and its reluctant guest, the Public Library. All three, however, were suffering from the chronic cultural weakness of the town.

The arrival of the Archaeological Society was heralded by a caustic and strictly impertinent leader in the *West Surrey Times* in March 1889. 'The Archaeological Society has presented as striking an example as could be found among Surrey Institutions of the power of lingering in suspended animation without any evidence of real vitality.' It was dying on its feet in London and the projected move might just about save it'.[18] The *Times* cordially welcomed the advent, however, and pilloried an unfortunate reader who, believing that the Society was to be rate-supported, wrote to protest against gentlemen of learning being subsidised by hard-working citizens. 'We publish the letter as a curiosity, a specimen of the peculiar narrowness of vision . . . which is just a little out of date nowadays. The Society was self-supporting but, even if it were not, the duty of town councils was to support culture as well as commerce.'[19]

The Society was founded in Southwark in 1854, product of that wave of interest in local history which brought many other similar societies into existence from the mid-century onwards. Directing its interests towards Surrey, rather than towards London, it fell victim to the amorphous nature of the capital: no one locality was necessarily its natural home. It migrated uneasily between Westminster and Croydon for some years before it took the decision to look outside London for a place to site its permanent headquarters. By a fortunate coincidence, in 1885 Guildford Corporation had acquired, along with the Castle, a handsome town-house of considerable historic interest which was ideally suited for the purpose of housing a learned institution. George Williamson led the local movement to attract the Society to Guildford and, after prolonged negotiations, the Surrey Archaeological Society in 1898 made its final home in the building called Castle Arch, so named from the great gateway that abuts it.

The arrangement made with the Corporation was that the Society should pay a nominal rent of £12 per annum and, in return, would allow the public limited access to its collections. In 1905 the Corporation itself began collecting items – a timely decision, for it saved the carving of the great White Hart when the inn that it had adorned was demolished – and two years later an agreement was made whereby the Council would erect a museum on the site in which the Society could place its collections. The town's first museum was then endowed with a guaranteed income – of £40 per annum.

In 1919 an entry in the minutes showed exactly how the system was working. It was reported that 'Mr Luck, custodian of the Museum on free days, had struck work in November for an increase in pay. That Mrs Edwards was [paid] 11/6 a week, including free days, and that she paid Mr Luck' and that an anonymous member of the Society had been paying Luck the additional money he demanded.[20] The system limped along for another fourteen years, during which the Corporation raised its contribution to £100, before it was rationalised in 1933 when the town accepted all responsibility for the institution. The Society still maintained its interest, together with the greater part of the available administrative space.

The vital archives and record section followed a similar development, encouraged by the fact that in 1928 the construction of an adequate muniment-room resulted in the Museum's recognition by the Master of the Rolls as a depository for manorial documents. The subsequent small but steady inward flow of hitherto scattered records – including valuable collections from the neighbouring great houses of Clandon and Losely – at last created the basis of a civic archive system.

Nevertheless, the first professional Curator Archivist was not appointed until 1947. Throughout its formative years, the Museum suffered even more from public indifference, amounting at times to hostility, than did the Library. During the discussion as to the future use of the Guildhall after the construction of the new municipal buildings a councillor, legitimately protesting against a suggestion that it should be used as the Museum, summed up the local public concept of such an institution by scornfully remarking that they did not want stuffed owls in the ancient building. The remark was echoed a few years later by a governor of the Grammar School, in his turn objecting to the proposed use of the School's buildings as a repository for 'platypus skeletons and ostrich eggs'. A museum was a place to put odds and ends, travellers' curios and the like, and had no conceivable value as an instrument of education. It was particularly unfair to Guildford Museum which from its early days had established a disciplined policy of acceptance, politely declining such gifts as the poisoned arrows and the model of the Garden of Eden which Gordon of Khartoum desired to present in 1918. It was designed to present a coherent picture of local life, and maintains that objective.

The Archaeological Society currently pays £100 per annum as a combined rent and fee for secretarial services, the sum covering the use of a large and handsome room for its library and other smaller rooms for storage. It is an uneconomic rent but 'The work of the Museum and the Society is so closely integrated that the utmost care is needed if justice is to be done to both parties. Both derive great advantage from the association or, to put it crudely, have a stranglehold on each other,' the last report of the official Curator declared.[21] The Society's own publications of official Surrey records, together with its magnificent series of *Collections* containing an immense range of papers on local history, make that symbiosis almost indissoluble, a nineteenth-century concept of municipal scholarship flourishing vigorously in the twentieth-century university town.

In 1962 the town obtained its first library building – 112 years after Parliament had enacted that local authorities could pay for library buildings but not library books: thirty-eight years after the first temporary library had been established by the Borough under threat of losing its powers to the County, and some twenty years after protests from the involuntary war-time guests of the town had resulted in a new, if reluctant, approach.

Paradoxically, the tardy provision of a universally recognised public service was due, in large part, to the fact that the town already possessed a library. On 11 March 1834 the Guildford Mechanics' Institute was founded 'for the promotion of useful knowledge among the working classes'. Dissension seems to have been one of its primary talents, for almost immediately internal quarrels resulted in a split in 1835, a union was effected in 1840, more quarrels led to another split in 1860 and it was not until 1892 that a finally unified society established itself in a handsome new building, complete with library, reading-room, magazine room and ladies' room.

Despite its theoretically humble purpose, the Institute was sociably fashionable. In 1880 its president was the Earl of Northumberland, and the long list of its vice-presidents included many of the wealthy families of the locality. Long after the coming of the Archaeological Society it maintained its position as the major academic organisation of the town. In addition to a well-stocked library, it provided a meeting-place for local cultural societies, published an excellent little magazine, *The Keep*, ran public lectures and even established a little museum of its own.

There was no one cause or specific date that marked its decline.

Regularly through the twenties and thirties it published appeals for increased membership, but its numbers of members remained fairly constant and well in excess of 1000. Subscriptions were low, amounting to £464 in 1933. But it possessed property and the terms of its constitution forbade any move towards dissolution that was not supported by nine-tenths of the membership at two successive meetings. But proportionately it lost ground, being essentially a static society in a rapidly growing town, and gradually sank into the background as the Public Library developed.

In 1924 the Institute agreed to let part of its premises to the Corporation for the establishment of a reference library. The embryonic public library was a meagre, haphazard collection of books, run on the barest possible minimum of money which later was made to provide for an even less enthusiastic lending library. Public demands for a viable system were almost completely ignored by the Council. It is difficult to assess accurately the public reaction in this matter. The indignant letters in the press might indicate a general public desire, but they came from a relatively small section of the community. The Council's massive indifference must have been based on the sure knowledge that the bulk of the townspeople held firmly to the belief that those who wanted books should buy them. In 1935 the Council made a remarkably tactless move, proposing to take over the Guildford Institute – buildings, library and all, for the public good. '[It] did not propose to make any payment and took up the attitude that this organisation [the Institute] had been provided in the past for the good of the town, and was now serving the interests of the few, and was not a particularly lively service. Negotiations broke down amid a good deal of bad feeling on both sides.'[22]

Then the war brought hundreds of evacuees into the town from London – people who had been brought up to expect, as a matter of course, that a self-respecting community should possess a communal library. Displaying the common energy of the immigrant, they by-passed the local Council and enlisted the powerful aid of the County Council. Prodded from all sides, Guildford Borough Council moved reluctantly into action. In

1942 the first qualified Librarian was appointed – thriftily, the Librarian was later made responsible for the Museum – a small staff established and a book-stock of 10,000 volumes hired from the County. The rented accommodation in the Institute proved inadequate and for the next twenty years the Library migrated from one temporary home to another. In 1957 the Council, pursuing its ambivalent policy towards culture, acquired a beautiful seventeenth-century house on the High Street as an exhibition centre. Behind it was the characteristic long garden of the Guildford burgher's house – an ideal site for a public building. In 1960 work began on the site and in August 1962 the town had acquired a permanent public library.

The long delay had eventually worked to the Library's benefit for advantage was taken of the considerable development in library construction that has taken place since the war. The architects were faced with the problem of fitting the building into a long, narrow area and the shape of a seventeenth-century garden eventually dictated the shape of a twentieth-century building. The building was integrated, not forced, into its surroundings. An ancient brewhouse in the garden was left intact, later to form a small milieu for public meetings, and the space between the Library and the back of the house on the High Street was turned into a paved courtyard. The various elements became one, creating a quiet, accessible public place that has all the attractions of a private garden. In the Library itself a room additional to the usual library departments was set aside for local material: many of George Williamson's own books and manuscripts form the backbone of the collection, a reciprocative honour that would doubtless have pleased him.

In marked – and, indeed – startling contrast to the community's long indifference to its literal and graphic records is its loyalty to a theatrical tradition that, extending over two centuries, culminated in a theatre that can be judged not in a local but in national terms. That contrast was clearly pointed out in February 1970 when, at the same Council meeting, a plea to increase the Borough's contribution to its Library to at least the national level was rejected, while it was agreed to increase the Borough's annual grant to the Theatre. It is probable that the tradition owes its strength to the same factors that have made of the town the trading centre for a scattered population whose fragments are located in rural areas. Again, the town's position relative to London – just far enough to develop an independent life and close enough to be influenced by the social movements in the capital – would provide a powerful impulse towards the establishment of a theatre even while it hampered the development of its other cultural centres. The actor-managers of the nineteenth century would naturally include such a conveniently located town on their circuits, and even in the twentieth century the fact that a London-based actor can travel to and from the town for an evening's performance has contributed substantially to the present high standard of the Theatre.

By the end of the eighteenth century, the casual and un-sophisticated entertainments organised by the guilds was giving ground to a more formal system whose impulse was financial. In 1789 an enterprising manager, Henry Thornton, judged that the town was ripe to be exploited and established yet another theatre in a rapidly growing circuit which was run on the modest principle of small profits, quick returns and the very minimum of expenditure. The town's first theatre was a humble structure, of red-brick, tucked away in a side street next door to the old Cockpit but an index of Thornton's self-confidence, as well as an indication of the regional nature of the town's position, was provided by the fact that the theatre was capable of seating 400 people although the population of the town had not yet reached 3000.

Thornton's confidence, and that of his successors, was justified and over the next sixty years the theatre enjoyed an unsophis-ticated but vigorous existence under a series of managements irresistibly reminiscent of that of Vincent Crummles, complete with endless 'final benefits', child prodigies and advertisements for low comedians. By the mid-nineteenth century, however, the theatre had obviously begun to run into difficulties for in 1860 it was described simply as a warehouse and was finally demolished in 1889. The theatrical tradition nevertheless continued, though at an ever lower standard, a series of third-rate companies putting on performances in an inconvenient hall in North Street. By the end of the nineteenth century Guildford theatre was indistinguishable from a low-class music-hall.

In 1909 a letter from a resident to the local *Free Press* sparked off an unofficial enquiry into the present position of the theatre that incidentally threw considerable light on the rapidly changing social conditions of the town. The writer of the letter bewailed the lack of a true theatre particularly in the long, dark winter months when there was nothing whatsoever to do in a small town. Wealthier citizens could afford to travel to London for an evening's entertainment but such an evening, the writer calculated, could cost as much as 15*s* and was therefore out of reach of the majority. Was it not possible to resurrect the theatre?

The *Free Press*'s enquiry into the possibility elicited replies from two clearly distinguished categories. The older members of the community were unanimous in their belief that the town could no longer support a proper theatre – the quality just would not rub shoulders with the increasing number of artisans and it was the quality upon whom a theatre must depend for its financial success. The other extreme was typified by John Dennis, the energetic head of the rapidly growing engineering works. He made the point that the workers of the town, creating the wealth of that town, were at the least as entitled to entertainment as their social superiors and clinched the argument with the unassailable economic fact that the combined spending power of this new class of artisan was quite capable of maintaining a theatre. His firm alone paid out nearly £1000 per week in wages, and some of his higher paid workers were earning thirty shillings a week or even more.

Ultimately, the economic argument prevailed and in 1912 a local group – the County and Borough Halls Company – opened in North Street a theatre that was capable of seating 1000 people. The size of the new venture was matched by a far higher standard of production than that which had prevailed over the previous half-century, and found justification in an enthusiastic local support for some twenty years. Its decease in 1932 was brought about suddenly and by external causes: under the new licensing acts Surrey County Council, the responsible authority, demanded physical changes in the building whose ultimate costs were calculated at some £20,000. The Co-operative Society, the new owners of the theatre, was sympathetic but declared itself incapable of underwriting the relatively immense sum and, despite massive local protest against what was seen as a rigid bureaucratic application of regulations, a continuous theatrical history of nearly 150 years came to an abrupt end.

It was revived again immediately after the Second World War in a manner that gave indication of the town's rapid future development as a regional centre. In 1945 two young men – Patrick and Roy Henderson – were seeking a venue for their own theatrical enterprise and were advised by a leading actress to 'try Guildford': in the following year two more immigrants came to the town. The licensing restrictions that had destroyed the old theatre were still in force, and it was only under the guise of a club that the brothers were able to avoid the otherwise crippling costs. But that very limitation provided a clear indication of the extent of public support for a theatre – a support proportionately far stronger and far less equivocal than for any other cultural project: in a month 3000 members were enrolled in the club. During the fifteen years of its life the Guildford Repertory Theatre was able to draw upon a similar enthusiastic support as that which attended its birth: among its members were people of a national standing in the theatrical profession, a fact which at once contributed to the standard of its productions and proved of immense significance in the future development of the dramatic tradition in Guildford.

In 1963 the theatre again came to a sudden ending, this time by fire. But the physical destruction was merely the dramatic underlining of an expected conclusion for the lease was due to expire that year and, for some time previously, the theatre's directors had been considering its future position. Their ultimate decision was, in the context of the town's theatrical tradition, astonishing. Over the previous century and a half Guildford's theatre, though progressing steadily from crudeness to sophistication was nevertheless essentially local: within that context an expected decision would have been to create another modest, local theatre and in the early stages of their deliberations, indeed, the directors were considering a sum of some £70,000 as the absolute maximum that it was possible to raise for the purpose. It was eventually decided, however, to build a theatre whose final cost was to be well in excess of £300,000.

The theatre's ability not merely to make, but implement such a decision, was its association with an actress of international fame. In 1958 Yvonne Arnaud had died in the town where she had spent the last months of her life. She had been one of the warmest supporters of the modest theatre, giving to it something of the aura that clung to her name as well as contributing a very high degree of professional critical ability. Even allowing for theatrical hyperbole she seems to have been genuinely loved in her own profession and, through her ability to project a sense of intimacy even through electronic media, immensely popular with a very large national audience. An appeal launched in her name therefore almost automatically moved on to a national level, a fact well demonstrated both by the choice of milieu – the Dorchester Hotel, London, and the list of guests at its launching in October 1961. Exactly a year later one half of the initial appeal for £200,000 had been collected: four months later the first subsoil tests were made and in June 1965 occurred the first performance of the completed Yvonne Arnaud Theatre.

> we are an island people
> And in our natures earth and ocean couple
> Begetting other islands, such as those
> We knew in childhood: Daniel Defoe's,
> Ballantyne's or Stevenson's, Crichton's or Prospero's
> 'Come unto these yellow sands
> And then take hands . . .' For here has been created
> An island theatre. . . .
> A theatre charming as a country favour
> Lying between the mill stream and the river.

Christopher Fry's *Prologue,* spoken upon the first opening night, had an immediate and powerful significance relevant to the town's explosive twentieth-century growth. This island theatre 'charming as a country favour' was a few yards distant from the commercial heart of the town and its immediate locality, known as Millmead, was perhaps the most beautiful and certainly the most vulnerable area of a town increasingly hungry for land. The fact that the river still entered the town inviolate on the south was due in part to the town's slowness of development in its historic period, in part to the Borough Council's restraint in the 1930s – but mostly because the land protected itself. The ancient road entering the town from the south swung away from this low-lying, marshy area to climb the solid high ground before the Castle. The subsoil was relatively unstable, as Henry Peak found when he built his houses abutting the town bridge. There, the desire to build along the line of the High Street made it economically feasible to build the massive foundations required: further down the river the economic argument failed. There was little incentive to build upon ground, always liable to flood and at considerable distance from the only road: Millmead therefore presented, in the late twentieth century, substantially the same appearance that it must have presented when the river first carved its way through the impelling chalk spine.

Then, in 1961, the southern road was realigned and widened, becoming a major highway a few feet distant from the river bank: immediate and continuing pressure was placed upon the planning authority to allow this suddenly valuable land to be developed commercially. Such development was inevitable: public protest was later able to prevent the building of a massive hotel and carpark along the river bank but it failed, signally, even to modify plans for an immense department store whose present bulk obliterates, in a featureless wall, what had been a natural and distinctive meeting point of town and country. But though development was unavoidable its form could, perhaps, be controlled – a powerful contributory factor to the Borough Council's decision to lease, at a purely nominal rent, a peninsular site to the Theatre's management.

Ideally located though it was both in terms of communication and aesthetics, the site posed a major problem to the architects: in solving it they gave the Theatre a unique form. The small, water-confined area dictated the ultimate size of the building even while the shape – irregular but roughly rectangular – argued the final horse-shoe shape of the Theatre itself, with the curve following the termination of the peninsula. To the casual eye, the external walls of the greater part of the building seem to be all of glass so that the natural elements of the waterside side and the contrived elements of the Theatre flow visually one into the other. The ancient town mill, whose operation was almost co-existent with the recorded history of the town, latterly producing electricity where once it had produced flour, was incorporated into the over-all design, its plain nineteenth-century brick acting as foil to the twentieth-century glass and concrete. Within the Theatre, the stage is immense, for it is the seating accommodation that has been sacrificed to the limitations of size, and not the production facilities. The *Illustrated London News,* reporting the opening performance, remarked pertinently that the stage was almost as large as that of the London Palladium, but where the Palladium seats 2500 the Yvonne Arnaud Theatre seats only 568. The limitation is an asset from the point of view of the audience, for it enables productions of a national standard to be enjoyed in the comfort and intimacy of a small theatre. But it presents a very real economic problem to the Theatre management, for an auditorium of appropriate size should seat in the region of 750 people: in the absence of those additional 200 seats, the Theatre is heavily dependent upon its grants – some £20,000 annually from the Arts Council and £1750 from Guildford Borough Council itself. The Borough Council's grant is minute compared with the massive injection from the Arts Council but is proportionately very high in terms of local expenditure – a clear enough indication of the community's valuation of a permanent home for its favoured culture and the creation of a building which posterity will probably rank with the Guildhall and the Hospital.

CHAPTER FIVE

The Governance of the Town

On Christmas Day 1835 the ancient constitution of the town came to an end, swept into history under the surge of national reform. The old world had died in considerable uproar as the sweeping measures of the Reform Act of 1832 widened the parliamentary franchise, reducing the privileges of the few in favour of the many. In Guildford, John Mason, as an old man, remembered

> the consternation which the passage of the Bill produced among those opposed to it in the town. One had abundant opportunity for hearing of the desolation and ruin predicted from the passing of this measure. It was with reluctance that the lumps of clay were prepared in which to place the candles for the lighting up of our windows, as a general illumination was decreed in honour of the event. It was the fear of having our windows smashed that inclined us to go with the stream.[1]

Parliamentary reform led inexorably to local reform. In 1834 royal commissioners reported that

> There prevails among the inhabitants of the great majority of incorporated towns a general and in our opinion just dissatisfaction with the municipal institutions – a distrust of the self-elected municipal councils, whose powers are subject to no popular control and whose acts and proceedings, being secret, are not checked by the influence of public opinion . . . a discontent under the burthen of local taxation, while revenues are diverted from their legitimate use.[2]

Guildford came out well in the long tale of municipal corruption and inefficiency: the commissioners found that the town was both respectable and prosperous, with only two bankruptcies and twenty cases of felony in thirty years. Nevertheless, the town received a new corporate identity – the 'Mayor and Burgesses' in place of the ancient 'Mayor and Approved Men' – expression of 'the undoubted right of every burgess to select for himself from the burgess role the names of those persons he would wish to be councillors of the town'.[3] Open, if noisy, politics had taken the place of secret, if quiet, arrangements.

One of the results of the turbulence of the early 1830s was to activate a long-dormant element of violence that grew steadily over the following two decades until it threatened the very fabric of the community. The violence found a focus in Guy Fawkes Day, and hence gained the popular name of the Guy Riots. But the municipal elections occurred in November, too, and it seems likely that behind the lawless violence was a political intelligence using the mob for its own purposes. 'You must remember that if anybody had said or done anything which offended the mob during the year, it was all scored up and vengeance was sure to visit them on November 5th,' an eyewitness told the *Surrey Times* in 1889.[4] It would have been a simple task to ensure that political transgressors were included in the list of victims.

Henry Peak has left the most vivid and complete description of the opening of the saturnalia. Peak had come to Guildford, a stranger in the February of 1851, and the riot of the following November therefore had all the impact of novelty.

> I left my office rather late in the evening to go to my lodgings, and upon crossing the Bridge an imposing spectacle presented itself. There in the distance at the steps in the roadway opposite Trinity Churchyard a great fire was burning, brilliantly lighting up all around, and the whole town was as if in a state of siege. Every shop window not protected by shutters was barricaded, and wet straw and manure heaped over the areas and gratings . . . to prevent the penetration of fireworks. These were formidable and dangerous things, being immense squibs many of them 12 or 15 inches in length and $1\frac{1}{2}$ to 2 inches in diameter, and being chiefly loaded with gunpowder and heavily rammed, their force of explosion when discharged was tremendous and notwithstanding the precautions taken, I saw several mount to a great height and some actually entered the upper windows of houses. Curiosity drew me to the bonfire where a great and lawless crowd was gathered. The chiefs,

fantastically dressed, were members of the Guys' Society, an organised body defying the police and officials of the town, and a saturnalia of mob rule was being carried on. The whole place was at the mercy of the Guys, who gave orders by means of a horn.[5]

Peak did not usually exaggerate, and his opinion that the Guys were an organised body was probably not far from the truth. Three years later, in the riot of 1854, they executed what amounted to a military manœuvre requiring exact timing. A bonfire was lighted on Mount Street, the steep continuation of the High Street which climbs the Hog's Back, to draw the police. Sections of the mob were stationed in the streets and alleys leading on to the main thoroughfare and as the police hastened to the new bonfire the mob charged out and, armed as it was with heavy nail-studded clubs, totally routed them.

Year after year, as dusk fell on 5 November, the town would resound to the eerie rallying-cry of the Guys – 'Phillaloooo Muster'. 'Their cry will never be forgotten by anyone who ever heard it. It was a thrilling, piercing note of peculiar intensity, and was a warning for all peaceful citizens to be on their guard.'[6] Some few citizens, notably builders, made a small profit from the occasion, for wooden shutters and barricades were in heavy demand. But the vast majority complained vehemently at the damage, the terrorisation, the powerlessness of the police, the infamy that the town was earning. In desperation, the Council made an unprecedented decision: it looked outside the normal ranks of conciliar material for a man who could restore order. In 1863 Philip Whittington Jacob was elected Mayor with the fullest powers to bring the disorders to an end.

Jacob was neither a native nor a merchant. Born in Somerset about 1804, he came to Guildford in the mid-century as a qualified surgeon. But it was to linguistics rather than the medicine that he devoted his time. He was credited with knowing most European languages as well as Hebrew, Persian and Hindustani and to him fell the sub-editorship of a major section of Murray's epochal *Oxford English Dictionary*, then in course of compilation. Murray gave him unstinted praise: 'Of all the band of voluntary workers who have done so much to the work in the preliminary stages, Mr Jacob was *facile princeps* in the enthusiasm and energy with which he worked for several years and in the amount of work he accomplished."[7] In his adopted town, the respect in which he was regarded seems to have been tinged with awe. Peak remembered him as 'a man of learning and a great linguist, acquainted with the Sanscrit but also a man of great force of character. (He was, I believe, a brother of the Jacob of the Light Horse in India and at Balaklava.)'[8]

Jacob's preparations for the expected riot of November 1863 were on a military scale. Troops were brought into the town in the late afternoon of 5 November and patrolled it until the small hours. Assisting them was a large body of special constables, numbering some two or three hundred, sworn in for the emergency: they were issued with handsome batons of office, a few of which are cherished in private houses today. Troops and constables patrolled the town nightly until 21 November, when the military were withdrawn. The Guys erupted on that same night, causing widespread damage and coming near to murder when they threw a regular policeman on the great bonfire. Jacob appeared and read the Riot Act in three localities, the police and special constables gradually gained control and quiet returned by morning.

November 1864 passed quietly, but the following year brought evidence that the Guy Riots had very little to do with celebrating the delivery of Parliament from the Gunpowder Plot. The Guys emerged on 1 November, the day of municipal elections: they numbered only about thirty, however, and were quickly dispersed. They remained quiescent on 5 November, but on 26 December erupted in the most violent of all the riots when a policeman was so severely cudgelled that four men were later charged with attempted murder.

The fact that three of the men ultimately served prison sentences was indicative of the success of Jacob's tough policy. Hitherto, the ringleaders of the Guys had been inviolate – in 1863 a reward of £500 had been offered for information leading to their arrest but no such information had ever been laid, despite the fact that their identities must have been known to hundreds of their fellow citizens to whom the reward represented a dazzling fortune. Intimidation had been commonplace: one local reporter claimed that his life had been threatened because he had written detailed reports of the riots. But with confidence restored in authority more witnesses came forward, and their identification of some of the ringleaders not only contributed to the collapse of the Guys, but also gives posterity a clue to the nature of the riots. After the danger had passed, a number of citizens, too, put their experiences on record – though none in so detailed a form as did Henry Peak – and the sum of the information points to the conclusion that a very large proportion of the actual instigators of the riots were drawn from the upper levels of the town's society. The riots were by no means confined to Guildford: a living citizen of the town remembers the Lewes Guy Fawkes Day riot of 1904 when a barrel of blazing tar was rolled down the High Street. But the presence of prosperous citizens of Guildford in the mob, disguised in the conveniently fantastic costume of the Guys, argues that the local discontent with the Reform Bill of 1832 was not fully spent until the late 1860s. By 1867 5 November was again a day of ordinary, if boisterous, celebration in the town, and a grateful citizenry presented a handsome gift of plate to Jacob in commemoration of a signal act of public service.

But though Guildford had lost the annual excitement of the Guys – and Mason, for one, regretted their passing – it possessed still the scarcely less tumultuous events of the municipal and parliamentary elections. The election of a Member was still a matter of immediate and personal civic pride, for the small town was itself a constituency in its own right until the Redistribution of Seats Act of 1885 merged it with the county. It was one of only thirty-eight boroughs, too, which possessed the right to return two Members until the Reform Act of 1867 put them into line with the majority of constituencies. An unusually marked degree of election fever was therefore concentrated in a town of some 8000 inhabitants, and before bribery was effectively eliminated an unusually large proportion of the community consequently regarded elections as a legitimate means of supplementing their scant luxuries. In 1841 the successful Liberal candidate, Mangles, issued a card to his supporters in which he 'respectfully requests those of his worthy friends who may be disposed to celebrate his return to Parliament by their own firesides, to send the enclosed dinner ticket to Mr —— who will in exchange for such ticket give the bearer therof an order for 12 lbs beef; 1 gallon of strong beer; 2 quartern loaves; 3½ lbs of flour; 2 lbs of suet; 2 lbs raisins; 1 lb of currants two bottles of wine (port or sherry)'.[9]

Before the passing of the Ballot Act of 1872, the practice of publishing the results of the poll ensured that parliamentary elections had a direct and sinister effect on the town. Everyone knew exactly who had voted for whom and Peak, a confirmed Liberal, noted that 'there were not lacking proofs that the same was used as a blacklist against tradesmen and others'.[10] He had personal experience of the result: he lost a handsome commission for restoring a church very largely because a leading church-warden was the defeated Tory candidate who now took the opportunity to exact vengeance on the supporter of his opponent.

The local Liberals had little difficulty in returning their candidate – usually one of the members of the Onslow family – even after the 1867 Act deprived the town of one Member. Their later troubles, indeed, were largely caused by the bizarre character of Guildford Onslow 'so named from his being born on the day that his father was returned for the Borough'.[11] Guildford was himself returned in 1858 and again in 1868 but rapidly thereafterwards became deeply involved in the unsavoury Tichborn case. He was a fanatical supporter of the claimant, the grotesque Arthur Orton, creating a breach with his family so that in 1874 the Onslows put forward his cousin, Denzil, as the Liberal candidate. The normal election fever in the town was heightened by 'a family conflict which was marked by extreme bitterness and even sank to the level of savage indecency'.[12] Denzil was returned, but was later dropped after the borough was merged with the county, and Peak was convinced that the decline in the Liberal fortunes began when Guildford Onslow was discarded.

Despite the fact that the town returned one, and sometimes two, Liberal Members, Peak discovered, 'I had only been a very short

time in the town when I learned that to be respectable or prosperous – to be *anything* at all, one must needs be Conservative
or Tory as then more popularly called and I soon discovered
that the ruling power of the town was almost entirely that way'.[13]
It is doubtless due to his jaundiced view as a Liberal that his diary
is freely spattered with dark hints regarding Tory machinations,
but a clear picture of the conduct of nineteenth-century municipal politics is provided by his account of how, during his period
as Borough Surveyor, his staff was regularly put under pressure
at election times in an attempt to discover charges against him.
In the last decades of the century, November again became a
period of civic upheaval, no less troublesome because it was due
to legal electioneering rather than illegal hooliganism. Peak, now
a senior member of the Council and an influential figure in the
town, was among those who preached the virtues of civilised
compromise – a dangerous trend, in the *Times*'s opinion. 'If local
self-government is to be a reality, what can be more absurd than
the notion that a dozen men should arrange or "compromise"
with a dozen other meeting in another chamber that the four
individuals they select shall rule the roost for a term of three
years. All this hole and corner business is as much out of date
as sedan chairs as a means of locomotion.'[14]

It was the concept of secret arrangements to which the *Times*
objected, not the attempt to end faction and its product, canvassing. In 1891 its columnist 'Brother John' lightheartedly regretted the passing of the old system with the creation of four
electoral wards in the town. 'How awfully dull the elections
would be – a kind of street fight instead of a good all-over-the-
town-fight that we have now.' More soberly, the leader on the
same day regretted that the ward system would stimulate the
existing trend towards personal canvassing and was convinced
that the end-product would be a sterile parochialism.[15] Nevertheless, the unprecedented expansion of the town's size at the turn
of the century, in particular that of 1904, ensured that a more
ordered electoral system would push out the tumultuous, vulnerable if essentially homogeneous system of the past.

The Guild Merchant, for all its varied and manifest defects,

had been the symbol of social and political unity: every master
in the town had been a craftsman; every craftsman could hope –
in theory at least – to become a master and so join the governing
body. With the disappearance of the guild system, employees and
employers embarked on separate courses, the first trade union
appearing in the town by 1842. The unions, in their turn, created
their own federated body, the Trades Council, the local Trades
Union Congress. The national pattern was faithfully reflected in
the town with a new radical party flourishing in the soil prepared
by the unions – a party which, again reflecting the national trend,
grew as the Liberal fortunes declined. Despite heavy and increasing political pressures in the town, genuine Independents were
still returned over a wide area, providing a natural representation
for the very large proportion of the electorate who had small
liking for either Liberal or Conservative but even less for an
untried Labour Party. It was therefore not until November 1929
that the first Labour councillor took his seat.

The Labour Party had arrived – but only just. In 1933 the
expansion of the town was so great that it precipitated a local
'general election'. For months beforehand there was widespread
apprehension that the new party would achieve not a majority,
perhaps, but certainly a commanding position. And what would
be the effect on the town? The Chelmsford Incident was brought
out as warning: there, it was reported, a Labour councillor had
declined to show a Council agenda to his party or to vote as
instructed and was consequently expelled. 'We wonder what
happens in Guildford? Are Labour members free to exercise
their own discretion, or do they receive instructions how to vote
from a political junto sitting in secret?'[16] The Town Association
came into being, allegedly a non-political body existing solely to
advise the electorate as to the best available candidate for each
ward. In one ward, however, only one name was given, followed
by the remark '(The remaining candidates in this ward are
Labour nominees)'.[17]

The fears were ill-founded for only three Labour councillors
were returned. In 1936 more alarm was created when the party
gained two more seats – one of them creating an historic prece-

dent, for the successful candidate was a woman and so became the first woman councillor the town had ever known. Despite, or perhaps because of, this, 'In some quarters there is an air of apprehension at the slow but steady growth of the Labour nucleus . . . people holding anti-Labour views are discussing the advisability of co-ordinating their efforts.'[18]

The tiny Labour group undoubtedly created an impact out of all proportion to its size. In 1931 the three newly elected Labour councillors entered the chamber without their robes, precipitating a debate based on the motion that the wearing of robes should be optional – trivial enough in its substance, alarming in its implications of change. Even the scarlet aldermanic robes had, in fact, been one of the sweeteners which James II had given the town when he took away its ancient charters and at the debate now a defender of the robes echoed something of the English hatred of uniforms, and their embarrassment when robed even in the interests of tradition. 'It might be that sometimes they had felt a little conscious when they had gone through the streets in these garments and had been alluded to by someone who had pointed a finger of scorn.'[19] Nevertheless, the overwhelming opinion of the Council was that the robes were not merely traditional but were democratically proper, all councillors being clothed alike. The incident ended happily. The Mayor gently remarked that three robes were awaiting the new councillors and invited them to don them: they withdrew and returned 'amid applause' wearing them. More fundamental was the motion that the same three councillors put, three years later, that 'in future no firm or limited liability company in which a member of the council is financially interested shall tender for materials or execute work of any description for the Corporation.'[20] They made it clear that they were implying neither general nor specific accusations, and the long and serious debate that followed was evidence that the Council welcomed the opportunity to establish a basic principle at the beginning of a period of considerable Council expenditure. The unanswerable objection was that, because the Council necessarily drew a large proportion of its members from the merchants of the town, such a measure would either place an unfair limitation on them or, more likely, would result in even greater difficulty in obtaining recruits to the ranks of the Council.

The new party had rapidly established itself as a positive force in the town, but its conciliar representation was rarely to rise above its modest initial strength of four or five members. Unlike its major opponent, it was directly affected by the fortunes of its national party, a fact clearly shown in the post-war years when its support rose and fell according to the popularity of the Labour governments. In 1969 the number of Labour councillors had again fallen to three, but there was no corresponding expression of triumph on the part of its opponents. The *Surrey Advertiser*, again accurately reflecting the opinion of the majority of its readers, deplored the declining strength of the party, both the newspaper and its Conservative correspondents emphasising the need of a healthy opposition. In the previous year the *Advertiser* had congratulated the town, not the Labour Party, on the return of the Labour leader after a close-run election. The generous gesture was due in part to the recognition of the qualities of an outstanding councillor but in part, too, to the knowledge that one-party government was as undesirable in civic as in parliamentary affairs. Liberal representation became increasingly sporadic, despite the existence of a vigorous Liberal Association in the town, and Independent councillors had dwindled from the twenty-seven returned in 1936 to three in 1968. Locally, as nationally, politics had polarised on Conservative or Labour principles. Their support in the town runs along clearly defined areas of property ownership. The main Labour strength is drawn from the large Council estates on the north and west while the southern section of the town is almost wholly Conservative in loyalty. Within this area, however, the old suburb of Charlotteville clearly illustrates the basis of affiliation. The suburb, composed mainly of rented houses, is a small Labour stronghold within the Conservative area: within that stronghold, however, are dotted groups of owner-occupied houses and these, in their turn, are almost wholly Conservative in loyalty.

*

On Tuesday 28 July 1931, Guildford Borough Council sat for the last time in the ancient Guildhall. There was no ceremony to mark the end of a centuries-long association: at the end of the meeting the councillors merely walked out and, in September, assembled in a larger, nondescript 'temporary' building bearing the non-committal title of 'Municipal Offices' a few hundred yards up the street.

The decision to expand into larger quarters had not been taken hastily. In 1913 a debate that had gone on for over a decade, regarding the urgent need for more room for the expanded Council, had ended with the acquisition of the Corn Exchange across the road. The councillors had been at some pains to let their electors know that, in moving into the Exchange, 'they are not contemplating [building] a municipal palace. Other towns have felt the need of municipal offices with some architectural pretensions but Guildford was more fortunately circumstanced.'[21] The Council was spending only £4000 to acquire the Tunsgate buildings which would be run in the cheapest possible manner.

It was the Council's servants who were affected by the councillors' thrift. The Corn Exchange, known popularly as Tunsgate from an inn that once stood near by, had been built for totally different purposes in another century. Even the acquisition of eight adjoining cottages and the sum of £300 spent on fittings had done little to make the complex an adequate centre whence to run the affairs of a rapidly expanding town. The Medical Officer complained that it was almost impossible for him to run his vital office, and his complaints were echoed by every other department forced to grapple with an increasing mass of paperwork in a cramped ill-lit warren.

The Council discussed the matter for another fifteen years when it was decided that temporary municipal buildings should be acquired until such time as Guildford, doubtless in the near future, would acquire a modern town hall. In 1928 an existing building on the Upper High Street was purchased and £34,000 spent on enlarging and modifying it. By the time the work was finished, the word 'temporary' had ironic overtones and when the building was formally opened in September 1931 the Deputy

Mayor pointed out that it contained '304,000 new bricks, 2161 panes of glass, which did not suggest a temporary building'. In any case temporary was only a relative term.[22]

Meanwhile, the buildings behind Tunsgate were razed to disclose an immense area whose size and potential seems to have taken everyone by surprise. The opportunity was too good for the Council's tormentor, Brierly, to miss and in April 1932 the *Outlook* carried a blistering summary of the events.

> The extent of the space provided by the clearance has amazed those inhabitants who were unable to visualise the picture which would present itself when the buildings on the site had been razed. The aspect renders more remarkable than ever the action of the Town Council in deciding to provide 'temporary' municipal offices before determining what should be done with the Tunsgate area. On its own land the Corporation could have erected a larger and better building for the municipal offices, and with it the town hall which Guildford so sorely needs. The £19,000 to £20,000 which was spent on acquiring the site occupied by the temporary offices could have been saved and that sum, with the £15,000 or £16,000 more which has been spent in adapting the old building could, with probably £20,000 added have been used for the erection of a creditable and commodious building.

The decision had been made by one vote – the casting vote of the Mayor – and the Council now had not the faintest idea what to do with the Tunsgate site. 'In its quandary it has decided that it shall be a car park, and a car park it will remain.'[23] Brierly liked juggling with public sums and his financial calculations regarding the cost of a 'creditable and commodious building' are not necessarily accurate. But he proved a good prophet regarding the fate of the site: thirty-seven years later it was still a car-park.

The new Council buildings acquired, attention was turned to the future of the ancient Guildhall and it was then that proposals to turn it into a museum were properly defeated. Throughout the debates on the subject the councillors were obviously moved by so genuine an affection for the ancient building, an affection amounting to veneration, that they could use for it the term 'sacred' which reads not as a rhetorical adjective but as precise description. Even today there is no town hall in Guildford, the Guildhall's young successor being described either as the Council Chambers or the Municipal Offices, depending upon the function envisaged, colourless titles which at once adequately sum up its role and the citizens' attitude towards the building still known as the Guildhall.

The ancient home of the Guild Merchant has become the ceremonial home of the modern town. The monthly meetings of the Council take place in the new building, but the annual ceremony of mayor-making is performed in the Guildhall. It remains a court and here, too, visiting dignitaries are entertained, creating considerable problems for the caterers. Until 1966 the results of the Borough elections were announced from the balcony, a ceremony which reinforced the town's strong sense of historical continuity. In the dusk of a May evening the accident of costume was obscured, and as each candidate was brought forward by his robed sponsor from out of the brightly lit Council Chamber to receive the cheers or jeers from the crowd in the street below a tableau of living history was unself-consciously re-created. Administrative convenience moved the ceremony to the new Civic Hall where it proved, if nothing else, that the builders of the Guildhall knew what they were about when they provided a balcony for civic occasions. The transferred ceremony has lost not only its dignity but its purpose for candidates, sponsors, and electors are all on the same physical level and only a handful in the front ranks of the milling crowd have the remotest idea of what is going on.

Throughout the Guildhall there is an air of homely grandeur, a sense of spaciousness and dignity out of all proportion to its actual size and substance, and yet at the same time a sense of being in a private rather than a public building. An ascent to the little turret creates an odd feeling of gaining great height and the open chamber at the top seems to be soaring above the town although, in fact, the tower of Holy Trinity and its neighbouring multi-storey car-park both overtop the Guildhall. On New Year's Eve the crowd naturally gravitates towards the building, and youths clamber up the friendly projections of the façade to gain the turret and ring the town bell. 'They are rougher now,' the custodian notes from the experience of a generation. 'Once they used to sing but now they are likely to do anything.' And he ensures that the trapdoor is closed.

Long wooden steps lead down from this trapdoor in the turret to the loft – and here nothing has changed for centuries. A piece of nineteenth-century angle-iron has, perhaps, been re-secured with a twentieth-century screw and worn-out timber replaced here and there, but the dimensions and form remain unchanged. It is a great waste of space, perhaps, but it is like the loft of any private house even down to the householder's odds and ends that may come in useful some day: leaning against a wall are the two huge discs used when the clock was gas-lit. Their proper place may be in the Museum but this is undoubtedly their natural home.

Dominating the loft is a rough wooden case that contains the machinery which drives the clock suspended over the street outside. It is remarkably simple, almost skeletal, in appearance, the motive power being provided by great weights that descend deep into the bowels of the building. Aylward – if he was the maker – did his work well, for the simple machinery keeps excellent time.

In 1935, however, the history of the clock came under official enquiry and some doubts were cast upon the traditional story of Aylward. The façade of the building had been renovated and the date '1561' placed upon the regilded clock-face. Who authorised the placing of such a date on a building known to have been erected in 1683, the Council demanded. In defending the decision, the chairman of the General Purposes Committee summed up the whole problem of dating a building which continuously renewed its parts over centuries. 'The date 1683 referred to the [clock] case and if they put the date on for the present case it would have to be 1935,' he explained. The clock machinery itself was the vital element, not the case. The Committee had therefore assumed that the date 1561, which, it was claimed appeared upon the machinery, could properly be said to include the clock face.

The Council debate initiated a newspaper correspondence which brought some odd facts to light. There stood in the

Museum a lantern-clock, known to have been made by Aylward and dated 'Guildford, 1695'. Britten's authoritative handbook *Old Clocks and their Makers* gave independent corroboration that a John Aylward was indeed making lantern-clocks in Guildford at that time, although it qualified the support with the information that a man of the same name was credited with a clock dated 'Braintford, 1710'. Were there then two Aylwards, or did the Guildford Aylward emigrate after gaining his expensive permission to work in the town? Even if he did make the face of the town clock in 1683, he could not possibly have made that piece of machinery allegedly dated 1561. An ingenious suggestion was put forward that he might have made use of a spare piece bearing that date, but the controversy as a whole[24] served only to deepen the mystery and a compromise was later made by placing 1683, the date on which the façade of the Guildhall was constructed, on the clock face itself.

The main hall of the building bears plain evidence of its original function: it is simply a large shed or barn, a Tudor structure that was itself the enlargement of a humbler market-building, and given the dignity of a few pieces of stained glass. The Council Chamber on the first floor at the front of the building is a product of the seventeenth-century reconstruction, a snug, handsome, panelled room as appropriate for a dinner-party as for a formal meeting. Here are the 'family portraits' – old John Russell, mayor and historian, painted by his son John, Royal Academician; 'Vice Admiral Sir Richard Onslow Receiving the Dutch Flag after the Victory, 1797' – also by the younger Russell; a stiff portrait of Speaker Onslow, whose virtues are recited in the church across the road; a sprinkling of monarchs, here and in the hall below – James II and Elizabeth II, William and Mary, Charles II. Set at an angle in the Council Chamber is a massive clunch fireplace which could be described either as booty or protected heritage for it comes from the vanished manor of Stoughton whose lands have long been absorbed into the town. It fits into its surroundings as though made for them, for its elaborate carvings of the Humours are in the same style of exuberant fancy as the building itself.

Physically out of harmony, yet in keeping with the spirit of casual accumulation, is a massive, old-fashioned safe in which the town's plate is housed. In the mass, the plate has the curiously tawdry, theatrical appearance of most ceremonial regalia; but in their intimate setting the items have the attraction of family possessions: Williamson's Remembrancer medallion, a mayor's staff, gift of the first Elizabeth: a basin and ewer, bequeathed by John Parkhurst, who also gave the town its first library although that was less valued than these: Mayor's and Mayoress's chains of office, the gifts of the town's friends, the Onslows of Clandon – tankards, a rose-bowl, maces, miscellaneous objects of widely varying value collected on various occasions over five centuries and now, by the force of piety, granted unity.

The rapid increase in the town's size had forced the Council to abandon its traditional home, for not only had the administrative problems expanded but there had, too, been a substantial increase in the number of councillors and aldermen. Nevertheless, the town's millennium-old status as a borough remained unchanged. It had been confidently expected that the establishment of a cathedral would automatically grant city status and the irrepressible Brierly promptly christened his journal *Guildford City Outlook*, a name it retained until his more cautious successor removed it. In 1933 George Williamson, performing one of his first duties as Remembrancer, formally approached Lord Onslow, the Lord High Steward and as such the traditional protector of the town, asking what steps were necessary to achieve the formality of a city status.

Onslow was in an ideal position to give a full and sympathetic answer for he had been chairman of the recent Royal Commission on Local Government and this precise question had been raised. The answer he gave was dampening: certain communities, some even smaller than Guildford, had held the title of 'city' from time immemorial and would therefore always hold that title. Others, grown immense during the nineteenth century, had successfully petitioned the Crown for the grant of the title: one of the most recent had been Portsmouth. But as more and more towns expanded in population and grew in wealth and the competition to acquire city status had consequently increased, the Crown had grown ever more reluctant to grant the requests. There were no clear-cut rules as guidance to the presenting of a successful petition: imponderable factors of culture, antiquity and local importance as well as the measurable conditions of size and wealth were taken into account. Onslow thought that Guildford had no real hope, but he would do what he could to help if a petition were presented. The matter was raised occasionally over the next few years but nothing concrete came of the tentative overtures.

Guildford did indeed seem to possess all the marks of a city. Traditionally, it was the county town in which the Assizes had been held for over 700 years: its antiquity and present prosperity were alike indisputable; it possessed an intangible but real urban self-consciousness and it formed the natural social centre for a wide surrounding area of country. Nevertheless, it had steadily lost ground to the northern communities of the county – in particular to Kingston-upon-Thames, a subordination which was accelerated when, in rapid succession, Kingston became the seat of the County Council and of the Assizes.

The loss of these courts was the biggest single blow to Guildford's prestige but the town had only itself to blame when, after nearly a century of endless complaints from the judges, the Assizes were transferred in 1930.

In 1818 the citizens had confidently assumed that their handsome new Corn Exhange could adequately perform the double function of a market-place and a court. They were very rapidly disabused: regularly the judges complained, both formally and informally, that it was at times impossible to hear evidence because of the continual noise emanating within and without the building. The complaints came to a head in 1860, sparking off an explosion that echoed in the House of Commons and brought into question the constitutional power of a judge to exclude the public indefinitely from a court, and the corresponding power of the county Sheriff.

It began trivially enough on 2 August, and was probably precipitated by an elderly judge's simple bad temper on a hot day. The Sheriff, William Evelyn, had already aroused the judge's anger on a question of court etiquette and he became increasingly irritable, complaining of the noise. 'This is a barn. It's a disgrace to the county. I must clear the court if the noise continues.' Later, according to Evelyn's account,[25] the judge abruptly ordered the court to be cleared. 'For the first time in the history of an English court of Justice, the entire part appropriate to the public was forcibly cleared of the public . . . I had the mortification of seeing the people of Surrey, during the trial of a prisoner, thrust out at the point of the javelin by the Sheriff's officers, reluctantly obeying the orders of a judge who thus put an affront both on the County and on the Sheriff.' At the end of the session Evelyn again came into conflict with the judge and was summarily fined the very large sum of £500.

The public continued to be excluded from the court for over a week and at the end of that period Evelyn, after legal advice, took a determined and courageous action. He issued a proclamation stating 'As your Sheriff it is my duty to record my protest against the unlawful proceedings. All persons, so long as they conduct themselves with decorum, have a lawful right to be present in court and I hereby prohibit my officers from aiding and abetting any attempt to bar out the public from access to the court.'

During the next trial, the public asserted its right without opposition. But at eleven o'clock on that same night a messenger arived at Evelyn's home at Wooton some nine miles from Guildford, summoning him to court to answer a charge of contempt. In Guildford the following day, arraigned before the Lord Chief Justice and his brother judges, Evelyn defended himself with ability and dignity. 'My object was to assert the principle that no judge of this land has a right to clear an audience from any court of justice and that if any judge commands a sheriff or his officers to do so, those officers and that sheriff are bound to disobey the unlawful mandate.'

'In a very solemn tone and amidst the deepest silence', the Lord Chief Justice challenged Evelyn's basic contention. '[The judge's] primary purpose is the efficient administration of justice and so far as the exclusion of persons from any part is necessary to that object, the public must submit for the sake of the greater good.' He then turned to the particular aspect, the inadequacy of Guildford's Assize court: 'In this inconvenient court the noise from the street was found by my learned brother to be very much aggravated by that which proceeded from the lower part of the court. It did not rise from the disorderly conduct of the people assembled there, but as no seats were provided for them much movement naturally ensued and a stone floor added to the disturbance.' He acknowledged the altruism of Evelyn's protest, but nevertheless confirmed the summary fine of £500.

Evelyn appealed both against the fine and the concept that 'a sheriff is the minister and officer of the Judge. I deny the propriety of that description of the office. Both Judge and Sheriff are servants of the Crown. Judges are not viceroys.' But he received little backing in Parliament. The delicate affair was discreetly discussed in Committee, and a legitimate if convenient way out was discovered: the Guildford Assize courts were found to be grossly inadequate and the judge was therefore acting perfectly properly under the circumstances. A strong recommendation was made that the courts should be brought up to standard — but no indication was given as to who should pay for the improvement. *Punch* had the last word — a remarkably cruel one, considering its radical sympathies:

> In the Commons Mr Cochrane wished to know if Mr Evelyn, the 'Fined Old English Gentleman' would on account of his high character be let off paying the £500 imposed for his late lark at Guildford. He should petition the Home Secretary and not bother the House, but his better plan would be to make two notes in Evelyn's Diary. *Mem:* to fork out the £500 and *Mem.* Don't insult a judge again.'[26]

The ripples of a constitutional issue had subsided again, but it still left unresolved the question of the Assize accommodation in the town itself. The affair had been discussed widely in the national press, and on 22 August *The Times* carried a long letter from the Deputy Clerk of the Assizes, describing the remarkable conditions in Guildford which had brought about the controversy.

> During many Assizes . . . I have on no one occasion been there without hearing most grievous and oft-repeated complaints of conducting the Public business, owing to the disgraceful state of the 'Barn' provided as a court for the administration of justice. Without a plan it is very difficult to convey a notion of this 'Barn' which, at one end – consisting of two arches – is open to and actually adjoins the Public paved road. . . . About one third of the whole area of the Barn is separated from the rest by a wooden barrier, and is appropriated as a standing room, there not being a single seat in it for a continually changing and noisy crowd finding ingress and egress through the open end of the Barn.[27]

The reiteration of that word 'barn' stung local pride and the following day 'An Inhabitant of Guildford' protested against the slur.

> The building thus designated was erected in 1818 at a cost but a trifle less than £5000 – a tolerable substantial proof that it must be something more than a barn. That portion of it which is specially appropriated as the Crown court of the Assizes is also usually used as a storage for unsold grain, but when used as a court of justice everything is cleared away.[28]

In the defence which he published later, Evelyn, too, attempted to justify the Corn Exchange as an Assize court, using a curious mixture of sarcasm, scholarly allusion and local patriotism. 'The Crown Court, a temple sacred to Ceres and Themis, though its proportions might not satisfy a Vitruvius or a Ruskin, is yet a substantial and confessedly airy building and the Lord Chief Justice himself might have discerned some merit in the four stately columns of its portico. As to the Nisi Prius Court, even Surrey's Sheriff must admit that the Town Hall of Guildford is not quite so grand as the Town Hall of Carthage, and certainly the wars of Troy are not pictured on its walls: instead, there may be seen the portraits of three Stuart kings, of William and Mary and of two eminent members of the Onslow family . . .', so the defence died away rather weakly.[29]

It is not wholly clear why the description of Guildford's portrait gallery should buttress its claim of providing adequate Assize courts: certainly the judges remained unimpressed. The complaints continued regularly, even after the Crown Court had transferred itself from the Exchange to a hall in North Street. In 1914 Mr Justice Darling gave unequivocal warning of the likely result of official indifference. He had been obliged to call three times for silence and at length burst out, 'This is the worst court of justice I know. It is not a court of justice at all – it is a ball room. Every footfall is heard: there is not even a piece of carpet.' If Guildford could not bother to provide decent accommodation it deserved to lose the Assize.[30]

The only truly remarkable aspect of the ultimate loss of the Assize was the long patience of the judges that preceded it. Presented with what was virtually an ultimatum, the Borough Council began to consider the possibility of building a public hall. Nothing came of it – nothing, in fact, was to come of it for nearly forty years. Inevitably the first suggestion was made that the Assize should migrate permanently to Kingston, whose Council was eager to provide suitable accommodation. But even then the judges favoured Guildford, one of them making the point that if the Assize removed to Kingston it might just as well go on to London. It was then discovered, somewhat tardily, that the Local Government Act of 1888 placed the responsibility for Assize accommodation in the hands of the County Council – and the County Council was already established in Kingston. The rest was a foregone conclusion, only nine councillors voting for its retention in Guildford.

It did not need Brierly's outburst to tell Guildford that the town 'through its Town Council, has only itself to thank for the position. It is another case of "Dilly" and "Dally". The Council realised what was needed when Kingston, instead of Guildford, was chosen as the seat of the County Council and yet it did not exert any effort to satisfy the need for a hall for utilisation as an Assize court until ... their lordships' patience had been exhausted.'[31] In 1936 the Lord Chancellor reviewed the Assize circuits and there was a determined local attempt to regain the privilege. Substantial citizens offered interest-free loans towards the building of a hall, the Council discussed and accepted the possibility that the Assizes, far from contributing financially, might cost the community some £20,000 a year. But the Chancellor decided against a change. Kingston had been put to considerable expense: it was convenient to the bulk of the population. 'If a satisfactory court is built at Guildford and suitable judges' lodgings provided, this is a matter which some years hence might possibly be favourably re-considered.'[32]

From year to year, the role of the Mayor of Guildford is, as in all English towns, purely ceremonial in nature outside the Council chambers. The opening or closing of this or that function, the eating of innumerable public meals, the receiving or the addressing of innumerable and lengthy speeches – this appear to be the sum of the mayoral activities for which his fellow citizens are currently prepared to pay some £600 per annum in expenses. But occasionally, when a civic crisis coincides with the presence of a powerful personality on the mayoral bench, it becomes briefly but clearly apparent why a modern community needs what is, in effect, a tribal leader – a patriarch. Under the stress, office and community synthesise so that the holder of the office is neither mouthpiece nor representative but is the community itself speaking and acting as an entity. It had happened during the Guy Riots when the outsider Jacob correctly interpreted the will of the community and brought the disturbances to an end. It happened again when Leslie Codd, himself personally indifferent to the religious overtones, became the instrument that initiated the last phase of the building of the Cathedral. And it achieved its most remarkable local manifestation during the Depression of the thirties when William Harvey initiated an experiment in social co-operation which, incidentally, provided more effective advertisement for the town than any quantity of professional propaganda. By the time it had finished, communities not only in the rest of Britain but in Europe, North America and the Far East had heard of the means whereby a small Surrey township had coped with the twentieth-century hydra.

At the beginning of the unemployment crisis, local opinion was sympathetic but detached. In commenting upon the trend to-wards the organisation of protest by the unemployed the *Surrey Advertiser* remarked, 'We do not say a word against the unem-ployed themselves. They have our deepest sympathy in the posi-tion in which they find themselves. We believe nine out of ten would far rather be at work than drawing unemployment bene-fit.'[33] The remark, which reads as though it were referring to a worthy but essentially alien race of people, was an accurate ex-pression of local opinion in the early autumn of 1931.

The crisis in the town was to be brief but acute, achieving its peak a year later. By then, opinion had changed radically as the mounting total of unemployed, like the mounting death-roll of some medieval plague, warned the community that few were exempt from contagion. In November 1932 a correspondent in the *Advertiser* pointed out the double significance in urging that something should be done immediately for the unemployed. 'No decent person can sit down to his Christmas dinner knowing that good workers are deteriorating body and soul for want of work and, secondly, it is better for us to grapple with unemployment than for it to grapple with us.'

In that same month, Mayor William Harvey launched an appeal in a personal letter distributed to most households in the Borough. It was a simple, practical presentation of the problem and a means of local solution. There were about 700 men unem-ployed in the town. The Council had already given to the appeal fund a block grant of £3000 'taken from projects which are of less immediate urgency. This is a generous lead and they cannot do more without increasing our rates which would press hardly on many who are very near the poverty line.' The essence of the scheme was the disbursal of money in wages, not in charity doles. All work would be passed by the Town Council as 'necessary im-provements' to the town and the men engaged on such work would be paid thirty-five shillings a week. All money contributed would be used solely for wages – 'Every shilling provides an hour's work – or, as the *Outlook* put it succinctly, 'A bob for a job'.

Launching an appeal is a relatively simple business: a letter to the Press and the distribution of leaflets will attract the attention of the minority who contribute to charity as a matter of course. Making an appeal work by stimulating the charity of the passive majority, and coping with the complex administrative problems that follow success, is another matter. Harvey's appeal was successful because, long before he took it to the public, he had worked out every detail and once it was launched he devoted the greater part of his waking hours both to its encouragement and its administration. The target figure was immense in the context of a small town, approximately £1000 per week for the seventeen weeks from the date that the appeal was launched until 31 March – the minimum sum needed to keep 600 men in regular employment over that period. The citizens of the town were asked to assess themselves at one per cent of monthly income, or twopence in the pound weekly. The town was divided into districts, each with its collectors, and each householder was supplied with a 'promise' form on which he stated the amount he could regularly contribute. If a household just could not contribute anything, then the head of the house was asked to state this on the form and he was thereafter not troubled by the district collector. Statistics were compiled and published weekly showing how much had been collected, how many had contributed, how many 'responses' had been received – and the proportion of people capable of contributing who had not yet come forward. The statistics incidentally provided an interesting measurement of the charitable impulse: by the time the experiment had ended, one-third of those capable of contributing had done so, approximately one person in three believing himself to be his brother's keeper.

Three weeks after the appeal was launched £1700 had been collected. By 3 December the fund had increased to £2736 – 2070 people out of 21,000 possible had subscribed. The total increased steadily by something over £600 per week, receiving an expected acceleration over the Christmas period when a variety of suggestions were put forward to boost the fund. One proposal was that each family should raise a collection among themselves at the Christmas dinner, another was that each bridge four should contribute threepence per rubber.

But though the total of the fund and the consequent numbers of men at work increased encouragingly it was apparent that it would fall short of the gross sum required. Then help came from an unexpected source. The traditionally stony-hearted Treasury, moved by the strong social current, looked a little more closely at its ledgers and discovered a nest-egg of £8000 'rebate on tax'. It was added to the fund – but for a specific purpose.

In fulfilment of the promise that contributions would be used only to provide wages, work at the beginning of the scheme was of an unskilled nature, for skilled labour would have required outlay in materials. The men therefore had been employed largely in tidying the town's open spaces – long-neglected tasks and worthy, but contributing little of a permanent value. The massive infusion of the Treasury grant, however, enabled the town to acquire a long-desired amenity – an open-air swimming-pool. The project had been discussed at various times for many years, and a detailed plan had long since been in existence. It was now taken out of its pigeon-hole and the Council, moving with the municipal equivalent of the speed of light, put it into operation. On 29 November the Borough Surveyor received instructions to submit his report. By 10 December the report was ready for the Water Committee, on the fifteenth it was passed by the Finance Committee, on the twentieth ratified by the Council and on the following day, Wednesday 21 December, the first twenty men were working on the site in Stoke Park. Guildford, which habitually took decades rather than years to contemplate spending any sum that passed the hundreds, had taken just twenty-two days to put into operation a plan which ultimately cost £15,000, a record which is perhaps Mayor William Harvey's most impressive memorial.

The Mayor's Fund did not lack critics from either extreme, both from those who felt that the entire operation should have been rate-supported and those who were convinced that loafers were being kept by charity. In a series of vigorous public speeches Harvey refuted both points. An increase of rates would not only penalise those only slightly better off than the unemployed, but it would require full Council agreement – a tardy and cumbersome operation contrasting with the speed of an appeal which needed no other authority than the parable of the Samaritan. Regarding the opposite objection, forcefully the Mayor pointed out that he had direct experience of individual cases where a man was told that he would actually get less on the Fund than on unemployment relief but had replied, 'Never mind about that. Give us a job.' The best proof of the scheme's efficiency, perhaps, was the flood of enquiries that came from other stricken communities – particularly in the North – regarding the operation of the Fund. Ultimately, William Harvey received an O.B.E.: his fellow citizens, assessing his civic contribution at a rather higher rate, gave him the highest honour that lay in their collective power, making him an honorary Freeman of the town.

CHAPTER SIX

In Search of a Centre

In February 1961 the President of the West Surrey Association
of Building Trades Employers gave fair warning to the citizens
of Guildford of what was immediately in store for their town.
'Guildford . . . must be regarded as a building site in the process
of being "redeveloped",' he told a meeting of the Association.[1]
The immediate context of his remark related to the much overdue
rationalisation of the dilapidated station-approaches, but its
substance applied only too clearly to the town as a whole – particularly as viewed by the immensely powerful national organisations who saw in that site an opportunity of considerable profit.
Five years earlier the ancient Lion Inn had disappeared in a
cloud of dust and controversy: over the next four months planning applications were approved for the construction of an
immense car-park next to Holy Trinity Church, a massive new
road that would divorce the town from the river at Millmead, a
new theatre, a large departmental store on the river bank. By
1967 the supermarkets had established themselves on the High
Street, some as metamorphoses of earlier, more discreet forms,
others as new arrivals; the entire area around the ancient lane
known as Friary Street was scheduled for demolition; much of
the old extra-urban Bury Fields lay under an office block; tower
blocks of flats had arisen on the steep and conspicuous Mount.
Almost every one of the projects affected a greater area than any
single project had ever affected in the past, the Cathedral alone
excluded. The tempo continued so that by 1969 an area equal
in size to that of the old town-centre had been cleared down to
the primeval chalk, wiping out the traces of sometimes centuries-

long human occupation as though it had never been and sealing the amnesia under immense new structures. The town could have been taken as text-book illustration to the ministerial warning 'At the present rate we could rebuild every town in the country over again in 50 years – and the rate is still increasing. Large areas are taken for redevelopment, and a single new building may replace half-a-dozen new ones.'[2]

Again, it is probable that the lateness of the town's development saved its identity, for by the time the full onslaught of large-scale commercial 'development' had struck it there existed equally powerful parliamentary protection. Before that, the nature of the town's staple trade was itself an architectural protection. The nineteenth- and early twentieth-century shop-owners on the High Street were prosperous enough to maintain their ancient premises in good order, but there were no prospects of vast fortunes to tempt them to wholesale demolition and re-construction. The smallness and compactness of the town, too, early engendered in its citizens a lively awareness not only of its physical beauty but of their corporate responsibility. The awareness found specific expression in the foundation of the Old Guildford Society as early as 1896 and in that of its successor, the present Guildford Society, in 1936. Both societies achieved some positive results, but their greater value probably lay in their role of sounding-board. Official planning-approval is not necessarily synonymous with public approval, but by the time an unpopular major project has attracted general public attention it has usually reached such an advanced planning-stage that a massive co-ordinated reaction is needed to counteract its impetus. The existence of an amenity society both allows a potential developer to gain an unofficial but authoritative assessment of public opinion, and allows the public to gain an early indication of the projected development and, if necessary, take action in time. In Guildford, too, the presence of a genuine local newspaper extends public knowledge of impending changes both in breadth and depth, for the *Surrey Advertiser* usually gives the fullest coverage even to comparatively minor projects.

The preservation impulse continued strongly if sporadically

through the twenties and thirties. Brierly hammered away regularly at the need for a High Street Preservation Society and the Council did at length take powers to prevent some of the more drastic alterations, but by that time the greater part of the lower southern half of the Street had vanished to reappear clad in the anonymity of neo-Georgian. The eccentric 'Ferguson's Gang' briefly appeared to add a touch of colour to the cause of preservation, the members working under assumed names – Erb the Smasher, The Bloody Bishop, Red Biddy – to raise money in order to protect threatened historical buildings. Some buildings disappeared casually almost overnight – the Tudor lodge of the Royal Park was one such victim – others survived equally accidentally. In 1935 the great Corn Exchange was actually ordered to be demolished in order to improve the traffic flow but was reprieved at the last moment, an architect taking advantage of the fact that no plans for the development of the site had yet been prepared and so was able to make a plea for preservation in an altered form.

In the post-war years the sporadic campaigns were coordinated and strengthened by the national planning Acts of which the Civic Amenities Act of 1967 will probably have the greatest single effect. Hitherto, preservation orders had only too often resulted in the isolation of a favoured 'historic' building so that it survived uneasily in alien surroundings. Guildford, in particular, benefited from the new Act, for its major monument was the chance collection of buildings that formed the High Street, and the whole street could now be designated as a protected area forming an entity. The controls in general exerted a brake on a process that would otherwise have resulted infallibly in the destruction of the old town, but official attempts at preservation could have some odd results. It was insisted that the façade of the new Marks & Spencer's store should retain the characteristics of the building it replaced, even though that building had been erected only in 1904, and had been substantially altered in 1954, only eight years earlier. A few months later it was announced that Sainsburys' old store was to disappear entirely to allow the erection of a new structure. 'The present frontage is not, in fact, very old, for it was put up in 1904.'[3] There seemed to be no logical reason why the façade of one building should be laboriously re-created while that of another, erected at the same period and generally considered to be superior, should vanish completely. Even odder was the mummified fate of the ancient Bear Inn. Friary Street, in which it stood, was to be wholly demolished and a massive complex erected along its length. The Royal Commission on Historical Monuments and the Surrey Archaeological Society together pointed out that the interior of the Bear was a genuine early sixteenth-century building of considerable interest but that the façade was of recent date and of little importance. The whole should be preserved, or none at all. 'We see little value in retaining the façade only.'[4] The building was demolished and part of the façade painstakingly incorporated into the new complex.

The planning-powers invested in a distant Ministry could prove a two-edged weapon, as likely to be used against the community as in its favour. In 1955 the citizens of the town, their Council and the Council of the county itself were unanimously opposed to the destruction of the White Lion Inn to allow the erection of a new department store for Woolworths'. 'The Lion was one of the only two survivors of the famous series of Guildford inns and posthouses,' the Borough Council declared. Not only did it discharge a social as well as historical function, but the erection of yet another major store in its place would add to the already serious congestion in the vicinity. 'A better place for such a store would be in North Street, where the amenity and traffic difficulties of the High Street did not apply.'[5] Despite the immense popular feeling which backed the official opposition of the councils, the Minister overrode the county prohibition and another ancient building vanished into history, largely because it did not possess obvious external marks of antiquity. A concession was made to public opinion by preserving the figure of the White Lion that once stood high on the Inn, and it crouches now un-happily over the swinging doors, suffering a more humiliating fate than that of its ancient competitor, the White Hart, logically at rest in the Museum. Sainsburys', which stands upon the site of the Hart, records the association with a twentieth-century engraving of a hart, a gesture in harmony with a façade that is as original as that of the Guildhall which faces it.

In 1930 the shock of the loss of the Assizes brought home sharply to both citizens and Council the fact that they were trying to run the affairs of an ever growing urban community with facilities designed for a small market-town. The shock acted as a stimulus, evidenced by the private offers of substantial loans to build an adequate hall if the Assizes could thereby be brought back. The problem could be simply stated: the town needed a complete new civic centre or, at the very least, a substantial hall.

Tunsgate seemed the obvious first choice. The Exchange was in the very heart of the town, it possessed historical continuity, was of large size and of imposing – indeed, almost overwhelming – dignity and behind it was a considerable area of vacant land that seemed predestined for a civic complex. The Exchange itself had survived almost miraculously after it had ceased to be a market and had demonstrated so strikingly its inability to be a court. Its existence was threatened when the development of the southern regions of the town created the demand for an access road to the High Street. In 1901 the Old Guildford Society declared that it was better to demolish the Exchange than its neighbouring houses. 'The Exchange was built in the time of the worst taste in English architecture in the days of the Regency.'[6] Taste in architectural fashions changed, but Tunsgate still lay under threat, intensified when the Council abandoned it as a municipal office and was constantly reproached for its lack of decision regarding the future of the site behind it. The fact that its use as a car-park was contributing substantially to public funds increased the Council's reluctance to do anything about it. 'Properly laid out there was no reason why the parking place should not be a thing of beauty,' the Planning Committee claimed. Preparing plans for Tunsgate became a popular diversion, the local journals publishing a variety of suggestions from architects and laymen alike. In 1933 the incoming mayor produced an elaborate scheme to create a new entity with an ancient name, Castle Square: it would require the demolition of the Exchange but this could be used as a ceremonial entrance to the Castle grounds. In 1935 the Council's patience exploded and it decided, almost without dissent, to demolish the building in order to create the desired access-road. 'Year after year they had listened to the same story. They were living in days of rush and bustle and practical business. "We want to get into Tunsgate car-park and the quicker the better." '[7] But the traditional procrastination now worked in the building's favour and a timely plan to create an access road to both the car-park and the southern suburbs by turning the Exchange into an arch, enabled the building to survive with its proportions relatively undamaged though finally eliminating its potential as a hall. On 29 November 1968 – thirty-eight years after the site first became available – planning permission was granted for a major development which curiously echoed the 1933 proposals to create a central square.

On 23 February 1935, the *Surrey Advertiser* brought to the attention of its readers 'a vision of a noble civic centre for the borough' prepared by three young architects of the town and backed by the approval of the now legendary Sir Edwin Lutyens.

The plan differed radically from all the other enthusiastic schemes dreamt up by both professionals and amateurs for it recognised the immediate, practical need for a major meeting hall while yet allowing for a flexible, long-term development of a major project that could proceed as money became available. The site chosen was the house and grounds of a large seventeenth-century building called Allen House, which stood opposite the Grammar School, and which was at the time being used by the School as an annexe and as playing-fields. The plan envisaged a series of buildings on the grounds with the handsome house preserved as a nucleus. 'The advantages of grouping public buildings are so well recognised that it would be redundant of me to enumerate the obvious merits,' Lutyens wrote. 'In my considered opinion, Allen House is ideally suited for a group of civic buildings and Allen House would become the natural hub of the city.' Turning to the fact that the site belonged to the School, Lutyens went on, 'I suggest that the Royal Grammar School should seize its opportunity of securing playing fields in close proximity to the town so that the transfer of the School itself could be carried out at some future date. There are not many public schools adjacent to their playing fields.'[8]

The authors of the scheme ably defended themselves against the critics who claimed that, aesthetically, it was better to distribute important public buildings around the town rather than to mass them.

> To erect public buildings in various parts of the town may be the line of least resistance, but it is uneconomical, inconvenient and aesthetically undesirable. It is uneconomical because it means the duplication of services . . . it is equally uneconomical, in the present stage of the development of the town, to purchase separate sites for each building as the need arises, particularly as this would almost certainly involve the acquisition of land already occupied and built upon. It is inconvenient because it forces the inhabitants to cover unnecessary distances in order to reach the various centres. And it is aesthetically undesirable because only a range of buildings will give the fullest architectural value in return for capital invested.'[9]

Their plan did not require heavy initial expenditure beyond that needed for the acquisition of a site that would allow a steady and rational development until the town at last possessed those administrative and cultural centres for which it had so long awaited. They followed up the defence with a courteous but barbed reference to the Council's ostrich-like habits.

> We are sure that the Council will not continue a policy of procrastination and temporary expediency, so that in 20 or 30 years time we shall find ourselves devoid of permanent buildings and in precisely the same situation as we are today. Do the Council believe that they would be discharging their responsibilities by merely meeting immediate needs, with a gross disregard for the future?[10]

Onslow of Clandon lent his considerable weight to the project. 'The Allen House site is an ideal one, and if it can be acquired without detriment to the school do not let us allow this chance to slip. We may be sorry for it later.'[11] In its own files, too, the

Council possessed a six-year-old report, from a major firm of London architects commissioned to assess possible localities for a municipal centre, which strongly recommended this site.

> The Allen house site has the openness of Stoke Park, it is almost as close to the centre of the town as Tunsgate. . . . Although [our] scheme necessitates the removal of a certain number of buildings for the new loop road the site for the proposed Municipal Buildings is an open one, and presents no difficulties of level. It has the further advantage of being considered in the future as part of the development with the proposed public garden in Foxenden Quarry.[12]

That report had gathered dust, along with so many others, but the new Allen House plan so gripped the public imagination that, in response to steady pressure, the Council compromised, inviting Professor Patrick Abercrombie to inspect again all the sites that had been canvassed and to give his own opinion as to the ideal site for a public hall. Abercrombie did so, and his report of March 1936 was a brief but vivid sketch, from the hand of a widely acknowledged expert in town-planning, of Guildford at a crucial stage of its development.[13]

He dismissed outright the possibility of developing the Tunsgate area as a public hall. It was too near the High Street, for he estimated that fifteen per cent of all audiences in such a building would possess private cars: it was not capable of being expanded in the future, and the intrusion of buildings of different scale and character would adversely affect their surrounds – a consideration which did not deter the siting of the giant car-park in the same area a generation later.

> The question as to where the exact centre of gravity of a town like Guildford is, is a difficult one to answer. It [is] not necessarily the same as the geometrical centre of the municipal area. I feel strongly that in whatever direction the outskirts of Guildford might develop, the High Street will remain the real centre of life.

It was for this reason that unreservedly he too recommended the Allen House grounds as a potential site not merely for a hall but for a complete centre. 'The northern boundary of the site beyond the greens is the real surprise of the site to a stranger: Foxenden Quarry! This is indeed a marvellous place that recalls the famous Buttes Chaumonts at Paris. Not enough has been made of it perhaps. A faint idea of the possibilities of a terrace overlooking this abyss is gained from the archway into the wall: here is a background to a group comparable to the quarry foreground of Liverpool Cathedral.' Time has given a touch of irony to more than one aspect of Abercrombie's report: a generation later the abyss served to house a permanent car-park.

Abercrombie's more detailed proposals for the site envisaged a cloistral development, an enclosed but accessible complex. He therefore saw no need for any additional roads – in particular the expensive and destructive eastward continuation of North Street that was being canvassed. There was no need, either, to demolish the 'temporary' municipal buildings 'which had on two sides a very adequate façade and whose rear could be made presentable'. Allen House itself, together with the municipal buildings, would be part of a group of separate buildings, each to be erected as opportunity presented. On the delicate question of the Grammar School's future he, too, felt that a removal would be in its interest. The sale of the site could contribute towards a new building and the ancient school building itself 'could become one of Guildford's show places', possibly in the role of museum.

Initially, the School's reaction was an indignant rejection of the whole idea. It had displayed to the full the Guildford talent for surviving under the most adverse conditions, declining almost to vanishing-point in the nineteenth century but emerging, strengthened, to assume its place as the major academic institution not only of the town but of a wide surrounding area. Local patriotism, however, combined with the knowledge that it had long outgrown its sixteenth-century buildings, brought its governors at length to a qualified assent. They had plans to construct a new junior school on the Allen House grounds but were prepared to sell the entire site for a civic centre. The Borough Council quaked: it planned to buy only a part of the site, just large enough to erect a hall. As for the rest – time would tell. The School governors replied firmly that they were selling all or

nothing. 'The whole school must remain a physical and educational unit: from this it follows that unless it is possible for the
new junior school to be built in close proximity to the old school,
the whole school must be moved to a new site.'[14] Stoke Park had
been chosen as a possible new home and the governors were perfectly prepared to move the School there and pass the old buildings over to the town, provided it was made financially possible for
them to do so. The Borough Council enquired about costs.
Approximately £60,000, it was told, of which half would be
provided by the county and the other half by the town. The
Borough Council remained silent.

Six months afterwards, Guildford learned that it had at last
acquired a new hall – but it was neither Allen House, nor Tunsgate
nor any of the various sites and buildings that had been canvassed
over the past forty years. The building was a large mansion,
known as The Firs, placed at the extreme end of the Upper
High Street. 'The Firs was sprung very much, if not entirely, in
the nature of a surprise . . . at least two thirds of the Council were
utterly unaware of this site entering the scheme of things at all
until it was presented as a piece of practical politics.'[15] There
were dark hints as to back-stage negotiations resulting in
dubiously legal profits, hints which at length required public
denial. There were bitter protests at the waste of public money
in paying Professor Abercrombie 200 guineas and then ignor-
ing his advice. A group on the Council initiated an action that
was only marginally constitutional, attempting to execute their
own referendum in order to overthrow the Council decision. Protests, referendum and hints were alike unavailing and irrelevant.
Finance had dictated the Council's decision, for the new house
and grounds had been acquired outright for £12,265 after the
owners' valuation had been reduced from £23,000 by arbitra-
tion. Patrick Abercrombie, hastily consulted, replied that if The
Firs had been within his terms of reference he would have had
no hesitation in recommending it. In 1937, ambitious plans were
drawn up to create for the site a complex similar to that which
had been envisaged for the Allen House grounds. Nothing came
of the plans. Nothing, indeed, was to become of the limited plans

for a public hall until the building-surge of the post-war years brought it into existence. It stands today surrounded by the inevitable car-park that was to have been the site for a twentieth-century heart for the medieval town.

In March 1969 the Town Clerk of Guildford, looking back over his years of office, came to the conclusion that 'the worst thing to happen during his twenty-one years as Town Clerk was the rebuilding of the Royal Grammar School on the High Street site. It should have been moved to a site where it could expand.'[16] Whatever the effect upon the School, the long-term effect upon the town is incalculable, for the loss of the Allen House site was also the loss of Guildford's last chance to establish its ancient centre as the natural heart of the modern town. Abercrombie's opinion that the High Street would remain the centre of gravity has been substantially modified by unpredictable factors. The County Development plan for the town envisages the establishment of a civic centre on the old Friary lands when the gasworks and the immense brewery have been demolished. Work has already commenced there on the construction of part of an ambitious sports-centre, and proposed additions include law courts, Crown offices and a police station. Commercial and social buildings of considerable distinction will take the place of the squalid structures that fringe the area and, within a short distance, the Cathedral and University have established an immense new centre of gravity. The long-neglected area is suddenly arising to challenge the dominance of the old centre. So long as the Council maintains its ceremonial link with the Guildhall and its officers discharge their duties in the forty-year-old temporary buildings on the Upper High Street the High Street will still remain the centre. But the town's steady growth makes it virtually certain that the existing municipal offices will demonstrate their inadequacy beyond argument. In that event, municipal piety would yield yet again to administrative convenience and the heart of the town would shift to the new centre of gravity on the banks of the river – a few hundred yards downstream from where it all began.

The broad picture presented by the Council's planning activities in the twentieth century is one in which the procrastination endemic in any public body charged with spending public money, was raised to a chronic degree by most unusual circumstances. For nearly a century the governing body of the town struggled to provide social services for a residential population expanding at an unprecedented rate – far above the national average – while compensating development in industry and related occupations lagged far behind. The asynchronisation preserved the historic heart of the town but it contributed to the cultural poverty: each proposal to spend money in order to raise the standards commensurate with the population immediately and intimately affected the individual citizen and aroused proportionate opposition.

The development in the years following the Second World War began, very slowly, to alter the balance. Industry was rigorously controlled, but still increased at a rate sufficient to warrant the establishment of an industrial estate. Office accommodation, insidiously capable of a greater degree of destruction than industry, fell under general metropolitan control. The town, nevertheless, was included in the localities listed by the Location of Offices Bureau and, from the 1960s onward, both national and international organisations migrated from London to establish their headquarters in Guildford: service industries, already established to supply the hinterland, increased under the new stimulus. Detectably, the burden of financing the town was being spread over a wider area.

Consequent upon the social broadening was the enlargement of the physical centre to provide additional accommodation – and here the town's essentially linear shape enabled the enlargement to be achieved at little historic cost and considerable civic benefit. Since its beginning, Guildford's life had been concentrated along the few hundred yards of the High Street with an extension south, forming Quarry Street, and another to the north, forming Chertsey Street, the whole forming a simple Z shape. Historic development had followed the lines of these three streets, reaching back no more than the few yards necessary to accommodate a house and a garden. The prolific but gimcrack commercial development of the late nineteenth and early twentieth century in its turn followed the line of these streets, crowding behind the established buildings, and it is at the expense of this highly expendable material that the new structures began to arise.

In the opening months of the 1970s became evident the results of the long-range plans for the town – in particular as they affected the highly vulnerable area of the High Street. It would appear that the lessons of the early 1960s have been learned: no new building here achieves that level of sheer brutality demonstrated by the megalith in Bury Fields which not only wiped out most of a long-matured community but effectively sterilised what remained. The major development is maintained in two blocks, one on either side of the Street, behind the established line and with entrances effected, in the one case, through the natural access of the Tunsgate arch and, in the other, through a brilliantly devised arch that was once a Victorian shop-front. The ancient appearance of the High Street is therefore unaffected, with the addition of a much needed increase in depth and visual change. The development here is epitomatic of the whole and it would seem that the town is approaching a physical equilibrium to match the social: whether, or for how long, it can maintain that balance can only be conjectured. But even as the town could, when it chose, defy the planners – obstinately increasing its size beyond the expected or currently desired limit, obstinately shifting its social centres in accordance to its own social rhythm, so it may defy the developers, obstinately maintaining into its second millennium the shape of the factors that gave it birth.

Notes

THE following notes are limited to the identification of quoted sources with the exception of (*a*) identification of source material on controversial topics and (*b*) identification of material to enable acknowledgment of recent research.

References to newspapers and similar periodical publications – including long runs of reports emanating from the same authority – are fulfilled here, together with certain classes of MS. material. All other references are fulfilled in the Bibliography on pages 220–4.

ABBREVIATIONS

An asterisk indicates location of rare or unique material, including that in MS., typescript or privately printed publications.

Arch. J.	*Archaeological Journal*
BE*	Guildford Borough Engineer's files
DNB	*Dictionary of National Biography*
EHD	*English Historical Documents*
MR*	Guildford Muniment Room
OGS	Old Guildford Society
P*	Private custody
PL*	Guildford Public Library
SAC	Surrey Archaeological Collections
SAS*	Library of the Surrey Archaeological Society
VCH	*Victoria County History*

CHAPTER 2. THE SHAPING OF THE TOWN

1. Margary, p. 40.
2. Belloc, p. 107.
3. *Surrey Advertiser*, 28 October 1933.
4. Nevill, SAC, xvii.
5. Russell, p. 18. This printed version is slightly different from the original: B.R. D IX 10 MR.
6. The Surrey Domesday in *VCH*, 1 295–328.

7. Quoted in Russell, p. [4].
8. The whole letter in Russell, pp. 11–16.
9. Russell, p. [161].
10. Aubrey, *Surrey*.
11. Russell, p. 58.
12. Laurence, p. 198.
13. *Surrey Advertiser*, 25 August 1893.
14. MoH Report for 1911.
15. *Surrey Advertiser*, 14 October 1933.
16. MoH Report for 1936.
17. Surrey County Council, 2:12.
18. The enquiry in Russell, pp. 201–5: MS. in BR/OC/1/2 MR.
19. Russell, p. 175*.
20. *West Surrey Times*, 28 February 1891.
21. Ibid., 9 May 1891.
22. MoH Report for 1901.
23. *London Argus*, 30 April 1904.
24. *Surrey Advertiser*, 28 November 1931.
25. Ibid., 5 December 1931.
26. Ibid., 12 December 1931.
27. *West Surrey Times*, 4 November 1927.
28. *The Times*, 25 May 1931.
29. Verbatim in *Surrey Advertiser*, 4 June 1932.
30. Ibid., 28 July 1934.
31. Ibid., 20 August 1931.
32. Surrey Development Plan, 12:6.
33. *West Surrey Times* Extra No. 1, pp. 7, 26.
34. Quoted in Jellicoe, p. 28.
35. YMCA, p. 7.
36. MoH Report for 1903.
37. Ibid., 1908.
38. Ibid., 1933.
39. *Surrey Advertiser*, 28 March 1969.
40. Ibid., 16 January 1932.
41. Ibid., 9 February 1935.
42. File No. 866 BE.
43. *Surrey Advertiser*, 21 September 1935.

CHAPTER 3. THE CATALYSTS

1. Quoted in Laurence.
2. Ibid., p. 23 n.
3. Brayley, 1 95.
4. Lowther, SAC xxxix.
5. Florence An. 1036.

6. *Encomium*, quoted *EHR*, p. 323.
7. For a summary of the theory, see *VCH*, 1 228.
8. Pipe Roll 20 Hen. II.
9. Malden (*Shell Keep*), who provided evidence of the existence of the shell keep, could cite only three others so established: those at Clun, Christchurch and, possibly, Norwich.
10. Tupper, preface.
11. Quoted in Laurence.
12. Liberate R. Chancery 30 Hen. III.
13. Ibid., 40 Hen. III.
14. Ibid.
15. Froissart, 11 270.
16. Bax, SAC, xviii.
17. Laurence, p. 29.
18. Quoted in ibid., p. 33.
19. Peak, H, f. 634.
20. *The Builder*, 9 July 1888.
21. Peak, H, f. 634.
22. Preamble to Hen. VIII charter: Russell, p. [i].
23. Ibid., p. [iii].
24. Ibid., p. 197*.
25. Ibid., p. 171.
26. Ibid., p. 199*.
27. Quoted in ibid.
28. Quoted in Gross, 1 52.
29. The clearest account of the function of these local courts in Dance, *Records*, pp. xx–xliii.
30. Court Leet, 16 January 1542: Dance, *Records*, p. 47.
31. Russell, p. 213.
32. Ibid., p. 200.
33. Ibid., p. 208.
34. Court Leet, 17 January 1536: Dance, *Records*, p. 33.
35. Aubrey, *Surrey*.
36. Russell, p. [11].
37. Ibid., p. [18].
38. Ibid., p. [20].
39. Ibid., p. 160.
40. Turner, *Arch. J.*, xlvii.
41. Peak, D.
42. Malden, *S. Nicolas*, p. 6.
43. Russell, p. 74.
44. Malden, *S. Nicolas*, p. 7.
45. Smith, p. 8.
46. Holling, SAC, lxiv.

47. 'Act for settling Augmentations . . .' in Russell, pp. 48–9.
48. Ibid., p. 51.
49. Laurence, p. 60.
50. Nairn, p. 231.
51. Palmer, *Statutes*, p. 16.
52. Russell, p. [11].
53. Palmer, *Statutes*, p. 21.
54. Ibid., p. 54.
55. Nairn, p. 237.
56. Mason, p. 60.
57. Austen, f. 35.
58. Ibid., f. 49.
59. Vine, pp. 10–13.
60. Laurence, p. 201 n.
61. Quoted in *VCH*, II 115.
62. The whole text in Brown, *Friars*, p. 7.
63. Russell, p. 145.
64. The petition verbatim in Powell, *Billeting*, SAC, XXVII.
65. Mason, p. 67.
66. *West Surrey Times*, 11 August 1888.
67. *Pearson's Weekly*, July 1905.
68. Laurence, p. 200 n.
69. The poster in Peak, G, f. 565.
70. *Outlook*, September 1931.
71. Ibid., December 1928.
72. *Surrey Advertiser*, 22 June 1935.
73. Ibid., 6 July 1935.
74. Ibid., 3 December 1932.
75. Both letters verbatim in *Surrey Advertiser*, 2 December 1933.
76. Quoted in ibid., 18 July 1936.
77. Nairn, p. 230.
78. Letter in *The Times*, 22 April 1936.
79. BBC, p. 9.
80. *Guildford and Godalming Times*, 29 April 1961.
81. Ibid., 15 April 1961.
82. Ibid., 22 April 1961.
83. Ibid., 29 April 1961.
84. Ibid., 27 May 1961.
85. *Surrey Advertiser*, 6 May 1961.
86. *Guildford and Godalming Times*, 29 April 1961.
87. *Surrey Advertiser*, 20 May 1961.
88. Ibid., 19 May 1962.
89. Ibid., 7 November 1964.

90. *Guildford and Godalming Times*, 2 June 1962.
91. *The Times*, 16 May 1964.
92. *Surrey Advertiser*, 27 June 1964.
93. Ibid., 3 April 1967.
94. *Guildford and Godalming Times*, 8 January 1966.
95. Press Report No. 1, December 1964.
96. *Surrey Advertiser*, 29 October 1966.
97. Ibid., 10 January 1969.
98. University, *Union Handbook*, p. 15.
99. *Surrey Advertiser*, 17 January 1969.

CHAPTER 4. THE CORPORATE MEMORY

1. Dance, *Records*, p. xv.
2. Quoted in Russell, p. 187.
3. Powell, p. 7.
4. Quoted in Russell, p. 17.
5. Dance, *Records*, p. xx.
6. Palmer, *Statutes*.
7. *Surrey Advertiser*, 20 April 1936.
8. Russell, p. [17].
9. Williamson, *Guildford*, p. 165.
10. *DNB*, II 1150.
11. Bray, SAC, XLVI.
12. Peak, A, f. 2.
13. Ibid., C, f. 248.
14. Ibid., C, f. 254.
15. Ibid., D, f. 302.
16. Cf. Myson, introduction.
17. *Outlook*, July 1933.
18. *West Surrey Times*, 16 March 1889.
19. Ibid.
20. Museum Minutes, 1 February 1919. BR/CTM/Mus 1–4 MR.
21. Museum and Muniment Room: Report, 31 March 1968.
22. Guildford Public Library: f. 2.

CHAPTER 5. THE GOVERNANCE OF THE TOWN

1. Mason, p. 15.
2. Quoted in *Encyclopedia Britannica* (1877), VI 435.
3. Quoted in Williamson, *Guildford*, p. 14.
4. *West Surrey Times*, 23 February 1889.
5. Peak, D, ff. 273–80.
6. Williamson, *Guildford*, p. 184.
7. *Surrey Advertiser*, 4 January 1890.

8. Peak, D, f. 279.
9. The card quoted in *Outlook*, October 1925.
10. Peak, E, f. 410.
11. Ibid., 407–10.
12. Vulliamy, p. 263.
13. Peake, E, f. 402.
14. *West Surrey Times*, 27 April 1890.
15. Ibid., 14 February 1891.
16. *Surrey Advertiser*, 18 March 1933.
17. Ibid.
18. Ibid., 7 November 1936.
19. Ibid., 30 April 1931.
20. Borough Council Minutes, 27 February 1934: No. 15.
21. *Surrey Advertiser*, 1 November 1913.
22. Ibid., 12 September 1931.
23. *Outlook*, April 1932.
24. Britten, p. 145.
25. For what follows, see Evelyn, *passim*.
26. *Punch*, 1 September 1860.
27. *The Times*, 22 August 1860.
28. Ibid., 24 August 1860.
29. Evelyn, p. 45.
30. *Surrey Advertiser*, 4 July 1914.
31. *Outlook*, December 1928.
32. *Surrey Advertiser*, 22 August 1936.
33. Ibid., 5 September 1931.

CHAPTER 6. IN SEARCH OF A CENTRE
1. *Surrey Advertiser*, 11 February 1961.
2. Ministry, *Historic Towns*, p. 5.
3. Report in *Surrey Advertiser*, 18 February 1961.
4. The letters in file Gui/8950/80/67 BE.
5. Ministerial letter dated 9 June 1956 BE.
6. OGS: Minute Book, 1901.
7. *Surrey Advertiser*, 3 August 1935.
8. Ibid., 23 February 1935.
9. Leighton, p. 6.
10. *Surrey Advertiser*, 27 April 1935.
11. Ibid., 30 March 1935.
12. Richards, p. 6.
13. For what follows, see Abercrombie, *passim*.
14. *Surrey Advertiser*, 6 June 1936.
15. *Surrey Weekly Press*, 16 October 1936.
16. *Surrey Advertiser*, 28 March 1969.

Bibliography

Patrick Abercrombie, 'Guildford: Site for a Civic Centre. Report and Plan, February 1936'. Borough Engineer's file 866.

Anglo-Saxon Chronicle, a revised translation edited by Dorothy Whitelock (1962).

John Aubrey, *Miscellanies* (1969).

—, *The Natural History and Antiquities of the County of Surrey*, vol. III (1718).

George Austen, *A monument for the schole of Guldeford . . . wherein is added the principal matters in an olde booke called the Black Booke*. Muniment Room BR/OC/7/1.

C. J. Barlow, *Archbishop Abbot's School, Guildford* (Guildford, 1924).

Alfred Ridley Bax, *Parliamentary Survey of Guildford Castle in 1650*, Surrey Archaeological Collections, XVIII (1903).

Hilaire Belloc, *The Old Road* (1948).

William Bray, *Extracts from the Diary: with a Foreword by F. E. Bray*, Surrey Archaeological Collections, XLVI (1938). The complete diary in Muniment Room BR/85/1/1–76.

E. W. Brayley, *History of Surrey*, edited and revised by Edward Walford, vol. 1 (n.d.).

British Broadcasting Corporation, *The Building of Guildford Cathedral* (1960).

F. J. Britten, *Old Clocks and Their Makers* (1919).

J. F. Brown: *The Black Friars of Guildford* (Guildford, 1952).

William Camden, *Suthrey and Sussex* (Reigate, 1905).

Hector Carter (ed.), *Guildford Freemen's Books 1655–1933* (Guildford, 1963).

Cathedral Council, *see* New Cathedral Council.

Chamber of Trade, Minute Book, 21 March 1911– . Private custody.

J. W. Clark, *On Libraries at Cesena, Wells, Guildford and Clare College, Cambridge*, Cambridge Antiquarian Society Proceedings, October/November 1891.

William Cobbett, *Rural Rides* (1826).

COPEC Council, *Guildford Housing Problem* (Guildford, 1926).

Enid M. Dance (ed.), *Guildford Borough Records 1514–1546*, Surrey Record Society, vol. xxiv (1958).

— (ed.), *The Borough of Guildford 1257–1957. Catalogue of an Exhibition of the Borough Plate and the Borough Records* (Guildford, 1957).

— (ed.) *The [Surrey Archaeological] Society's Collection of Antiquities and Records*, Surrey Archaeological Society, liii (1954).

De Guldeford: a true state of the poll and proceedings at the general election of two burgesses or members to serve in Parliament for Guildford (Guildford, 1796).

Encomium Emmae Reginae, trans, A. Campbell, Document 28 of *English Historical Documents*.

English Historical Documents, vol. i, *c.500–1042*, ed. Dorothy Whitelock (1955).

William John Evelyn, *A Letter Addressed to the Magistrates of Surrey* (1861).

Florence of Worcester, *Chronicle*, trans. Joseph Stevenson (1853).

J. K. Green, Manuscript notes on Guildford history. Guildford Public Library.

—, *Sidelights on Guildford History, I–IV* (Guildford, 1952–6).

Charles Gross, *The Gild Merchant*, 2 vols (Oxford, 1890).

Guildford Institute, *The Keep*, nos. 1–24 (Guildford, 1912–18).

Guildford Public Library, 'History of Guildford Library' (1962). Guildford Public Library.

Guildford Theatre Club Ltd, Board minutes 1946–63. Guildford Public Library.

Frederic Harrison, *Annals of an Old Manor House: Sutton Place, Guildford* (1899).

C. Hernihough, 'Archbishop Abbot's School', in *The Outlook*, June/July 1931.

F. W. Holling, *The Early Foundation of St Mary's Guildford*, Surrey Archaeological Collections, lxiv (1967).

Wilfrid Hooper, *The Pilgrim's Way and Its Supposed Pilgrim Use*, Surrey Archaeological Collections, xxxiv (1936).

Hospital of the Blessed Trinity, *see* Philip G. Palmer.

G. A. Jellicoe, *The Report Accompanying an Outline Plan Prepared for the Municipal Borough Council*, privately printed, 1945.

Alfred John Kempe, *The Losely Manuscripts* (1836).

[F. Laurence], *Guildford: A Descriptive and Historical View of the County Town of Surrey* (Guildford, 1845). Library of the Surrey Archaeological Society.

Brian Leighton, J. Garnett Harper and H. H. Norris, *A Civic Centre for Guildford . . . Revised from Proposals Submitted to the Guildford Borough Council on 12th February 1935*, privately printed in Guildford, 1935.

A. W. G. Lowther, *A Brief History of the Surrey Archaeological Society*, Surrey Archaeological Collections, LIII (1954).

—, *The Saxon Cemetery at Guildown, Guildford*, Surrey Archaeological Collections, XXXIX (1931).

H. E. Malden, *History of the Parish and Church of S. Nicolas* (Guildford, n.d.).

—, *The Shell Keep of Guildford Castle*, Surrey Archaeological Collections, XVI (1901).

—, *see also* 'Victoria History'.

Owen Manning, *The History and Antiquities of the County of Surrey . . . continued to the Present Time by William Bray*, vol. 1 (1804).

Ivan D. Margary, 'The North Downs Main Trackway and the Pilgrims' Way', *Archaeological Journal*, vol. CIX (1953).

[John Mason], *Guildford, 1897*, privately printed in Guildford, 1897.

Sir Edward Maufe, *Guildford Cathedral* (1968).

Ministry of Housing and Local Government, *Historic Towns: Preservation and Change* (1967).

—, *The South East Study: 1961–1981* (1964).

William Myson, *Surrey Newspapers: A Handlist and Tentative Bibliography* (1961).

Ian Nairn and Nikolaus Pevsner, *The Buildings of England: Surrey* (Harmondsworth, 1962).

Ralph Nevill, *The Place-name Guildford*, Surrey Archaeological Collections, XVII (1902).

New Cathedral Council, *Guildford Cathedral* (Guildford, 1959).

H. H. Norris, *Charities Act 1960: Review of Charities in the Borough of Guildford* (Guildford, 1967).

Old Guildford Society, Minute Book, 1897–1902. Guildford Public Library.

Earl of Onslow, *Thomas, 2nd Earl of Onslow and Guildford Onslow M.P.*, Surrey Archaeological Collections, XXXVII (1927).

C. F. R. Palmer, *The Friar-preachers of Guildford*. Guildford Public Library.

Philip G. Palmer, *Hospital of the Blessed Trinity. The Statutes Literally Transcribed with Introduction and Notes* (Guildford, 1927).

—, *Inventory of Abbot's Hospital, Guildford, 1635*, Surrey Archaeological Collections, xxx (1917).

Eric Parker, *Highways and Byeways in Surrey* (1950).

Henry Peak, 'Recollections and Activities as Mayor of Guildford', 16 vols lettered A–P. Guildford Public Library.

D. L. Powell, *Billeting in Surrey in the Seventeenth and Eighteenth Century*, Surrey Archaeological Collections, xxvii (1914).

— (compiler) and Hilary Jenkinson (editor), *Inventory of the Borough Records with Some Illustrative Extracts*, vol. iii (Kingston-upon-Thames, 1929).

Herbert Powell, *A Catalogue of the Old Library of Guildford Grammar School* (Guildford, 1900).

Remembrancer Reports, vols. i–v (1933–8) (scrapbook, 1958–(typescript). Guildford Public Library.

Richardson and Gill, Guildford: [Architect's] Report on Sites of Proposed Municipal Buildings (1967) (typescript).

John Russell, *The History of Guildford, the County Town of Surrey* (Guildford and London, 1801).

Thomas Russell, Manuscript notes on Archbishop Abbot. Guildford Public Library.

—, Manuscript notes on the history of Guildford. Guildford Public Library.

Edith Smith, *Church of St Mary the Virgin* (Guildford, 1930).

D. M. Stevens, *The Records and Plate of the Borough of Guildford*, Surrey Archaeological Collections, ix (1888).

—, *The Royal Grammar School of Guildford*, Surrey Archaeological Collections, x (1891).

D. M. Sturley, 'Allen House, No. 1 High Street Guildford: Some Notes on Its History'. Guildford Public Library.

Surrey Archaeological Society, *Surrey Archaeological Collections Relating to the History and Antiquities of the County*, vols 1– (1858–). *See also* Bax; Bray; Dance; Holling; Hooper; Lowther; Malden; Nevill; Onslow; Palmer; Stevens; Waller.

Surrey County Council, *Development Plan: Guildford and District Town Map. Report and Analysis of Survey* (1966).

Surrey Record Society. *See* Enid M. Dance.

'Surrey Times', *The Changing Face of the Past 100 Years*, 'Surrey Times' Centenary Supplement (Guildford, 1955). *See also* 'West Surrey Times'.

Richard Symmes, 'Collection for Surrey'. British Museum Ad. MS. 1617. Photostat copy of folios 193–208 in Muniment Room.

Martin Tupper, *Stephan Langton: A Romance of the Silent Pool*, 23rd ed. (Guildford, n.d.).

Thackeray Turner, 'Unusual Doorways in Old Buildings', *Archaeological Journal*, XLVII (1890).

University of Surrey, *Report of the Vice-Chancellor for the Session 1966–67 (Incorporating the 2nd Annual Report Presented to the Court of the University)* (1967).

—, *Union Handbook 68/69* (London and Guildford, 1969).

Victoria History of the County of Surrey, ed. H. E. Malden, vol. 19.

P. A. L. Vine, *London's Lost Route to the Sea* (Newton Abbot, 1965).

C. E. Vulliamy, *The Onslow Family 1528–1874* (1953).

J. G. Waller, *Wall Paintings in the Church of Saint Mary, Guildford*, Surrey Archaeological Collections, x (1891).

H. R. Ware and P. G. Palmer, *Three Surrey Churches* (Guildford, n.d.).

Paul A. Welsby, *George Abbot: The Unwanted Archbishop 1562–1633*.

'West Surrey Times', *Our County Town*, 'West Surrey Times' Extra No. 1 (Guildford, 1889). *See also* 'Surrey Times'.

Thomas Whitburn, *Local Pictures as Landmarks of History: together with (for the First Time) a Complete List of the Pictures Belonging to the Town and Full Information Concerning Them* (Guildford, 1888).

George C. Williamson, *Guildford Castle: A Chronological Survey* (Guildford, 1926).

—, *The Guildford Caverns* (Guildford, 1930).

—, *Guildford Charities* (Guildford, 1931).

—, *Guildford in the Olden Times: Sidelights on the History of a Quaint Old Town* (London and Guildford, 1904).

—, *The Royal Grammar School of Guildford: A Record and a Review* (London and Guildford, 1929).

Y.M.C.A., *No Room to Live in Guildford: A Statement of Facts Concerning the Housing Problem* (Guildford, 1902).

Yvonne Arnaud Theatre Management Ltd, *Opening Festival Handbook* (Guildford, 1965).

The $2\frac{1}{2}$ inch to the mile (1:25,000) Ordnance Survey map covers Guildford on sheets TQ 04, 05, and SU 94, 95.

Index